THE COST TO CLOSE
ReShawna Leaven

Real Estate Chronicles Publishing Group

This book is a work of non-fiction, the names, characters, places, and incidents are the product of the author's experience or are used fictitiously. Any resemblance to actual persons, living or dead, or actual events is purely coincidental. The purpose of this book is to serve as an educational resource, offering insights and practical advice to navigate the complexities of real estate transactions. It is designed to support real estate professionals and consumers by shedding light on common challenges and providing strategies to overcome them. However, it is crucial to understand that this book does not offer definitive solutions to real estate issues and should not be seen as a replacement for the professional advice of a licensed real estate broker or attorney. The content within these pages aims to assist in the real estate journey, however the author and publisher accept no responsibility for any misuse of the information provided. This book is not intended to act as legal, accounting, or professional advice in any specific real estate situation. As the author does not hold a license in law, accounting, or other fields requiring official certification, readers should not rely solely on this text for guidance on legal or financial matters. Instead, it is recommended that readers consult with a licensed professional in their jurisdiction for expert advice tailored to their specific circumstances. In sum, this book is a tool to enhance understanding and facilitate smoother real estate transactions, but it should complement, not replace, the expertise of qualified professionals in the field.

To Sharon, for being the best mother that a daugther could ask for.
To Edward, for stepping in as a father when I needed you most.

INTRODUCTION

This book serves as a beacon for real estate professionals, casting light on the myriad challenges and predicaments that can disrupt a transaction. It's a collection of real-life tales designed not only to educate but also to offer a dose of enlightenment, peppered with humor where appropriate, to those navigating the tumultuous waters of real estate. Through these narratives, drawn from the trenches of the industry, agents are equipped with practical knowledge to safeguard their deals, both present and future. These stories, rooted in actual events but with names changed to protect privacy, form a bridge between theoretical knowledge and real-world application.

In an industry awash with resources on lead generation, there's a noticeable gap when it comes to handling the hurdles that invariably pop up during transactions. The lack of a one-size-fits-all solution necessitates an "avoidance list" for agents, a toolkit for circumventing common pitfalls. The real estate realm is often reticent, with professionals wary of sharing their mishaps for fear of judgment. This silence stifles the spread of valuable insights, despite the evident need in a field where credibility is king.

Real estate is a domain of endless nuances, demanding agents to master not just the logistics of deals but also the delicate art of managing human emotions. The industry, despite its portrayed glitz on television, is grounded in the emotional and financial stakes of buyers and sellers, making each transaction a complex dance of negotiation.

Agents, whether focusing on buyers or listings, evolve through their experiences, learning lessons that refine their approach to the multifaceted real estate journey. This book aims to accelerate that learning curve, offering a wealth of lessons for both newcomers and veterans.

Real estate influences nearly every aspect of our lives, from the mundane to the monumental. It shapes our living spaces, affects our economic landscape, and offers opportunities for personal and investment growth. The sector's history is marked by dramatic fluctuations, from the high interest rates of the 1980s to the 2008 financial crisis, presenting both challenges and opportunities for those willing to navigate its complexities.

According to the National Association of Realtors (NAR), a staggering 87% of new agents exit the industry within five years, a testament to the sector's demanding nature. Success hinges on more than just skill; it requires resilience, a deep understanding of the market, and the ability to forge meaningful connections with clients. This book addresses these challenges head-on, providing scenarios and advice to arm agents with the necessary tools for success.

The key to thriving in real estate lies in belief, planning, flexibility, and continuous learning. By absorbing the experiences shared in this book, agents can enhance their transactional strategies and elevate their careers. It's not just about surviving in the industry but flourishing, by embracing the complexities with confidence and a touch of humor.

TABLE OF CONTENTS

1

THE CIRCUS

"*WELCOME, LADIES AND GENTLEMEN, to the mesmerizing world of real estate, where transactions unfold like a grand three-ring circus.* Picture this: a whirlwind of performers, each playing their part in a spectacular event of different acts taking place simultaneously. It rivals the awe-inspiring theatrics of a traveling big top. "*Step right up, for this is no ordinary show—it is one of the greatest transactions ever performed.*"

In our arena, real estate agents are like masterful magicians, deftly weaving through the intricacies of deals. They transform challenges into opportunities with the grace of a trapeze artist, soaring high and catching success with impeccable timing.

Buyers and sellers are the enchanted audience, captivated by the skillful juggling of contracts, conversations, and coffee. They watch, hopeful and eager, as their dreams are spun into reality, much like the harmonious coordination of a well-rehearsed circus act. This real estate world often mirrors the multifaceted nature of a circus, where different acts occur simultaneously, adding layers of complexity.

Imagine the unexpected, like the myriad of clowns spilling from a compact car, similar to the unforeseen surprises in a credit report when discoveries of unknown accounts like unpaid debts and delinquencies appear one-by-one.

During the event, negotiations sparkle like fireworks, details come together in a dazzling display, and strategic moves illuminate the stage, captivating the audience. One anticipates the usual "whoa!" and "yeah!" from the crowd.

As the circus reaches its finale, so do our real estate transactions. As the circus performers take their well-deserved bows amidst applause and cheers, in the same manner, real estate professionals and their clients celebrate their victorious closings, despite the myriad of obstacles encountered along the journey.

Their friends and family on social media as the audience, only seeing the joyous end. The snapshot shows them as our client beaming with an oversized key cutout at closing - one only knows what was going on behind the stage. This story invites you to pull back the curtain and go behind the stage, to delve deeper into the acts that take place on occasion with a closing. So, get a ring-side seat, grab some popcorn, and prepare to be mesmerized by this spectacular event that unfolds under this "big top".

Every week felt like navigating a maze with no exit in sight. Sundays, once leisurely and calm, turned into a vortex of silence – no callbacks, no emails buzzing with pdf's bearing offers. Just the Richardson family, grappling with strategies to leap from one home to the next. *"What haven't we tried?"* they asked, their minds weary from the relentless brainstorming. *"How about throwing in a new smart TV or the living room set? Maybe a hefty concession?"* Nia was the listing agent and daughter of the Richardson's. She was donned a strategy guru who always put on her thinking cap in times like these. With each brainstorming session, the list of considerations and trade-offs grew longer and more complex.

Nia's parents embarked on a journey in the frosty embrace of February, envisioning a seamless transition to a new forever home slated for completion by the warm embrace of August. Their timelines seemed ample—a comfortable span to sell and smoothly transition to their new haven. Yet, the unpredictable rhythm of the real estate market birthed its own impromptu performance, similar to the unexpected display of a contortionist introducing astonishing twists at every turn. The market bent and twisted with surprises that left everyone wondering, *"How are we going to do this?"*

ACT I: TRAPEZE ARTISTS

Suddenly, there's an unexpected change in the Act I. The builder sent an updated completion notice that they were on course to complete the home in June instead of August. Now they were faced with an additional task – not only selling their current home, but also ensuring everything aligned for a seamless transition. A new looming question hung in the air: *Could they pull off a smooth move in this tightened timeframe?"*

Navigating each week with the agility of a trapeze artist, Nia began to swing from one potential solution to another. There was a greater sense of urgency to sell the home. The trapeze was swinging and needed more momentum to reach the next point. She didn't just list the property on the MLS to stir up chatter; she went all out – vibrant color brochures, snazzy postcards mailed to all renters in the neighborhood – she did it all, short of broadcasting a prime-time TV ad (*ha, ha*).

Part of her strategy was always to hold an open house. To prepare, she made sure that the home was in tip-top shape inside and out. She was up at the crack of dawn, armed with a vacuum cleaner and a mission. As she whirled through each room, leaving perfectly straight vacuum lines in her wake, she flung open all the blinds, and walked through each room making sure every nook and cranny sparkled. After loading her car with a parade of "Open House" signs, she strategically planted them from the bustling highway right to the front door, creating a welcoming trail for potential buyers. In addition, for the pièce de résistance, she baked a batch of chocolate chip cookies so that visitors would step into the showing and be greeted not just by a stunning home, but by the irresistible scent of freshly baked treats.

As the open house commenced, it began more like a curious sideshow than a main event. The neighborhood onlookers and casually intrigued clients with their agents paraded through with immediate feedback about how great the home looked as though it had been professionally staged. But in this part of the ACT, no buyers took center stage. In a market that once resembled a frenzied circus tent with eager buyers tumbling over each other, offering hefty sums above the asking price all of a sudden things had dramatically shifted. *"Lions, tigers, and no buyers, oh my!"* Nia thought to herself. This metropolitan area had seen the trapeze bar swing before, but it was not swinging far enough to catch those buyers so that they could get to the other side. Instead, the high-flying trapeze act of increasing interest rates had swung into play, swooping down on affordability, and scaring away the crowd.

As the weeks turned into months, the price of the house somersaulted lower and lower, each reduction a tightrope walk over their financial safety net. Finally, it plummeted to the 'limbo line' of $800,000 - a figure that had them bending over backwards in disbelief. With each price cut, a slice of their equity vanished into thin air. Their thoughts could be compared to looking inside of the magician's hat, wondering what magic trick they could perform to make the crowd spark with excitement.

ACT II - MAGICIAN

ACT II begins with Nia pondering other potential tactics after she received no offers following the open house. With a twinkle in her eye and her brainstorming hat on, she wondered if luring buyers with tantalizing offers like buying down the buyer's interest rate to enhance affordability or paying HOA fees for several months. as a bonus. She swung into action, the way only a seasoned real estate pro could.

CONVERSATION AT THE DINING ROOM TABLE
(With Nia, Lawrence, and Imani)

Nia - Nia greeted her parents with enthusiasm, *"Hi Mom and Dad! I've been giving a lot of thought to your property. Despite the challenges, I believe there's still opportunity,"* she said, optimistic.

Lawrence - *"The house has been on the market for a while. Despite open houses and price reductions, we've had no contracts."*

Nia - *"I understand it's been tough. But sometimes a fresh perspective can make a difference. I've been exploring various strategies we may have overlooked."*

Imani - *"Ok, I'm open to hearing your ideas."*

Nia - *"We can consider concessions. Options include offering to cover closing costs, paying HOA fees, or buying down the buyer's interest rate to enhance affordability. We could also include the basement furniture in the sale, as you won't need it in the new house."*

Imani - *"Do you think that would really make a difference?"*

Nia - *"Absolutely. Buyers are often attracted to homes with added incentives. Our home presents well, so that's not the issue. It's more about affordability in the current market."*

Lawrence - *"We need to try something. The builder said our new house will be ready two months earlier than expected."*

Nia - *"The market is unpredictable, but that doesn't mean we can't find opportunities. We don't want our home sale to become the fire-eater's act – risky and unpredictable. Instead, let's aim for the grace and precision of the tightrope walker, balancing each step with skill and patience"*

As the meeting concluded, Nia retreated to her room to work on an action plan for her parents' house and her other business deals as well. A week after she implemented the new strategies, she received requests for several showing appointments and decided to host another open house. The results paid off with a potential offer.

HIGHWIRE - PHONE CALL
(With Nia Washington and Jenna Rivers)

After their greetings and salutations, Jenna potential buyer's agent and

Nia about the home.

Jenna - *"My clients are truly impressed with the Richardson's' work on the property. However, we need to have to talk about the price and the seller concessions being offered."*
Nia - *"Of course, Jenna. We're certainly open to considering reasonable offers. The Richardson's have put a lot of effort and resources into enhancing the property, and we believe that's reflected in its value."*
Jenna - *"The market's quite competitive these days, and we've done our homework. Our clients are ready to make a fair offer, but it needs to align with the current market conditions."* (Her tone and persona fit right into the squeaky wheel category).
Nia - (She thought to herself, can she just send me the contract so we can actually negotiate it. Right now, we are negotiating air)*"We understand how market trends play a role. Could you submit your clients' highest and best offer? I'll discuss it with my clients for consideration."*
Jenna - *"Ok. I'll prepare my clients' offer this afternoon and send it over late this evening after they've signed it. My clients are currently at work. I've got to pick up my dog from the vet, my kids from soccer practice and prepare dinner,"* (Nia thought to herself while listening, *"Wow, I don't really care about your laundry list of duties. I just need the contract!"* Nia knew that she had to be extra nice because this was the only potential offer, she had thus far).
Nia - *"Sounds good. We'll be waiting for your offer. Nice chatting with you Jenna, buy!"*

Nia's evening was interrupted by the ping of her inbox, revealing Jenna's email with an offer for her parents' home. She opened the attachment and reviewed the details. She quickly used her software to create an estimated seller closing statement. As she reviewed the numbers, a sinking realization dawned on her: the final numbers weren't going to cut it. But Nia, ever the problem-solver, wasn't one to back down from a challenge.

Before even bringing this conundrum to her parents, Nia conjured up a plan, her mind whirring with possibilities. It was then she metaphorically swung her magical wand - a flourish of decisive action rather than actual magic. With a determined glint in her eye, Nia decided to dive into her own reserves, contributing the necessary funds at closing to bridge the financial gap. It was a bold move, fueled by her unwavering commitment to turn the dream of her parents moving to their forever home into a resounding reality.

With a mix of anticipation and anxiety, she settled at the dining room table (which had now turned into the command center) with her parents. She began to discuss the details of the offer and go over the estimated closing statement line-by-line. Her parents understood what needed to be done and were grateful for her generosity.

After two days of negotiations, they came to agreeable terms and the offer was ratified. Though Nia knew that the journey was far from over, the next steps would involve inspections, appraisals, and the finalization of the deal, each phase another step on the path to closing.

ACT III: TIGHTROPE WALKERS

In the middle ring, there were things that needed to be completed for the new construction home while waiting for the old home to close. The lender for the new home made several requests to the Richardson's in order to get them fully approved.

A series of emails and requests through the online portal from the lender:

- interest rate

- rental verification,

- re-verification of employment

- updated bank statements

EMAIL (From Loan Officer to Buyer)

FROM: Danielle Roberts/TO: Imani Richardson/CC: Kelvin Montgomery
Subject: Next steps: Interest Rate Lock

Hi Imani,

My name is Danielle Roberts. I am stepping in to manage Kelvin Montgomery's client files while he is out of the country. There is a pressing item that needs to be addressed. It's time to lock in your interest rate. Interest rates have gone up in the time period since your initial pre-approval. With your qualifying ratios, you will need to buy-down your interest rate. To buy down your interest rate, you can use the closing costs that the builder is contributing of $25,000 to bring down your interest rate and come closer to a payment that will fit with your debt-to-income ratios.

Danielle Roberts
123 Tired Mortgage

It's important to note that a week prior, interest rates had dropped, but the loan officer failed to lock in the interest rate.

EMAIL (From Buyer to Loan Officer)

FROM: Imani Richardson/TO: Danielle Roberts/CC: Kelvin Montgomery
Subject: Re: Next steps: Interest Rate Lock

Hi Danielle,

We were under the impression that the interest rate was locked. However, we are ready to lock the interest rate NOW. Please let us know what's needed and we will get on it right away.
Imani

EMAIL (From Loan Officer to Buyer)

FROM: Danielle Roberts/TO: Imani Richardson/CC: Kelvin Montgomery
Subject: Re: Re: Next steps: Interest Rate Lock

Hi Imani,

I will attach the documents to the web portal by COB today for you to e-sign. Make sure your husband signs as well.

Danielle Roberts
123 Tired Mortgage

Imani diligently followed Danielle's instructions, uploading the necessary documents to the web portal. However, the process hit a snag when a new condition emerged: rental verification. The lender required confirmation of the Richardson's rental history, as their current residence of nine months wasn't enough. They needed evidence of consistent payment history over the past 12 months, so Imani reached out to the property management company of their previous rental. Unfortunately, their response was frustratingly slow, similar to a sloth's pace, delaying the process further. Imani decided to go directly to the office of the rental management company the next day after work (boots on the ground) to ask for the documents firsthand. She was able to gather the documents to scan and upload them when she arrived home.

At this time, many things are taking place under the big top. Back at 123 Previous Home Way, the closing of Richardson's home was completed on a Monday, and they negotiated a rent-back agreement for five days. This arrangement afforded them the time needed to seamlessly transfer their belongings to their new home and complete a thorough cleaning before handing over the keys to the new owners.

After closing, Imani uploaded the executed closing statement through the web portal for verification of the completed settlement. This was needed as a document for the new home. Forty-eight hours later, another condition surfaced in the web portal: proof of funds from sale of their home. In response, Nia promptly submitted the required proof of funds, hoping this would keep things moving smoothly.

456 Forever Home Lane was scheduled to close on the Wednesday of that same week. The family planned to move on their closing day, a Wednesday, but it was not just any Wednesday – it was whimsically dubbed "Stilt Walking Wednesday."

On the anticipated closing day of their new home, Lawrence, Imani, and Nia were met with unforeseen hurdles. Each had taken the day off for closing and the move. Yet they found themselves in a state of limbo, waiting for the lender's crucial "clear to close" confirmation. The moving company had arrived early, at 7:30 am, and the family was prepared to pitch in. As the day progressed, their optimism began to wane around 12:15 pm, no emails, no phone calls or text messages received. Despite their readiness, a sense of uncertainty hung in the air.

By the afternoon, their apprehensions were realized. At 3:00 pm, Nia received the disheartening email: the closing was officially delayed. The stand in loan officer said that there was a HUD rule with the financial credit being given by the agent to close on 123 Previous Home Way. She said that they were waiting on an answer from HUD on this issue. To add to their frustration, there was no indication of when this issue might be resolved, leaving them in an uneasy state of waiting and uncertainty. This delay didn't just throw a wrench in their moving plans; it also draped a cloak of uncertainty over their journey to the new home, turning what should have been a time of excitement into a sitcom of second-guessing.

The moving company, having nearly completed their job in anticipation of unloading at the new home. The family's belongings were packed into two 26-foot moving trucks, symbolizing their state of transition. The change of plans meant that instead of moving into their new home, they now faced the daunting task of finding storage space — and potentially multiple ones at that.

To compound their stress, the moving company presented them with a tight deadline. They needed to retrieve their wrapping materials within a week, or they would add a surcharge fee of $750. The movers offered a slight concession: if they could return and move the items within a week, the fee would be waived. This predicament added another layer of urgency and complexity.

Back at the house, disappointment hung heavily in the air. It was nearing 5:30 pm. Although moving everything into storage had been a swift process due to the close proximity of the units, a new challenge arose. Imani, attempting to open the garage, found it unresponsive. She wondered if a power outage was to blame, especially considering the recent community maintenance work.

CONVERSATION BACK AT 123 PREVIOUS HOME WAY
(With Nia, Lawrence, and Imani)

Nia - *"Mom, did you disconnect the service?"*
Imani - *"Yes, I did."*
Nia - *"Oh, no! You should have arranged for a transfer instead."*
Imani - *"Don't scold me, Nia. I am already under a lot of stress as it is. Can you look up hotels nearby? We can't stay here tonight since we have no beds and no electricity."*
Nia - *"Yes. How many nights should I book?"*
Imani - *"Just find something for one night for now. I'm tired."*

Nia faced the daunting task of securing two hotel rooms, a necessity born out of urgency rather than choice. She managed to find a hotel that met their standards at a steep $175 per night for each room. With no other options, they booked the rooms and settled in, their evening culminating with a simple dinner at a close fast-food restaurant near the hotel.

Imagine a ringmaster, complete with a top hat and a booming voice, running the show at the hotel refuge. With every elevator ding and door slam, it's as if he's announcing another act in this big tent of discomfort. *"Ladies and gentlemen, watch as this family battles the high-wire act of sleep deprivation!* or *Behold, the amazing appetite-disappearing trick!"*

After two more days at the hotel with no answer, they decided to give the loan company a week to get things in order. This meant scheduling the hotel stay for a week, where they would continue to experience the disconcerting uncertainty and inconvenience of being without a home and living out of their bags.

Here's where the plot thickens, it was like a circus act gone awry. In this unexpected twist, Danielle, the stand-in loan officer, introduced a new complication. She requested a gift letter for the funds used in closing 123 Previous Home Way. Nia found this peculiar, yet she obliged. She thought to herself, *"Why do I need a gift letter for the last home? The transactions are unrelated. Surely, they only require confirmation that the property was sold and an account of the fund's origin. Why should this be an extra hoop to jump through?"* Her thoughts echoed the bewilderment of a circus audience witnessing a performer's unexpected stunt.

Danielle sent several emails that laid out her points with the finesse of a juggler tossing flaming torches:

- The amount of the credit was too much

- The funds should have come from someone else

- The funds could not come from the agent on the transaction

A tense dialogue unfolded between Imani and the interim loan officer, Danielle Roberts. During their discussion, Danielle proposed the idea of seeking an alternative lender and loan program, a suggestion that carried significant implications. The builder had made it clear: the $25,000 concession, crucial for closing and reducing the interest rate, would not be available with an external lender. This presented a financial challenge for the Richardson family, as securing this concession was vital and they lacked the additional funds needed without it.

Amidst this predicament, Nia sprang into action, contacting every loan officer in her network to explore their ability to close the loan within the required timeframe. Her conversations with trusted mortgage professionals revealed a consensus: not only was the loan feasible, but the concerns raised by her parents' lender were unfounded. This revelation brought both relief and a renewed sense of urgency to find a viable solution.

A week later, as the dramatic events kept everyone in suspense, Kelvin, the primary loan officer, returned from his vacation. He swiftly made corrections and submitted the necessary documents to the underwriter. Finally, on the next Tuesday, Kelvin delivered the much-awaited news...your clients are "clear to close."

Eager to transition into their new life, the Richardson's decided to coordinate the move and the closing on the same day. They arranged for the movers to collect their belongings from storage, timing it perfectly so that by the time the closing was completed, they would be ready to start setting up at their new residence. Imani called upon her dear friend Patrice for assistance. Generously taking time off work, Patrice dived into the task with energy and dedication, working alongside Nia. Impressively, the moving company managed to transport the contents of four 10 x 15 storage units in just three hours.

Meanwhile, Imani and Lawrence set out for the final walk thru of their new home at 11:00 am and had their closing at 1:00 pm. By 4:00 pm, they were back at their new house, a testament to the efficiency and coordination of the day's events. In the warmth of their new home, Imani and Lawrence expressed their heartfelt gratitude to Patrice for her invaluable help and support during this significant transition.

In the grand finale of the circus story, Nia and her parents overcame a whirlwind of challenges and closed on their new home. Amidst the juggling of documents, the tightrope walk of negotiations, and the unexpected acrobatics of the market, they emerged triumphant. Their journey, peppered with moments of tension, humor, and sheer determination, mirrors the captivating acts of a well-orchestrated circus.

As the final curtain closes, we reflect on the invaluable lessons learned and the resilience displayed. The Richardson's' story is not just about buying and selling property, it's a testament to what goes on behind the curtain: the power of persistence, adaptability, and family support in the bewildering big top of real estate.

So, dear reader, as you close this chapter and ponder your own real estate ventures, remember the circus analogy. Whether you're an agent with a buyer or a seller, life in the real estate ring can be a thrilling and sometimes unsettling performance. But with the right mindset, a dash of humor, and a willingness to embrace the unexpected, you too can navigate this circus and emerge victorious.

THINK BEYOND THE STORY

- What was the cost of this real estate transaction? emotional, physical, or financial?

- What would have happened if Imani and Lawrence did not adapt Nia's strategies?

- Should Nia have managed the required funds for closing on the sale another way?

- How should you manage the misunderstanding with the interim loan officer?

CLOSING POINTS

- Remember that the builder gives incentives to buyer(s) to use their preferred vendors and usually will not allow the buyer(s) to go outside of that umbrella

- Timelines can change in a transaction. Be adaptable.

- Always ask your clients "What are you willing to do?"

- Clients should be cautious about planning for movers before the "clear to close" has been issued

- Create a list of strategies to take on your listing consultation that includes all possible outcomes and scenarios (as many as you can think of for their particular case).

- Always ask all the people (i.e., clients, loan officer, buyer's agent, seller's agent) involved in the transaction if they have any vacation plans during your closing period.

- Understand basic lender conditions.

- You need to have a list of trusted professionals that you can call on for help ("phone a friend")

2

BEFORE THE BELLS

"Before the keys, there are many fees."
ReShawna Leaven

REAL ESTATE AND DATING share a striking resemblance. Both involve a process of courtship in search of the perfect match. In the case of real estate, it's a quest for the ideal dwelling. Many real estate agents call themselves "matchmakers." They participate in similar dating processes. For example, the quest to find a new home requires a courting period. One must make a decision on the type of home and search (make dates for those that look good), and complete further research to determine whether the area and property meets their needs and preferences. In both cases, this careful assessment of qualities and character is necessary to ensure that a suitable match can be made.

THE MATCHMAKING GAME

- Showing appointments are <u>dates</u>.

- An offer is a <u>commitment</u>.

- The contract to close is the <u>engagement period</u>.

- The closing is symbolic of <u>marriage</u>. (this final stage of the process is the ultimate goal)

In the quest for the ideal home, there will be numerous properties that fail to meet the mark. These options may seem promising but fall short of the coveted title of "home." However, for those who are determined to own their dream residence, success is achievable with the right strategy and support team in place. This story explores how Nora Hill embarked on a captivating journey with her clients, as she unravels the art of finding a home to fulfill their deepest wants and needs.

The story delves into the potential loopholes and pitfalls that may arise when navigating the complex world of real estate sales. Nora Hill, a seasoned professional in the industry, was collaborating with clients who had specific requirements for their dream home. They were in search of a single-family residence with a spacious backyard, hardwood flooring throughout, and situated within a reasonable distance from their places of work and in a desirable school district (Nora Hill directed them to use one of the online sources to research school ratings themselves).

DATING PHASE: HOME TOURS

GROUP TEXT MESSAGE
(With Nora and her clients)

"Hi Nora. I wanted to see if we could go out to view homes on Saturday or Sunday. Are you available?" ***[Tracy sent at 12:00 PM]***
"Yes, I am available at 11:00 am on Saturday or 6:00 pm on Monday." ***[Nora sent at 12:12 PM]***
"Let's do 11:00 am on Saturday." ***[Tracy sent at 12:15 PM]*** *(Nora sighed to herself. She was hoping for a Monday appointment, but she pressed on.)*
"Can you send me a list of homes that you are interested in so that I can check availability and make a showing appointment?" ***[Nora sent at 12:18 PM]***
"Yes, I will have John email them to you this evening. Thank you. I really

*think we are getting closer." **[Tracy sent at 12:48 PM]***

Upon reviewing the addresses listed in the MLS, she was taken aback to find that the properties were townhomes, rather than single-family homes. Despite this change, her excitement and optimism remained undeterred as she eagerly scheduled appointments. Nora even added a few properties to the list that John emailed, because a few of those homes had come under contract. She was able to find suitable matches with a range of options within their budget and preferred location radius. They began viewing homes two weekends back to back (they went on 30 dates to be exact).

DATING PHASE: AFTER 30 VISITS

CONVERSATION AT A SHOWING APPOINTMENT
(With Nora the buyer's agent, and Tracy and John her clients)

Tracy - *"I love this house, John. This is it! This is the house I want!"*
John - *"Are you sure? We've looked at about 50 houses already."* John asked with a puzzled look.
Nora - *"We've seen lots of homes but not 50."*
Tracy - *"Right. We haven't seen that many yet."*
Nora - *"I think this is it. We have seen 30 or so homes. What do you think about this house, John?"*
John - *"What do we have to do to get this house? I am done looking and want to get this part of the process over."*
Nora - *"I am so excited that you guys have found something that you feel comfortable placing an offer on. We'll need to submit an offer to purchase to the seller right away. I can prepare the documents at my office. If you would like to take a break and have lunch, that will give me time to prepare everything and you can meet me at my office after you eat, say around 3:00pm."*
Tracy - *"That's perfect. You know that I'm eating for three now."* (Tracy was pregnant with twins)

COMMITMENT PHASE: OFFER

GROUP TEXT MESSAGE
(With Nora and her clients)

"Hi Tracy and John. I have good news. The seller accepted your offer with no changes. You are now under contract!" **[Nora sent at 4:45 PM]**
"That's great!" **[John sent at 5:20 PM]**
"Wonderful news, Nora. I know we have been a pain in the "you know what" to work with, I'm sure. Well... me at least." **[Tracy sent at 5:25 PM]**
"No, it's all part of the process. It takes time to choose the right home. I think you nailed it." **[Nora sent at 5:40 PM]**

ENGAGEMENT PHASE: CONTRACT TO CLOSE

Following the completion of the home inspection, the process of escrow continued. The appraisal of the property was successfully conducted, with the resulting value coming in at an impressive $570,000, exceeding the initial sales contract price of $560,000. However, the sale encountered yet another hurdle (this would be a misunderstanding between the couple during the engagement phase). The underwriter requested an additional appraisal due to recent renovations and flipping of the property within the last six months. The purpose of this request was to clarify the property's true supported value (this is asked of lenders sometimes after a short window when a house is purchased and renovated in a short period of time). The lender would accept the lower of the two values presented.

The buyers were understandably frustrated upon discovering this information, as neither the lender nor their agent had informed them of the possibility of requiring two appraisals. This unexpected expense amounted to $1,200, a cost that they had not accounted for. Nora failed to discuss this detail in their discussions.

Subsequently, the title company requested that the current property owner, an LLC, submit its Articles of Corporation and other required documents. With failed attempts to reach the seller and listing agent, the title representative asked the buyer's agent to assist with getting in contact with the listing agent to put pressure on the seller to submit the required documents to close on time.

EMAIL (To Listing Agent from Buyer's Agent)

FROM: Nora, Buyer's Agent/ To: Listing Agent
Subject: URGENT! 123 Main Street LLC

This is the 4th time that we are requesting documents from the seller's LLC. We need this for our files.

Nora Hill
Please Real Estate

In a matter of minutes after receiving the email, the listing agent replied with the required information, without an apology for the delayed response. This swift action was crucial to the process, as it involved the seller's information, which was necessary to issue a title commitment for the buyer's lender. Without the title commitment, the buyer would not be able to close on the loan.

Ultimately, the second appraisal revealed a value $5,000 higher than the original appraisal.

Sales Price	Appraised Value #1	Appraised Value #2
$560,000	$570,000	$575,000

Suppose the appraisal valued the home at $559,000. In that case, Nora would have suggested the Johnsons negotiate a reduced price with the seller. This negotiation would involve drafting a sales addendum outlining the new terms, coupled with the inclusion of the appraisal report.

WEDDING PLANNING

During the wedding planning phase there are many components that have to be coordinated. Some are difficult and challenging, while others tasks run smoothly. Similarly, in the world of real estate, not all deals end with a smooth exchange of keys and a mortgage agreement. Some may end with a release of contract and the seller may find a new buyer (s)...

To ensure a successful "happily ever after", it is essential for agents to thoroughly explain the process to their clients and highlight any potential hurdles that they may face. This way, clients are better equipped to navigate any challenges and approach the transaction with knowledge.

TEXT MESSAGE
(Between Listing Agent and Nora – Buyer's Agent)

"Can you send me the utility company information for transfer for 8352 Please Ct?" **[Nora sent at 10:00 am 5/1]**
"Sure. I will email it to you now." **[Listing Agent sent at 11:08 am 5/1]**
"Were you able to get the information?" **[Nora sent at 12:00 pm 5/3]**
"What information?" **[Listing agent sent at 12:08 pm 5/3]**
"The utility information for 8352 Please Ct." **[Nora sent at 12:10 pm 5/3]**
"Yes, I thought that I emailed it to you. Sorry, I have been busy with my full-time job." **[Listing agent sent at 12:35 pm 5/3]**
"Ok. Please send it as soon as possible. I do not want my clients to be without service." **[Nora sent at 1:05 pm 5/3]**
"Sent." **[Listing agent sent at 1:07 pm 5/3]**
"Thank you." **[Nora sent at 1:09 pm 5/3]**

As an agent, there may be occasions where you find it difficult or challenging to communicate with a co-agent. However, it is essential to assess whether this difficulty is due to a communication issue or something else entirely.

As Nora Hill, the real estate agent, gracefully navigated the delicate dance of matchmaking in the world of real estate, she understood the profound similarities between finding a dream home and finding a perfect partner. With a keen eye for detail and an understanding of her clients' desires, Nora adeptly arranged the "matchmaking game" for The Johnsons, the eager buyers. Showing appointments become meaningful dates, where potential homes and hearts are explored. As the Johnsons found themselves smitten with a special property, Nora guided them through the offer process, translating it into a heartfelt commitment.

The ensuing contract-to-close period acts as an engagement, a time of excitement and anticipation before the final union. And when the day of closing arrived, Nora proudly officiated the metaphorical marriage between her clients and their ideal home. In the end, Nora's true joy lies not only in closing deals but in bringing together two parties destined for happiness. The ultimate goal, achieved with a touch of finesse and a dash of intuition, is the creation of a lifelong and harmonious union between a family and their perfect abode.

THINK BEYOND THE STORY

- What was the cost of this real estate transaction? emotional, physical, or financial?

- What would have happened if the agent could not have provided the correct LLC documents for ownership of the property?

CLOSING POINTS

- You should always call after sending an email. It is possible that your email went to spam or was not read in a timely manner.

- Obtain permit records by checking the city or county records. Especially, when a property has been recently renovated.

- As in case, find out how long the property has been owned (from tax records or from agent)

- Inform the agent that you will likely need two appraisals and there will be a longer appraisal contingency period needed.

- Despite your best-efforts, clients will always remember what went wrong with their home purchase rather than what went right.

3

ASSURANCE

"Real estate sales can put the squeeze on you."
ReShawna Leaven

R EAL ESTATE SALES ARE like a tourniquet's grip
Squeezing tight and taking you on a trip
The entire process can be so intense
With twists and turns, keeping one's nerves in suspense

So, take a deep breath and hold on tight
The end result will be worth the fight
When the end is near, and the sale is complete
The tourniquet will loosen, no pressure no defeat

Like a tourniquet, the sale can be a challenge
But with the right tools you can find a balance
But with patience and persistence, the sale will be earned
The agent will boast, "I negotiated the terms"

With a reward at the end, you've accomplished the goal
The tourniquet will finally loosen and release its strong hold

Emergencies can come in an instant without notice in real estate. It makes one feel like being in an emergency room as a patient hooked up to a monitoring system, but instead of checking for blood pressure and heartbeat vitals, it monitors the stats of customer service.

Your knowledge and the ability to juggle a variety of tasks on a day-to-day basis with this analogy include:

You hear the sounds of the hospital monitoring equipment

Beep. Do we have what we need?
Beep. Is this the correct document needed for closing?
Beep. When will the file be out of underwriting?
Beep. Is the appraisal going to come in under the listed price?
Beep. Why wasn't the verification of employment already completed?

The drips of the IV administers saline and other required fluids to clients.

Drip. You have found a home.
Drip. The home inspection came back without any significant issues.
Drip. The appraisal supports the sales price.
Drip. Both agents communicate effectively throughout the sale.

This is a comparison of hospital staff to real estate industry professionals during a real estate transaction:

- Intake Specialists are compared to **loan processors**

- Nurses are compared to **loan officers**

- Doctors are compared to **underwriters**

- Discharge specialists are compared to **title representatives**

Hospital Staff	In Real Estate	Comparison of Roles
Intake Specialists	Loan Processors	Intake specialists gather initial information and set the stage for further medical assessment, loan processors collect and organize the borrower's financial information, preparing it for evaluation. Both roles involve organizing and preparing initial information for further processing.
Nurses	Loan Officers	Nurses are key to patient care, monitoring their condition and administering treatments, much like loan officers who guide applicants through the loan process, providing advice and managing their application. Both have frontline roles that involve direct interaction and care (or service) for the individual.
Doctors	Underwriters	Doctors make diagnoses and determine treatment plans based on assessments, similar to how underwriters analyze loan applications to decide on approval or denial. Both roles require specialized knowledge to make critical decisions based on the information provided by the preceding roles.
Discharge Specialists	Title Representatives	Discharge specialists coordinate the patient's departure from the hospital, ensuring all necessary steps are completed, much like title representatives manage the finalization of the mortgage process, ensuring all legal and financial steps are properly executed for the closing of the loan.

When you're hit with a crisis and need to dash to the emergency room, you're swept off in an ambulance with sirens blaring "wee-woo, wee-woo," as you race towards the hospital. Similarly, in the real estate world, when your loan process hits a snag, it's like needing urgent medical attention. There are hazards aplenty lurking in the network of lender processes. As a buyer, you're thrust into this maze, trying to decode various requirements and procedures. Even when you feel you have completed everything that the loan company has asked for, you may find your documents being rejected by an underwriter.

In this chapter the dwelling type was wrong. These are the moments where the loan process feels like an ambulance ride – urgent, loud, and disorienting. Such hurdles not only delay your closing, but also add layers of frustration and inconvenience to your experience. Now this story places you in the emergency room in suite #102.

BEEP, BEEP...

At a crucial juncture in the mortgage process, a seemingly minor oversight by the loan officer set the stage for a significant setback. At a quick glance, the loan officer viewed the property's outward appearance from the MLS and classified it as a townhome in the loan package that was submitted to underwriting. This assumption, seemingly innocuous at first glance, was actually a critical misstep.

Townhomes and condos, while sometimes have an exterior similar in appearance, differ fundamentally in terms of ownership and structure, which directly impact the loan terms and requirements. A townhome typically suggests individual ownership of the structure and the land it sits on, whereas a condo implies ownership of the unit only, with common areas jointly owned by the condo association.

This misclassification had far-reaching implications. When the underwriting team delved into the details and discovered the discrepancy. The property was, in fact, a condominium, not a townhome. This revelation not only necessitated a re-evaluation of the loan terms, but also prompted a thorough review of the entire loan package. The differences in insurance requirements, ownership structure, and association bylaws between condos and townhomes meant that the initial loan assessment was no longer valid.

For the buyer, this error was not just a bureaucratic hiccup; it was a major obstacle. It delayed the approval process, as the underwriters had to reassess the loan's risk considering the condo's specific characteristics and association rules. For the loan officer, it was a stark reminder of the importance of attention to detail in real estate transactions. In the same way, this situation could be similar to lying in triage in suite #102, shivering with chills, battling an upset stomach, feeling an unusual tightness in your chest, and enduring a low temperature. Initially this situation may seem perplexing, but you are in an emergency room where sometimes they can be shorthanded.

So, you are seen by a physician's assistant who assesses your symptoms and concludes that you have a stomach virus based on your symptoms. However, upon further review and re-examination by the senior physician on duty who carefully reviews your chart and x-rays, a more serious diagnosis becomes known, you have pneumonia. This revelation shifts the course of your treatment, addressing a condition that had been masked by symptoms misleadingly similar to a less serious illness. This scenario in healthcare, much like in real estate, underscores the critical nature of an accurate assessment and the far-reaching implications that can arise from initial oversights.

As we continue this closing process, once the mistake was corrected with the building type (townhouse to condo) the buyer received a request to switch hazard insurance policy type from an HO3 policy to an HO6 policy. The buyer promptly complied, and the process appeared to be back on track. Both the buyer and their agent were under the impression that everything was moving smoothly. However, this sense of progress was short-lived.

BEEP, BEEP...

With the insurance coverage for the property now properly established and approved, there is another lender requirement for this property type. Our attention turned to obtaining the Certificate of Insurance. This document represents the insurance coverage for the dwelling and serves as the master insurance policy for the community within a planned unit development. Despite its significance, it's not commonly known to buyers. In this particular case, the buyer was responsible for obtaining the insurance certificate and updating it with their information, including their name, address of the new property, loan number, bank name, and address.

To facilitate these necessary changes, the buyer's agent needed to formally request updated policy documents from the master insurance agent. This was submitted, reviewed, and approved. Many lenders typically manage this process on the backend, leaving buyers and their agents unaware of the task's completion. The lender for this transaction who we will call "Lender X" placed the responsibility on the buyer and their agent to rectify the issue.

It can be tough preparing a buyer for the exhaustive list of demands that may arise. Agents try in most cases to take on that burden, but some tasks need to be completed by the client. While this part of the transaction may not unfold in the manner that most stories have unfolded, it serves as an indispensable guide through the transaction's complexities. Being cognizant of the various approval conditions can brace the client for things to come. The underwriter's nod is the final key to closing the loan.

The moment the deal finally closes, it ushers in a sensation of immense relief, much like the feeling of being released from an emergency room after an intense and uncertain ordeal. It's that liberating moment when the doctor gives the all-clear, and you step outside, the fresh air washing over you, easing the burden of worry that had been pressing down on your shoulders. The unending beeps, glaring lights, numerous tests, and analyses during the long ominous process in the hospital are now a thing of the past.

THINK BEYOND THE STORY

- What was the cost of this real estate transaction? emotional, physical, or financial?

- How can you educate your clients on this process?

CLOSING POINTS

- When it comes to insuring a new home purchase, it's crucial to understand the distinct types of insurance policies available to ensure the appropriate coverage is obtained. The first step is to determine whether the property is a townhome or a condominium, as this will dictate the type of policy required.

- If the property is a townhome, a TYPE HO6 policy is likely needed, while if it's a condominium with an association, an HO6 policy is required. An insurance professional should always be consulted for guidance.

- For townhomes and single-family homes, an HO1 policy is an owner-occupied insurance policy that covers only specific perils listed in the policy, such as fire, lightning, hail, windstorms, and theft. Additional riders, like flood and earthquake coverage, can be added as well.

- On the other hand, an HO6 policy is designed for co-ops and condominiums and covers interior damage, improvements, and personal property. It also provides liability coverage and specific coverage for improvements made to the unit. The condo association's policy typically covers the outside building structure and common areas like hallways. It's important to note that personal property is almost always included in an HO1 policy.

- Ask the lender – how much coverage is needed, what type of policy is needed, do they need flood insurance, etc.

4

FROM THE GROUND UP

"Closing a transaction is like hitting a hole in one."
ReShawna Leaven

GOLF AND REAL ESTATE share more in common than you might think. Both require a blend of finesse and persistence. Each golf course offers a distinct challenge with its unique layout and varying topography, much like the world of real estate, where a planned unit development can have a section of homes that look alike on the outside but have different floor plans and distinct characteristics on the inside.

In today's fast-paced society, where instant gratification is often the norm, patience becomes a rare but crucial virtue in both arenas. Golf teaches the art of waiting for the right moment to strike, mirroring the real estate process where haste often leads to less-than-ideal outcomes. Both of these entities demand the resilience to see things through to the end, despite the modern world's relentless pace.

As this story "tees" off, let's see if the Moore's can pull off the process of their new home build without feeling like they had to yell "fore!" They'll need a lot of patience to make it happen, and we are all waiting to see how it turns out.

Having previously chosen their ideal lot and home style, the couple was now faced with the daunting task of selecting the interior finishes for their future abode. This brings us to the pivotal 9th hole, also known as The Design Center, where the couple must navigate an array of choices to create the home of their dreams.

Our adventure unfolds in the design center, where Naomi and Levi Moore were busy crafting their dream home, piece by piece with the design center coordinator. Evelyn Winstead, their real estate agent, who had haphazardly guided them through the first part of the new home buying process (getting the contract ratified) was not able to make it. The design center process was not easy for the Moore's. They were in the "green area" with this part of the process. It was like starting a round of golf without your trusted caddy.

THE DESIGN CENTER - The 3rd Hole

The design center became a canvas of possibilities as the representative unfurled the floorplan, inviting Naomi and Levi on a journey through each room. It was a dance of decisions, from the heart of the kitchen to the soul of the living spaces, she showed them choices that connected seamlessly from room to room of their future home. In this plethora of choices, the air was thick with excitement as they made every selection.

Unbeknownst to the couple, another obstacle lay hidden like a sand trap. As Naomi and Levi, with their can-do attitude, kept moving forward with help from the Design Center Representative, took a deep dive into the blueprint of the home and kept picking out the suggestions of the designer. They chose the floors, kitchen cabinets, countertops, and all the other bits and pieces, thinking hard about each choice. Naomi, who was always practical and careful with the family's finances, made sure they picked options that were not only appealing to the eye but also not too pricey. At the conclusion of their session, the design center's representative reviewed the chosen options, informing Naomi and Levi that a brief pause was necessary. This was to let the software crunch numbers, adding up their selections while factoring in the builder's credit. The air was thick with suspense as Naomi and Levi brimmed with eager anticipation. Time seemed to crawl until, finally, the representative handed them the printout. She methodically went over each detail, unveiling the grand total. An additional deposit would be required if their customization selections exceeded the builder's initial budget allowance.

CONVERSATION – DESIGN CENTER

Naomi - *"I didn't realize that the options would cost so much."*
Levi - *"It's ok honey. We can do it."*
Design Center Rep - *"Wonderful! Now, all we need is 30% of the option amount that's over the builder credit."*
Naomi - *"Wow 30%. How much is that?"*
Design Center Rep - *"It will be $7,500.* The representative began breaking down the numbers for Naomi and Levi. *"Let's start with the total amount for the options you've selected from the Design Center, which comes to $40,000,"* she explained. She then pointed out the generous builder credit of $15,000. *"Now, if we subtract this credit from your total options, we get $25,000 as the amount remaining after the builder's credit."* She paused for a moment to ensure they were following along, then continued. *"We calculate a 30% option reserve fee on the remaining amount. So, we take 30% of $25,000, which gives us $7,500. That's the amount you'll need for the reserve."*

Total Amount in Options (Design Center)	$40,000
Builder options credit	$15,000
Total amount after deducting builder options credit	$25,000
30% Options Reserve ($25,000 x 30%)	**$7,500**

Levi - *"Thank you for explaining it in detail. I have my checkbook and I can write the check now."*

When a buyer is hit with unexpected fees it is kind of like a tough moment in a golf game. The player hits the ball down the green and a strong wind sends it off course. For Naomi and Levi, their first big test came with the surprise amount they had to pay at the design center.

NEW HOME ORIENTATION - The 9th Hole

Now, Naomi and Levi were approaching a pivotal moment in their home-building adventure, reminiscent of being half-way through a golf game – intense with anticipation. Up next was the pre-construction meeting, a major checkpoint. Here, they would rendezvous with the construction manager to revisit the choices made at the design center.

Evelyn was present at this meeting. She sat down with Naomi and Levi and the construction manager, with the addendum they'd signed in hand. But since Evelyn hadn't seen the color and finish samples herself, it was tough for her to really get into the details or help out much. As they combed through the options and floorplan, Naomi and Levi placed their initials on each page, a symbolic nod of approval to every detail. They felt a mix of nerves and excitement. They had to check every little thing and make sure it was all just right. Any little mistake could be a big deal. Everything appeared perfectly aligned to forge ahead with the construction.

Time flew, and after several months filled with anticipation, the permits were finally approved. Naomi and Levi drove by their future home every weekend during the building process . They watched its exterior gradually take shape, capturing these moments in photographs. Finally, the anticipated day had arrived – the "New Home Orientation" meeting.

CONVERSATION – NEW HOME ORIENTATION

Naomi - *"There are so many mistakes in this kitchen. This kitchen is all wrong. The cabinets, granite and appliance package are not what we selected."*

Construction Manager - *"Let me get the selection sheet. (After reviewing his notes, he noticed several mistakes) "You are correct, Mrs. Moore. I am sorry that the site crew made this error. I will have to see how quickly this can be resolved."*

Levi - *"Are we going to be able to close next week?"*

Construction Manager - *"Ummm....that's highly unlikely being that it's Thursday afternoon and your closing is on next Tuesday. Though, I will see what I can arrange and get back to you later today."*
Evelyn - *"I wouldn't advise you to close before the items have been completed. After closing, it's your home and you are signing off that you agree that the home has been delivered."*
Naomi - *"Thank you."* (Naomi was in deep thought about Evelyn's comment. *"You should have been over here checking our home during construction, and maybe this wouldn't have happened. Hmmm!"*)

Naomi and Levi continued to walk through the home with the construction manager and she started to feel a bit upset. Even with all the excitement, it was pretty clear that things weren't perfect yet. The construction manager didn't let that stop him, though. He kept showing Naomi and Levi how everything in the house worked and made sure all the other selections were what they had chosen. They went through the checklist together, writing down everything that still needed to be fixed before they could move in. As they went through each room, they put blue tape on spots that needed some extra work or fixing.

Then, right before closing, Evelyn, their agent, received some really sad news about one of her family members passing away. Even though she was grieving, she reached out to Naomi and Levi to say congratulations on their new home and let them know she couldn't be there in person for the final steps.

THE CLOSING - The 18th Hole

At the closing table, everyone could feel the tension, kind of like being in an out-of-bounds area in golf. Without Evelyn there, Naomi and Levi felt a bit lost and worried about what else might go wrong. While Levi and Naomi sat in the waiting area, their glances flickered between hope and apprehension, each look conveying a silent question about what unexpected twists might still lie ahead. The journey to this moment had been a taxing one.

The receptionist called them to the conference room. They sat down at the table with the closing agent. He asked them for the identification and asked them to choose a pen for signing. They began to go through the papers sheet by sheet. Then that got to the HUD-1 and Levi spoke up, his voice laced with irritation and disbelief, *"I can't believe she didn't tell us about these fees. It's just not right."* Naomi, ever the optimist, tried to offer a possible explanation, *"Maybe she didn't know?"* But Levi was not swayed, his frustration mounting with each passing moment, *"That's not an excuse. She should've asked, or the site agent should have said something. We're the ones paying for this, after all."* It felt like navigating a golf course littered with obstacles, but now, as they signed the final documents, a sense of relief had come over them. The game was over, and against all odds, they had made the hole-in-one.

Construction isn't always a smooth ride. Misplaced lighting fixtures, cabinets that don't quite fit right – these are just a few of the hiccups that can occur. Thankfully, these issues are generally fixable. Buyers place their trust in the skilled hands of professionals, counting on their expertise to turn blueprints into reality. After all, if clients were experts at building, they wouldn't need us and they'd probably be out scouting for a plot of land and building their dream homes single-handedly - but let's be real, that's easier said than done!

As a real estate agent, it's crucial to guide your clients through the entire process, including the design center meeting and the new home orientation. It's also essential to be upfront and give as much information as possible (be knowledgeable) about all the costs involved in building or buying a resale home, so there are no surprises or misunderstandings down the line.

By doing so, you can make sure that the entire process goes smoothly without unnecessary tension or stress. Remember when this process goes well it can mean referrals for years to come and a good name in the business. Just like in golf, when you prepare and strategize properly, you can make the perfect shot and achieve a hole in one.

THINK BEYOND THE STORY

- What was the cost of this real estate transaction? emotional, physical, or financial?

- What could the agent have done differently throughout the process?

CLOSING POINTS

- The buyer's agent should go over some of the customary fees associated with a new home build. These may be different from purchasing a resale. (i.e., earnest money deposit, design center fees, closing cost).

- Rely on the site agent to give as many details as possible. Every community is different.

- Explain flexibility and adaptability to keep the stress down during the process

- Clients rely on the knowledge and experience of real estate professionals during the home buying process. Be present as much as possible. Careful examination of all elements, from design choices to contractual agreements, is essential.

- Buying or building a home is not just a financial transaction but an emotional journey.

5

FIRST TIME FOR EVERYTHING

*"Like a bowler aiming for the perfect strike,
success comes to those who align their strategies with
precision on their chosen lane of opportunity."*
ReShawna Leaven

THE REAL ESTATE MARKET operates much like the sport of bowling, where the objective is to achieve a **strike** with each new client and again when the transaction is successfully closed. The ultimate goal is to attain a **perfect game**, which involves completing the sale with satisfied clients who will also provide referrals. However, occasional missteps may occur, similar to a **gutter ball**, which could result from agents procrastinating or lacking relevant knowledge. When these setbacks happen, it's crucial to find a solution to save the transaction and secure a **spare**. In order to succeed in this field, it's important to adhere to ethical practices and avoid **fouls,** such as stepping on other agents' toes or mishandling important documents. Success in real estate requires a hefty investment, much like the weight of a bowling ball. When all industry professionals work harmoniously together, success is virtually guaranteed, and every agent is constantly striving for a STRIKE.

Like a bowler who encounters a gutter ball, real estate transactions can sometimes encounter setbacks. Unfortunately, the weight of the challenges can sometimes result in many gutter balls, which could be avoided if the agent possesses the skills to score a strike. Jaime Lee encountered numerous obstacles and struggled to keep all ten pins in play, leading to missed opportunities due to her lack of expertise.

As the days swiftly passed by and the clock ticked, she found herself stuck in a limbo. It had been a daunting 60 days since obtaining her real estate license, and prospects for a transaction seemed bleak. Despite being aware that it typically takes a minimum of 90 days to complete a sale from start to finish, she had mistakenly assumed that potential clients would be lining up to discuss real estate with her. However, she soon realized that building a successful business requires time and effort. She had to take the initiative to make phone calls, a process that she despised but had to do in order to succeed in the industry.

Even if she were to acquire a client at that moment, it would take a total of five months before she could expect any real estate income. To expedite the process, she placed an ad on a free online classified website, and after a two-week wait, she finally managed to secure her first buyer client. Recognizing that knowledge was key, she worked diligently to prepare for her upcoming business. She attended seminars, read books, and shadowed other agents in her office to gain valuable insights, demonstrating her unwavering determination to succeed in the real estate industry.

Jamie's enthusiasm and honesty earned her the trust of her first real estate buyer client, who sought an agent willing to go the extra mile. Her diligence paid off when her client's offer was accepted, but the next challenge was the home inspection. Without a ready list of inspectors, she had to turn to the Yellow Pages, a once-popular phone directory that listed businesses by category with their name and phone number. In today's digital age, there are plenty of websites and resources for finding reputable inspectors.

After contacting several companies, she finally secured an inspector who was available to accommodate the contract deadline and her client's schedule. Unfortunately, the chosen inspector lacked the latest technological advancements for the inspection and the report. Nonetheless, they completed the inspection within the timeframe, albeit at the last minute, leading to mounting anxiety, like pressure to obtain a diamond. As philosopher Thomas Carlyle stated, *"No pressure, no diamonds."*

INSPECTION DAY

Starting off on the wrong foot, the inspector arrived 45 minutes late, courtesy of a faulty portable navigation system, traffic, and poor planning. In the days before cell phones with navigation app, printouts were the go-to solutions. Nevertheless, during her visit, the inspector provided valuable insights and education to her clients about their home's functions and offered some useful tips.

With just one day left before the deadline, the inspector called David to inform him that the report was completed.

Inspector - *"Hi David, the report is complete."*
Jaime - *"Ok great, do you have my email address to send it to?"*
Inspector - *"I can't email it. It's on carbon paper. I can meet you somewhere to give it to you."*
Jaime - *"Wow, really! I thought the report would be available by email. Where can I meet you today? The home inspection report is due tomorrow to the seller.*
Inspector - *"I can meet you before my next appointment. I have the report in my briefcase. I will be at an appointment about 15 miles away from the property that I inspected for you. There is a coffee shop near there. Let's meet at 1:00 pm."*
Jamie - *"Ok. I will see you there. I will have to leave now in order to make it on time. Thank you."*

With haste, Jamie departed, determined to ensure the report's timely delivery. Jamie met the inspector at the local coffee shop a few minutes before 1:00 pm and he presented her with the written carbon copy with white, yellow, and pink sheets. He removed the yellow sheet to keep a copy for himself and gave her the remaining sheets and a SD card with the digital photos. She said "Thank you" to the inspector and on her way she went. It took a total of over an hour to get back to her office as she was in the boondocks. When she arrived back at her office, she looked at the report. She discovered that the inspector's handwriting was not legible. It was similar to that of a doctor's prescription note, which cause confusion during the interpretation process. *"How am I supposed to read this? Is this a home inspection report or a medical prescription?"* As a result, she had to decipher the report through several phone calls with the inspector (in between his inspections). Although the report identified a few minor issues and safety concerns, it was essential to address them appropriately to satisfy the buyer's expectations.

GUTTERBALL #1 - NEGOTIATIONS AFTER INSPECTION

Following an in-depth discussion with her clients regarding the inspection report, Jaime Lee sent an addendum for her clients to sign electronically. The addendum listed twenty requested home inspection repair items that the seller could either repair or replace. Jaime sent the addendum to the listing agent for the seller's review, along with a request for their acceptance of the items or counter with an alternative.

As expected, the sellers provided a counter option instead of making repairs. Instead of repairing any items in the home, the sellers opted to provide a credit of $10,000 towards closing costs. The listing agent created an addendum with the following verbiage that read, "[seller to credit the buyer $10,000 in lieu of repairs towards closing costs]." The buyers agreed to the seller's terms and all parties involved signed and sent the addendum to the lender for processing.

GUTTERBALL #2 - UNDERWRITING

A week later, the underwriter returned with a request for a copy of the home inspection report because of the closing cost credit addendum's verbiage **"in lieu of repairs."** This led to a text message exchange between the listing agent and the buyer's agent, about the new developments. A new addendum would need to be executed removing the closing cost credit and the seller to repair the safety issues on the home inspection report.

In the real estate industry, printed words carry significant weight, particularly when they are printed on a real estate contract or addendum signed by all parties. Therefore, one should be careful about overstating information in an addendum that is being sent to all parties. One should not attempt to bowl in non-bowling shoes, like Jaime did, but instead, use the shoes that are meant for bowling and the strategies to win the game. In real estate, your broker is an essential part of the team, who is responsible for the decisions of the agents in the company. The best approach would be to ask one's broker, "What's the best way to proceed with this issue?"

PHONE CALL
(With David Martin - Listing Agent / Frank & Deborah - Sellers)

Phone rings.

Frank - *"Hi . Frank here."*
David - *"Hi Frank. I have an important update for you and Deborah to share. Is she available?"*
Frank - *"Yes, Deborah is here."*
David - *"Ok, great. Well... the buyer's lender informed me that there is now a condition that must be met before closing can take place. The closing cost credit that you provided to the buyers cannot be used for their closing cost anymore. The lender requested a copy of the home inspection report and wants several items fixed."*
Deborah - *"What? Are you serious, ? We agreed on the closing cost credit because we couldn't afford to make those repairs. Weren't you the one who drafted the addendum for us to sign?*
David - *"I understand your frustration. Yes, I did create the addendum but the wording "in lieu of repairs" is the verbiage that was flagged by the underwriting department."*
Frank - *"Wait a minute, . I can't believe that no one caught this issue prior to this point.*

David - *"I apologize for the oversight, Frank. It was not my intention to create such a challenge. I have never had an addendum get returned with this condition so I did not think that it would be a problem."*
Deborah -*"This is really frustrating, . We were relying on that closing cost credit to cover the repairs, and now we're being told we have to do them ourselves. This is putting us in a tough financial position."*
David - *"I understand the impact this has on you both, and I'm terribly sorry for any distress caused by my error. Let's focus on finding a solution together. One option would be to fix the repairs that the lender is requesting prior to closing. Another feasible option would be to see if the lender will allow the closing cost credit of $10,000 to be escrowed and the buyer will be responsible for getting the repairs completed after they close on the home. I will have to confirm that this escrow option is viable. If those options are not viable, then a mutual release from the contract would be needed."*
Frank - *"We appreciate your willingness to fix this, , but we're still really frustrated."*
Deborah - *"We really need your support in navigating this issue. Please keep us informed and let us know if the escrow option will work."*
- *"Absolutely, Deborah. I'm committed to assisting you both throughout this process and finding a fair solution. I'll be in touch with updates as soon as possible. Once again, I apologize for any distress caused, and I appreciate your understanding and patience."*

IF WALLS COULD TALK CONVERSATION
(Between the sellers Frank and Deborah Banks)

Frank - *"Deborah, can you believe this mess? Now, we have to do repairs. I am so tired of this house"*.
Deborah - *"I know, Frank. This is CRAZY! So, we can't make any major plans now. I know you wanted to plan a cruise for our anniversary but now, we have to deal with this"*.
Frank - *"Yeah, I was ready for the cruise and to move to our new place, but this will be a big setback. My dad has a general contractor that owes him a favor that we may be able to use and pay him back after closing"*.
Deborah - *"Oh, yes Barry. I forgot about him. He should be able to fix*

the repairs on the list the lender gave us in no time".
Frank - *"But I still feel that we should get some recourse now that this is an issue?"*
Deborah - *"What do you mean recourse? From whom?"*
Frank -*"From . Can't he refund us some of his commission for this?"*
Deborah - *"Not sure. How much do you think we should ask for?"*
Frank - *"At least half".*
Deborah - *"Wow! $5,000. He wouldn't go for that".*
Frank - *"It's better than him losing the deal. We could easily say that we don't want to sell, get a release, and sell it ourselves".*
Deborah - *"You said a mouthful Frank. Send an email and request that as well".*

Frank composed an email to their listing agent, outlining their decision to proceed with the necessary repairs. However, they had two conditions in order to move forward. The first condition was a request for a two-week extension on the closing date. The second condition was that the listing agent provide a portion of his commission, specifically $5,000, to assist with the financial burden of the repairs.

Immediately, swiftly composed an email to his broker, seeking approval for the broker credit request. Thankfully, he was able to get a <u>spare</u>, the broker agreed without hesitation and promptly sent a broker letter confirming that $5,000 of the commission would be credited to the sellers at the time of closing. David felt relieved and satisfied with this resolution, considering it to be fair given the circumstances. As soon as he received the broker credit letter, he forwarded it to the title company for processing.

Following this successful development, David reached out to Jamie, providing all the necessary updates. He informed Jamie that the contract had to be extended and the home repairs would be made. The deal was going to be saved and go to closing. Jamie was relieved that her first deal was saved.

SOLUTION TO AVOID GUTTERBALL #2

Stating that the buyer will receive a credit in lieu of repairs will immediately alert the lender that there may be something wrong with the property. To avoid such a situation, Jaime could have re-drafted the addendum by stating, "(Seller will credit the buyer in the amount of $10,000 towards closing costs)."

When conducting home inspections, it's critical to be aware of common items that repeatedly arise. Such items include the absence of carbon dioxide detectors (if the house has gas), missing smoke detectors in the bedrooms, painted outlets (necessitating new outlets), painted windows that are non-operational (necessitating new windows), missing window screens, and the need for HVAC system maintenance. In this story, the buyers were overwhelmed with over eighty items on the inspection report, but it's not the number that counts; it's what was discovered. Typically, an inspection report includes a summary page, sections on the interior and exterior of the house, and recommendations.

In the game of real estate, just like bowling, it is important to focus on knocking down all ten pins without any gutter balls. By taking the time to re-draft the addendum and being knowledgeable about common inspection items, Jaime could have avoided potential pitfalls in the transaction. Just like a bowler who relies on their team and coach to improve their game, a real estate agent must rely on their broker and industry colleagues to excel in their profession.

THINK BEYOND THE STORY

- What was the cost of this real estate transaction? emotional, physical, or financial?

- Should David have asked his broker to review the addendum before her clients signed?

CLOSING POINTS

- Representing a first-time buyer can be challenging because they are unfamiliar with the process. It is crucial to educate clients on what to expect and the next steps involved. While some inspections may uncover problems, it is essential to determine whether they are significant enough to warrant walking away from the deal if the seller refuses to make the necessary repairs.

- Inform buyers of how credits work at closing. Make sure if you are requesting a closing cost credit in your negotiations, make sure you are not maxed out on all buyers' allowable credits.

- It is always important to be aware of the correct verbiage in all parts of the transaction, especially with addendums/and or amendments. Seek advice from the broker in charge.

- Don't assume that the same way you have been doing business is always the correct way in every transaction.

- Ask the inspector about their technology.

  - Do they have an infrared camera to check for moisture behind the walls?

  - Is the report typed and sent in an electronic format?

  - How soon will the report be completed after the

inspection?

- Will it only be one inspector or are there more than one inspector for the inspection?

- Do you complete any additional inspections other than the standard home inspection?

- What type of technology do you use in your business?

6

EQUATIONS

"Real estate is an equation with many variables."
ReShawna Leaven

NAVIGATING REAL ESTATE IS far from a straightforward algebraic equation, where A multiplied by B equals C. Instead, it often mirrors the complexities found in trigonometry, replete with numerous equations and intricate theorems. Overcoming the hurdles inherent in a real estate transaction is rarely a straightforward task. It demands adept critical thinking skills, like unraveling a convoluted equation that necessitates multiple steps, some of which may not immediately reveal the most apparent solution. This story compares to the complexities of a complex math equation that needed to be solved. This condo had a myriad of numerical variables that came into play during the transaction. While this is not a geometry lesson, the story will engage the logical side of your brain as you embark to solve the equations embedded within this scenario.

Edward Underwood's phone rang one day, a response to one of the many online marketing strategies he had employed. The caller expressed interest in selling a condo. He scheduled a listing appointment right away. Before the appointment he conducted extensive research on the surrounding neighborhood to identify comparable sales. This property was located in a highly coveted area of the city that attracted buyers quickly because it was located within walking distance to small shops, restaurants, and the city's mass transit system. After the initial appointment he was able to snag the listing and before long, it was under contract. The process now entered the realm of multiple moving parts, including inspections, obtaining condominium resale documents, and conducting an appraisal.

FIRST EQUATION ...

Sales Price < Appraised Value = Solution

Edward took on a challenge when listing this property for sale. The owner wanted to list the property above supporting comparables in the area at an asking price of $200,000. However, after the property went under contract, Edward needed to have an honest conversation with his client, warning him that the likelihood of the property appraising at the inflated sales price was slim. Edward had already conducted an analysis of the property's condition, taking into account the outdated formica countertops and worn carpet. Unfortunately, his initial recommendations had not been heeded, and now he had to explain the reality of the situation to the client.

EMAIL (From Lender to Listing and Buyer's Agent)

From: 123 Mortgage Co./To: Edward Underwood, Ivy Roberts
Subject: Appraisal for 234 Main Street

I hope this email finds you well. I am writing to inform you of an important update regarding the appraisal for the property located at 234 Main Street. Regrettably, the appraisal report does not support the current sales price. The appraised value of the property has been determined to be $189,500, while the agreed-upon sales price stands at $200,000.

In order for the transaction to proceed, we kindly request that you provide an addendum indicating a change in the sales price, duly signed by both the buyer and the seller. Alternatively, the buyer will need to cover the difference in the sales price to meet the appraised value. To support this new condition, the appraisal report has been attached for your review.

Thank you for your attention to this matter. Should you have any questions or require further clarification, please do not hesitate to reach out to us.

Best Regards,
Sara Smith, Senior Underwriter
123 Mortgage Co

Possible solutions for the deficiency amount

- Buyer pays the deficiency amount

- Buyer and seller split the deficiency amount

- Seller lowers price to appraised value

SOLUTIONS	BUYER	SELLER
1	PAYS OVER THE APPRAISED VALUE BY $11,000	SELLER KEEPS THE PRICE AT $200,000
2	PAYS OVER THE APPRAISED VALUE BY $5,500	SELLER LOWERS PRICE TO $194,500
3	PAYS THE APPRAISED VALUE	SELLER LOWERS PRICE TO $189,500

PHONE CALL

(Edward Underwood – Listing Agent and James Yancey – Seller)

Edward - *"Hi James. It's Edward. How is your Thursday going?"*

James - *"Hi Edward. All is well. Is the appraisal back yet?"*

Edward - *"Yes, James. The appraisal is in and that's the reason for my call. The appraisal came in at $189,500."*

James - *"Wow! That's almost an $11,000 difference. What do we do now?"*

Edward - *"One option is to lower the price to the appraised value. The second option is to start over again with a new buyer, but with the comparables it's not likely that it will be sold at the current listing amount of $200,000."*

James - *"So, is the buyer unwilling to come up with the difference in price?"*

Edward - *"I spoke to their agent already and unfortunately; they are not willing or able to at this time."*

James - *"Ok. I'm ok with lowering the price. I need to get this home sold as soon as possible."* (Unbeknownst to Edward, James was behind on his mortgage 60 days)

Edward - *"Great, I will send you the new sales price addendum to sign."*

James - *"That works for me. I just want to get this sold, so that I can move on."*

After having a frank discussion with his client, Edward promptly drafted an addendum reflecting the new sales price and presented it to both the buyer and seller for signature. Once the addendum was signed by both parties, Ivy, the buyer's agent, took the initiative to send the revised document to all relevant parties involved in the transaction.

FIRST EQUATION... solved

Condominiums require a resale package (sometimes called "condo docs" in slang terms) to be given to the buyers so that they are informed about property restrictions. This package is an essential tool to inform potential buyers of the property restrictions and other critical information they need to know before making their purchase decision. Typically, the seller pays for and orders the resale package, which contains up-to-date financials, meeting minutes, articles of incorporation, and details about monthly dues, special assessments, community violations, and any other items associated with the property.

Edward, being a seasoned real estate professional, understood the importance of the resale package and promptly ordered one for his client's condominium. He sent the package to the buyer's agent, which had no community violations or pending lawsuits, thus satisfying one aspect of the equation. However, unknown to Edward, there was dark cloud just about to move in the area, adding another layer of complexity to the already intricate transaction.

SECOND EQUATION...

Condo Questionaire ≠ Lender Guidelines = Solution

The condo questionnaire or sometimes called a lender questionnaire is a crucial document that provides a comprehensive analysis of the stability and financial health of the condominium complex. It's used by lenders to evaluate the lending potential of the property being sold. In this particular case, the condo questionnaire was received by the lender and sent to underwriting for a detailed review. The information provided would be evaluated by this department to determine the viability of the condo development and whether to proceed with funding or deny the loan request.

The underwriting department scrutinized the questionnaire and made detailed notes on the findings. It's crucial to pay attention to these details, as any issues may lead to the denial of the loan application, and the transaction may fall through. Let's summarize what the underwriter noted below:

- The reserve funds were found to be extremely low, which is a cause for concern as it indicates insufficient funds for necessary repairs and maintenance.

- Additionally, the ratio of investors to owner-occupied dwellings was not balanced, with 52% of the units being owned by investors and only 48% by owner-occupiers.

- Finally, the community had a high delinquency rate of 22% on their monthly dues, meaning that a significant number of owners were not paying their homeowner association dues in a timely fashion and were 30 days or more delinquent. All these factors could pose significant risks for the lender and affect the loan approval.

LENDER QUESTIONNAIRE

Description	Questionnaire Results	Underwriter Analysis	Results
Pending Litigation	No	OK	PASS
Reserve Funds	$40,000	(Should be $200,000 for community)	FAIL
Condo Dues Delinquency Rate	22% - 30 days late on condo dues	Above the lender's maximum requirement of 15%	FAIL
Owner/Investor Ratio	52% investors and 48% owners	Investor ratio to high	FAIL
Master Insurance Policy	$2,000,000 policy	OK	PASS

A review of this information was relayed to the selling agent from the buyer's agent in an email.

EMAIL (From Buyer's Agent to Listing Agent)

FROM: Ivy Roberts /TO: Edward Underwood
SUBJECT: Loan Denial for 1234 Main Street

Dear Edward,

I hope this email finds you well. I regret to inform you that, after careful review, the underwriter has made the decision to deny the loan for the property located at 1234 Main Street. This decision is based on the information obtained from the condo questionnaire. The following factors contributed to the loan denial:

Investor/Owner Ratios: The investor/owner ratios provided in the condo questionnaire did not meet our lending criteria.

Delinquency Rates of Condo Payments: The delinquency rates of condo payments within the community exceeded the acceptable limit set by our lending institution.

Low Reserve Funds: The reserve funds maintained by the community were deemed insufficient to meet our requirements.

In light of this decision, please find attached the denial letter and an addendum to release the contract. I apologize for any inconvenience caused by this outcome. Sometimes, certain factors are beyond our control, and we must adhere to strict lending guidelines.

Sincerely,

Ivy Roberts

99 Homes Sold Realty

attachment <<letter.pdf>>

SECOND EQUATION ... not solved.

FINAL EQUATION...

Condo Questionaire ≠ *NO SALE*

The transaction came to an end as the equation was unable to be solved. The seller made the difficult decision to terminate their listing agreement. To complete the termination process, Edward drafted and sent a listing termination form to his client and broker for signatures. As the assigned agent for the listing, Edward had played an integral role in marketing the property and advising his client throughout the process with no sale at the end.

Several months later, while conducting research for another client, Edward stumbled upon the address of his old listing in the MLS. Initially feeling upset, he clicked on the listing and discovered that the property was now an REO (real estate owned) being sold by the bank. Unfortunately, the condo had gone into foreclosure just two months after the termination of the listing agreement. Edward has mixed emotions about this transaction and his former client.

Thus, as this narrative draws to a close, the individuals involved had to realize that despite the experience and accumulated knowledge of the industry, the outcome can still yield negative results.

This transaction somewhat resembles an irregular quadrilateral, all sides not equal in this case. Sometimes there are unwitting variables needed to solve those sides that have information.

THINK BEYOND THE STORY

- What was the cost of this real estate transaction? emotional, physical, or financial?

- Could Edward have helped his client avoid a foreclosure sale?

CLOSING POINTS

- In a condominium transaction the seller pays and provides the resale package, but it's important to inform your buyers that the lender will require a condo questionnaire that the buyer must pay for. The fee is typically between $250 - $350.

- Condo appraisals and questionnaires are the biggest deal killers whether you are representing a buyer or seller.

7

THE HEIRS "AIR" THEIR DIRTY LAUNDRY

"Get your affairs in order."
ReShawna Leaven

CLARE, AN ACCOMPLISHED AGENT affiliated with the prestigious WWW Real Estate Firm, enjoyed a long-standing friendship with the Williamson family. This esteemed family unit was composed of six boys and four girls. It was with a heavy heart that Clare learned of their mother's passing, after having battled a lengthy and debilitating illness. Without hesitation, Clare made arrangements to attend the funeral and extend a comforting hand to the bereaved family. She knew all too well the challenges that lay ahead, as grief and sorrow set in after the loss of the matriarch of a family.

This family was also known to have a chaotic colorful relationship with one another as families of this size often do. She put on her seatbelt because she knew that the journey in this aftermath would ultimately be riddled with trying to get everyone on the same page with final wishes. Clare remained steadfast in her resolve to guide the Williamson family through the difficult period and help them get their affairs in order.

Since there was no will in place, the ownership of the family home would now pass to the surviving children as per the laws of the residing state. This means the demise of a person without a valid will (intestate) results in joint inheritance of property and possessions by the heirs. The probate process, which is a legal procedure for settling the estate of the deceased, typically takes around 60 days for ownership to transfer. Upon learning of this situation, Clare generously offered to assist the Williamson family with exploring viable options for overseeing their inherited property. In light of the options presented by Clare during a family meeting, the siblings collectively decided to sell the family home and equitably distribute the proceeds amongst themselves.

By operation of law, the residence located at 12302 Main Street, belonged to the ten heirs of the Williamson family, namely James, Paul, Henry, Ronald, Earl, Clarence Jr., Patrice, Sharon, Vera, and Renee. However, since some of the heirs did not reside in the local area, it was necessary to nominate a family representative to oversee the selling process. Following a collective deliberation, the siblings concurred that Vera, who lived in close proximity, would be the ideal candidate to assume Specific Power of Attorney and manage the sale proceedings.

Clare conducted a comprehensive and thorough competitive market analysis (current market conditions and recent sales of comparable properties in the area) along with the home's physical features, including its size, age, and location. She evaluated the current condition of the home, taking into consideration any necessary repairs, renovations, and maintenance to provide a detailed and accurate assessment. Clare's assessment was grounded in her deep understanding of the real estate industry and her ability to use data-driven insights to determine the optimal listing price for the property.

Let us delve into the pertinent facts regarding this property:

- Built in 1968

- This split-level home comprises 4 bedrooms and 1 ½ bathrooms. The number of bathrooms makes this property obsolete in today's market.

- The property had a considerable amount of deferred maintenance and was in need of repair (old gutters, power wash, faucets, etc.)

- It was listed and sold in "as-is" condition.

- Based on the current condition and no new upgrades, the market value for this property was estimated in a range between $165,000 to $172,000

- The siblings reached a unanimous decision to list the property at a price point of $165,000.

Prior to the listing of the property, it was necessary to declutter the home and prepare it for sale. Working in tandem, Clare (the listing agent) and Vera (Williamson sibling) jointly undertook the arduous task of sorting through the items in the house, categorizing them into distinct groups such as keep, donate, or sell. To ensure that the home was primed for sale, they enlisted the services of a team of contractors, composed of a junk removal company, an estate sale company, as well as a skilled handyman. Following a comprehensive preparation process, the property was finally ready to be listed on the market. After several weeks of extensive showings and rounds of negotiations, the property received a compelling offer and was promptly put under contract. On the surface, it seemed that the transaction was proceeding seamlessly. Upon ordering the title for the property, a few issues came to light.

PHONE CALL
(With Title Company and Listing Agent)

Rachel - *"Hello, Clare. This is Rachel calling from 123 Title."*
Clare - *"Hi Rachel. I trust everything is proceeding well."*
Rachel - *"Well...I have some information that I need to convey to you. Do you have a moment to discuss it?"*
Clare - *"Certainly, Rachel. What's happening?"*
Rachel - *"We have received the title report, and it seems that there are some outstanding issues that must be addressed. As this is an inherited*

property, it's possible for liens held by any of the heirs to be attached to the property. After conducting research on each of the heirs, we've discovered that a few of them have outstanding liens. I'm uncertain if there will be enough proceeds to pay off all the creditors and make the deal viable. I'll send the report to you for review."

Clare *- "That's quite surprising. I've never encountered a situation where liens could be attached to an inherited property from the heirs themselves."*

Rachel *- "Unfortunately, creditors are always eager to recoup their funds, and if they discover that there is real estate involved, they may attach liens to the title. I'm hopeful that we can come to a resolution and complete the transaction. I'll send over the report promptly."*

---

123 Title Company

1234 Title Way | Suite 123

Anywhere, USA

Title Officer: Rachel Holland
Escrow Officer: Nicole McLean
Escrow No.: **11-25421**-NK
Property Address: 12302 Main Street, Anywhere, USA
Effective Date: March 2, 1998, 8:30 a.m.

The following are the requirements that must be met.

Purchase Money Mortgage	First Trust: $105,000
Mechanic's lien	Roof replacement $2,500.00
IRS lien	Sister #1 - $1,200.00
Judgment Lien	Son #1 - $50,000.00
Judgment Lien	Son #2 - $20,000.00
Judgment Lien	Son #3 - $5,265.00

Rachel Holland
Title Officer

It was discovered that the heirs of the property, namely James, Paul, and Henry, were facing outstanding debt of a combined amount of $75,265 that needed to be settled. Renee was found to have an outstanding tax lien of $1,200 from the IRS, and an additional mechanic's lien of $2,500 was also discovered for a roof job that had been completed two years prior. With these new expenses, in addition to real estate brokerage commissions and closing costs, the grand total owed was a staggering $88,865.

Upon conducting thorough research and validation of each lien attached to the property, it was discovered that all liens were legitimate and needed to be paid. The total amount exceeded the expected proceeds from the sale of the property, and therefore posed a significant obstacle in making the deal work and providing clear title to the buyer. It was unfortunate that Vera's brothers' past skeletons had resulted in a situation where the amount of the debt exceeded what was possible to make the sale a reality.

Unfortunately, due to the multiple liens and debts owed by the heirs, the transaction had to be canceled. The Williamson family's property went into foreclosure due to the circumstances that were discovered. The news of the failed transaction and foreclosure was heart-wrenching for the family. The property was more than just a house; it symbolized their parents' memories, hard work, and the beginning of their family's legacy.

Despite Clare's best efforts, there wasn't anything that she could have done to assist with this transaction. As a seasoned real estate agent, Clare invested a significant amount of time and effort into the probate home sale. When she learned that the sale would not be able to proceed, Clare likely felt a range of emotions, including frustration and disappointment. She may have also felt a sense of responsibility for not identifying the issues earlier. Despite the unfavorable outcome, Clare learned important lessons about the importance of due diligence and research when working on probate home sales, and the need for a thorough understanding of all components involved.

THINK BEYOND THE STORY

- What was the cost of this real estate transaction? emotional, physical, or financial?

- How could the agent have managed things differently?

CLOSING POINTS

- Build a relationship with a title company or abstract company to check the land records on liens before you list a transaction

- To achieve success in probate home sales, it is crucial to have a deep understanding of the various components involved, including legal and financial matters. This is a specialized area that requires extra knowledge and skills, and it is recommended to take additional Continuing Education (CE) courses to stay up to date on this area of sales. By acquiring the necessary expertise, a real estate agent will be well-equipped to provide the highest quality of service to their clients and navigate any potential challenges that may arise.

- It is essential to have a "will" in place to avoid complications and confusion regarding the transfer of property and assets after someone's passing.

- Inherited properties can have hidden debts and liens attached to them, which can become a hurdle in the sale process.

8

A GUT FEELING

"Trusting your intuition is one of your greatest assets."
ReShawna Leaven

I N A WORLD WHERE logic and rationality are often prized over emotions and feelings, the concept of "intuition," as defined by the Oxford Dictionary means (a thing that one knows or considers likely from a feeling) serves as a powerful reminder of the importance of listening to our instincts. With the potential to be a lifesaving asset, possessing an intuitive nature is an invaluable trait to possess. Staying attuned to our environment through heightened awareness is an excellent way to harness our intuition. The compelling story illustrates and highlights the connection between having the knowledge to think about a situation and acting on it based on a gut feeling.

On a balmy September afternoon, Shelly Roberson was engrossed in updating her real estate website in her home office when an email pop-up notification gave an alert of a new lead. The email included the individual's name, address, phone number, and email address, along with a request for a list of homes priced between $700,000 and $750,000. As a recently licensed real estate agent, this lead elicited euphoria, with thoughts of the potential commission that she could possibly earn. Drawing upon knowledge gleaned from the rigorous real estate training sessions and seminars that she had attended; Shelly instinctively dialed the lead's number within the first five minutes of receiving the notification.

PHONE CALL
(With Shelly – Buyer's Agent and Robert – Potential Client)

Shelly - *"Hi, is this Robert James?"*
Robert - *"Yes, this is Robert."*
Shelly - *"This is Shelly Roberson from Intuition Real Estate. I wanted to thank you for signing up on my website to view homes."*
Robert - *"Yes, I am looking to buy a home. I want to find something near the courthouse as I am an attorney."*
Shelly - *"Great. When would you like to purchase your home?"*
Robert - *"I'm looking to move in the next 60 days. I have a new court case that I am working on that will dominate my time in the next couple of weeks. When can we schedule a meeting to view homes? I have a list of homes that I want to see. Also, I don't need financing as I will be a cash buyer."* Shelly and Robert had a few additional words and the call ended.

Upon concluding the call with Robert, Shelly's mind raced with the potential implications of securing the sale. *"This could be a game-changing moment for me,"* she pondered, *"a commission of $14,000, which is the most significant amount I have ever made in my life at one time!"* Shortly thereafter, Robert sent Shelly a detailed list of criteria that he would like for his new home, specifically requesting four bedrooms, two to three bathrooms, and a living space of 3,500-4,000 square feet. Shelly realized that since Robert was a cash buyer with a pressing need for a quick move-in, finding a vacant property would be ideal, as it would eliminate the hassle of negotiating with a seller for a smooth transition out of the home.

That night as Shelley lay in bed, a passing Nor'easter rudely disrupted her slumber. Unable to fall back to sleep, she turned to her trusted ally, the internet, to pass the time. Being inherently inquisitive, Shelly's natural instinct was to research anything that caught her attention with rigor and great detail. Despite her excitement about the new business opportunity that had seemingly "fallen into her lap," a seed of skepticism had taken root in her mind, causing her to question the situation further.

She typed the name of her new customer, *"Robert James"* with the words *"attorney and lawyer"* into the search bar along with different word queries (bar association, Robert James attorney at law). This led her to several webpages, but there was no connection to her new customer. She thought to herself, *"hmmm, maybe I will type in this query - sex offender, crime solvers..."* To her dismay, the page she landed on revealed a shocking truth about her potential client - a mugshot of someone with the name Robert James III with the address and information he had emailed her had an accusation of a violent sex offender with a pending trial date. Her heart skipped a beat as she realized the gravity of the situation. Robert had been truthful about his upcoming court case, but he wasn't an attorney - he needed one urgently.

Upon uncovering this disturbing information, Shelly promptly consulted with her brokerage firm and was provided with crucial safety recommendations. Consequently, she opted not to schedule any property visits with Robert James III. Despite his insistent attempts to contact her via various platforms such as emails, phone calls, and even text messages. Shelly remained firm in her decision to maintain distance. Although this particular story concluded with a positive outcome for this real estate agent, there have been numerous others across the county that have culminated in tragedy.

In the realm of real estate, every prospective buyer is considered a mere customer without a signed buyer agency agreement in place. It is only after a buyer signs such an agreement, which outlines the obligations and responsibilities of both the buyer and the agent, that they are elevated to the status of a client. Unfortunately, in the haste to avoid losing a potential buyer to a competitor, some agents may disregard the need for such an agreement and hastily proceed with showing properties. However, it is crucial to always adhere to established protocols, not only to safeguard personal safety but also to maintain a level of professionalism in the long run. Trusting one's intuition is vital in this line of work, as this story demonstrated, ignoring your intuition can lead to unfavorable outcomes. It's ok to put on your detective hat like Sherlock Holmes if you feel something is not right. The story will end with this quote from the author. "We must use our intuition as a compass to be a curious investigator to guide us through the uncharted territories of discovery."

THINK BEYOND THE STORY

- What was the cost of this real estate transaction? emotional, physical, or financial?

- What process should Shelly have followed from her training?

- What if Shelly had met Robert at one of the homes that he was requesting to view?

CLOSING POINTS

- There are apps and websites that real estate agents can use to check the validity of a customer.

- Ensure to copy the client(s) driver's license(s) for record-keeping purposes and to verify their identity.

- Meet the client(s) at your office first before going on a tour.

- When touring homes, always have an easy escape route and lock your car with no valuables showing (sometimes ladies leave their purse on the seat).

- Before getting out of your car or returning to it, scan the area for any potential dangers.

- Always inform someone when you are going to show homes or make appointments and share the client's information with someone.

- Avoid working with clients that make you feel uncomfortable.

9

DEFENSIVE POINT OF VIEW

"Don't wear your emotions on your coat sleeve."
ReShawna Leaven

IN BYGONE YEARS, WOMEN hand-washed clothes in wash tubes, employing ribbed washboards to rid garments of embedded soil. However, the 1970s ushered in the affordability of more households to have a modern washing machine. This revolutionized household chores and eased daily life. Fast forward to today's real estate transactions, where buyers exploring a prospective home often pay close attention to the washroom amenities. The presence of a washer and dryer that conveys with the property becomes a key consideration, sparing the buyer the need for this additional purchase post-closing. This offering from the seller often delights the buyer, presenting an added convenience and a welcomed perk in the home purchase journey.

As we jump into this story, real estate agent Shirley Newsome is faced with the unpredictability that can arise during a transaction. We begin at the final walkthrough of a home Shirley was selling. As she opens the door for her client, Shirley gestures for Vanessa Larkin to go ahead and enter the home. *"Here's a tape measure for your measurements. I will go to the basement to begin to check things out while you get the measurements that you need."*

Shirley and her client headed to different parts of the house to begin their tasks. While Shirley went to the basement to ensure that everything was in order, Vanessa went upstairs to take measurements for furniture and blinds. Shirley made her way to the laundry room area and was surprised to find that the bi-fold doors opened easily, as she remembered them being difficult to open during the home inspection. *"Hmm...that opened easily. I remember these doors having a tight grip during the home inspection."* - she thought to herself. Upon checking the laundry room, Shirley was surprised to discover that the front load oversized washer and dryer that had been present at the showing appointment and home inspection was missing. Shirley checked the contract to verify whether the appliances were to convey with the home. She opened the email app on her phone and looked at the list of conveyance items, and it stated that the washer and dryer were to remain with the home. Both the buyer and seller had signed off on these items. As a result, Shirley contacted Barbara, the listing agent, to inform her about the missing washer and dryer.

PHONE CALL
(With Barbara – Listing Agent and Shirley – Buyer's Agent)

Shirley - *"Hi Barbara. This is Shirley with Convey Real Estate. How are you?"*
Barbara - *"Good and you."*
Shirley - *"I'm well. I don't know whether you are going to be upset or not but there is a problem. I am at the walk thru with my client and the Red LG front load washer and dryer are missing."*
Barbara (said in a snappy tone) - *"Shirley, you don't know what you are talking about! The washer and dryer were never supposed to stay with the home. READ your contract, dear. You need to make sure you read your contract thoroughly."*
Shirley - In her mind she was thinking *"Barbara! Who do you think you're talking to?"* but she really said *"Barbara, that tone is not necessary. I would not have called you if I had not checked the documentation first. The conveyance section stated that the washer and dryer is part of the items that remain with the home. Your clients signed off on it. It's on page*

3 of the contract. I am sending it to you as we speak. (Shirley, the queen of multi-tasking forwarded the conveyance page of the contract to verify her statement) and she began to say... "This is a quick fix. Just have the sellers bring back the washer and dryer."
Barbara - *"No, that's not possible. It's on its way across the country with their moving company."*
Shirley - *"I see. So, what are we going to do about this Barbara? My client will close an hour from now."*
Barbara - *"Oh. I am reviewing the contract now and it does state that the washer and dryer is supposed to remain with the home. Ok, I will have to credit the buyer for the washer and dryer. The seller was not aware that the washer and dryer were to be conveyed."*

They both exchanged additional words of how the credit would be given to the buyer and ended the call. Shirley explained the final analysis to Vanessa who was overjoyed because she would use part of the funds for a washer and dryer and other items that she needed in her new home such as batteries, a fire extinguisher, toolbox etc.

During the phone conversation, Barbara did not offer an apology for the oversight and her tone. It is common for apologies to be left unsaid, as a person's responses are often based on their personality and mindset at the moment. It is important to maintain professionalism and composure in such situations. Just before the closing, Barbara presented Shirley with a gift card worth $2,500, equal to the value of the missing washer and dryer.

It turns out that Barbara's clients, the sellers, were unaware that the washer and dryer were supposed to be included with the home. It was Barbara's responsibility to remind them of all the conveyance items and to ensure that they were aware of their obligations under the contract. It is always a good idea to have two checkpoints with the sellers, both at the time of offer signing and before they move out, as a way to reinforce the terms of the contract and avoid misunderstandings. In real estate, it is important to be clear and concise in your communication. In this case, Shirley had to think fast on her feet and protect her client's interest.

THINK BEYOND THE STORY

- What was the cost of this real estate transaction? emotional, physical, or financial?

- What if Shirley had not mentioned the missing washer and dryer during the walk-through?

CLOSING POINTS

- Stay professional even when the other agent raising the unprofessional bar

- Be knowledgeable about the items that are supposed to be conveyed in your contract. As a real estate professional, you should be able to back up your claims with facts and evidence. Some agents may try to challenge your assertions, so it is important to be prepared. This is sometimes referred to as "the King Kong mentality," as people may try to assert their superiority by pounding their chest and making grandiose claims. It is important to avoid this mindset and to approach every transaction with professionalism and objectivity.

10

THE UNTOLD CHAPTER

"Peel back the layers to uncover the real truths."
ReShawna Leaven

I MAGINE THE NERVOUS ANTICIPATION before an annual checkup just before stepping into the doctor's office. You feel an uneasy feeling all over. Many thoughts run through your head, such as, *"I hope my blood work comes back with positive results"*. This feeling is parallel to the anxiety felt during a real estate transaction. You're afraid that revealing certain details could lead to unforeseen consequences. At your annual checkup when the doctor finally arrives, after the nurse has completed all of the preliminary things, there's a hesitation to disclose any ailments, aches, or pains that you may have been feeling. You don't want to say that you had chest pains last month. Similarly, in real estate, a seller might omit mentioning a negative financial situation because they believe it's inconsequential. In the same manner, at the doctor's appointment, an inclination to withhold any signs of irregular body dysfunction or abnormal growths, assuming it holds no relevance, mirrors the dilemma of withholding critical financial history during a property transaction.

We will turn our attention to our real estate agent in this story, Gwen Dodson. She was a person of strong resolve, with a no-nonsense demeanor. She was a child of divorce at an early age and was raised solely by her father. They developed a strong relationship as a result. However, despite their closeness, there were certain subjects that remained unspoken, like a veil of silence. Let's follow Gwen as she embarks on a journey of juggling the relationship of a close family member and the sell of a home.

Gwen's father, contemplating downsizing, reached out to her to evaluate his property for listing. Unlike her previous casual visits, this time Gwen approached the task with a business mindset. Armed with a pen and clipboard, she systematically went through each room, carefully noting the improvements required to make the home "listing ready." After a thorough walkthrough, Gwen and her father sat down to strategize a swift plan, encompassing exterior and interior enhancements. Tasks such as decluttering unwanted items, power washing the siding, painting the front door and trim, refreshing interior paint, upgrading bathroom fixtures, updating stainless steel appliances, and cleaning carpets were outlined. Staging was a "must have" component on Gwen's list of "to do" items. She would enlist the expertise of her own stager, who not only utilized some of the client's existing furnishings but also collaborated on the decluttering and design plan for the client.

Remarkably within 30 days the home underwent the transformation process. Gwen arranged for a professional photographer to capture the property's essence, ensuring stunning visuals. She crafted a compelling and detailed description, harmonizing it with the captivating photos, and promptly listed the property, marking the culmination of a well-executed plan that showcased Gwen's dedication to presenting her father's home in its best possible light.

Within three days, there were over thirty showings, which garnered a whopping five offers. After careful consideration, the most attractive offer was accepted, and the process of finalizing the sale began. The standard procedures were followed - inspections were conducted, contingencies were removed, an appraisal was ordered, and HOA documents were scrutinized.

All seemed to be going smoothly until the title work was ordered, and a problem arose, casting a shadow over the process. With just a week left before the scheduled closing date, Gwen received an alarming email from the title company. The shocking news was relayed to her about the seller (her father), that he had recently declared bankruptcy, which would cause a significant delay in the closing process.

EMAIL (From Closing Company to Listing Agent)

FROM: Closing Company/ TO: Gwen Dodson
Subject: Closing update

Good Afternoon Gwen,

We regret to inform you that there is an issue with the title. Apparently, the owner filed Chapter 13 bankruptcy and the court has to approve the sale. It will likely take up to five weeks to receive approval from the court.

Sarah O'Malley
Closing Company

The revelation was a heavy blow to Gwen, who now found herself caught in the crosshairs of a difficult and emotional situation. As she read the email, her mind raced, and she knew that she had to make a difficult call to her father. Gwen picked up her phone, scrolled to her "favorites" section and hit "Dad." It was a difficult conversation, filled with raw emotion and hard truths. But through it all, Gwen remained steadfast and resolute, determined to see the sale through to the end.

This heart-wrenching scenario underscores the delicate nature of familial relationships and the emotional complexities that can arise when business and personal relationships collide. It takes strength, courage, and a strong sense of purpose to navigate such difficult waters, but with determination and grace, anything is possible.

PHONE CALL
(With Gwen Dodson – Listing Agent / Eric Dobson – Seller/Father)

Gwen - *"Hi Dad. I just received an email from the title company. They stated that after pulling the title report, the house was included in a bankruptcy and that this would cause a delay with closing."*
Eric - *"Yes, that's correct. I should have told you, but I thought I would take care of it without involving you."*
Gwen - *"Ok. I understand, but it's important to share legal matters with your agent. This can be difficult sometimes when a family member is conducting business, but it helps to know so that we can be proactive and plan for situations like this. We will need to get an extension and send it to the buyers since we won't be able to close next week. This could put them in a difficult situation if they had planned on moving from a rental and have nowhere to go."*
Eric - *"I understand. I didn't know it was this complicated. Just let me know what I need to do now. I am sorry that I didn't tell you sooner. I am used to taking care of things myself, you know. Send me the paperwork and I'll sign it and do whatever else needs to be done to get this thing resolved."*

Next, Gwen had to speak with the buyer's agent to tell her the news. Beth was a "squeaky wheel" (it's similar to the sound that your brakes make when they have worn down to the rotors. Annoying!). It was not a pleasant conversation.

PHONE CALL
(With Gwen Dodson – Listing Agent / Beth Roder – Buyer's Agent)

Gwen - *"Hi Beth. Just calling to give you an update on the closing. Unfortunately, the closing will not take place for a few weeks due to an issue with the title."*
Beth - *"Gwen, I can't believe that we can't close on time! Why wasn't this issue caught earlier? The title company that I use finds issues out early."*
Gwen - *"It's really nothing that can be done and it's beyond our control. I will do everything in my power to expedite the process."*
Beth - *"My clients have already turned in their notice at their*

apartment and have nowhere to go. What's the issue?"
Gwen - *"I can't disclose that information to you. All I can say is that it could take up to three to five weeks to clear up."*
Beth - *"This is unexceptionable! My clients need to be compensated for this delay in some manner. (Gwen was quiet for a moment. She wanted to regroup to keep her professional tone). Hello! Are you still there? I don't hear anything."*
Gwen - *RADIO SILENT... for 30 seconds. "Well... I will have to speak with my client about this. Can you speak with your clients to ask about a requested amount so I can present it to my client?"*
Beth - *"YES! I will call as soon as we finish this call. I will email the details to you."*
Gwen - *"Thank you Beth and sorry for the inconvenience."*

Gwen thought to herself that Beth was speaking for her clients without asking their wishes first. Beth's conversation seemed to be a familiar one, playing out in countless real estate transactions where unexpected complications arise. It's an unavoidable fact that in the world of real estate, anything can happen. However, emotions can run high, especially for real estate agents who rely on their commission for each successful sale. It's essential to remain level-headed and not let emotions cloud negotiations.

Following the initial shock of learning about her father's bankruptcy, Gwen found herself thrusted into a whirlwind of legal proceedings and bureaucratic hurdles. Her father had filed for Chapter 13 bankruptcy, which is a type of bankruptcy that allows individuals with real estate to create a repayment plan to pay off their debts over a period of time.

Gwen's father had a court-appointed attorney who was in charge of the bankruptcy case. The attorney worked closely with the bankruptcy trustee, whose job was to administer the repayment plan and ensure that the debtor complied with all of the requirements of the bankruptcy court. As part of the Chapter 13 process, Gwen's father was required to attend a court hearing to confirm his repayment plan. This court date added another layer of complexity to the already challenging situation. Unfortunately, the bankruptcy filing put a hold on the sale of the property. Gwen and her father had to work with the bankruptcy trustee and the court-appointed attorney to ensure that the sale would not jeopardize the bankruptcy repayment plan.

After weeks of back and forth with the bankruptcy trustee, Gwen and her father finally received court approval to proceed with the sale of the property. The judge overseeing the bankruptcy case gave his blessing, and the sale was able to move forward. For Gwen, this journey was more than just a real estate transaction; it was a profound lesson in resilience, the art of communication, and the delicate balance between personal and professional realms.

The final chapter in this saga wasn't just about closing a sale, but about closing a chapter of uncertainty and opening a new one filled with possibilities. Gwen's experience serves as a reminder that amidst the tangles of laws and the unpredictability of human emotions, lies the heart of real estate – the people and their stories.

THINK BEYOND THE STORY

- What was the cost of this real estate transaction? emotional, physical, or financial

- How could Gwen have discovered the untold layers to assist her dad?

CLOSING POINTS

- When developing a relationship with the seller, during your initial consultation, your questioning style or a paper or electronic questionnaire will allow you to ask the tough questions (i.e., bankruptcy, delinquent payments, any unpaid liens etc.)

- Request a copy of the latest mortgage statement. By requesting the latest mortgage statement, you can see if the mortgage is being paid on time and give the information to the title company to order the payoff.

- Request a copy of the homeowners' association/or condo association statement. If you have a recent bill from the HOA/and or condo association, you will find which company manages the association and if it is delinquent.

- Find out if there are any unpaid judgments that could be attached to the property.

11

WOOD, WOOD, WOOD

"Your awareness is the armor in the realm of real estate,
protecting your path to prosperity."
ReShawna Leaven

"**W**HAT LIES BENEATH THE *foundation of a home? Carpenter bees, termites and ants, oh my!"* Despite our aversion to insects using our homes as a source of sustenance, it's essential to remember that all living creatures require nourishment. Unfortunately, some of the damage caused by these pests can go undetected, manifesting as an unknown defect that remains hidden until an official inspection is conducted. In such cases, the costs of repair can amount to thousands of dollars, an expense that is not covered by insurance.

Americans often engage in litigation to address various issues that concern them or when they believe their rights have been infringed upon. However, it is not possible for a person to file a lawsuit against an insect for "consuming" their dwelling. The only recourse is to bear the burden and pay the bill. Instead of waiting for unexpected expenses to arise, it is prudent to adopt a proactive approach towards maintaining the structural integrity of a home, thus avoiding potential headaches and unwanted surprises. "While we all love surprises," uncovering defects that pose a risk to the safety of your home and loved ones can be a dangerous and costly ordeal. There are many pest control companies that have a regular maintenance program to keep a homeowner aware of these dangers. However, many homeowners view this as an extra cost. They usually only become aware when an inspection is done during the sale of their home.

The real estate industry has named this inspection the "termite inspection," despite it serving as a comprehensive examination for evidence of wood-destroying insects, which includes carpenter bees, among other insects. This story commences with a parallel to the stock market on Wall Street, with the pest inspection serving as the closing bell for homeowners.

- The inspection concludes at 12:00 pm. Ding, ding, ding.

- The closing is scheduled for 4:00 pm. Ding, ding, ding.

With the inspection completed on the same day as the closing, there is no need to worry, right? Well... Although the inspection was conducted at noon, the property was slated to close at 4:00 pm the same day. The closing bells at the stock market are ringing, indicating that time is of the essence. Ding, ding, ding.

Upon completion of the pest inspection, the pest inspector's recommendation for treatment was forwarded to Andrew Thompson, the listing agent. Following a thorough review of the report, Andrew contacted his client to deliver the unfortunate news. Here's a snapshot of the conversation.

PHONE CALL
(With Andrew – Listing Agent and Nancy – Seller)

Andrew - *"Hi, Nancy this is Andrew calling in reference to 555 Miller Rd."*
Nancy - *"Hi Andrew."*
Andrew - *"How are you?"*
Nancy - *"I am well and you."*
Andrew - *"I'm good. I received the pest inspection report today and the*

company found carpenter bees underneath the deck and termites at the foundation of the home at the right corner of the basement."

Nancy - *"(In an upsetting tone stated). "Uhhhh. Wait a minute. Why am I just being informed on this? This is upsetting. Who was supposed to order the inspection?"*

Andrew - *"I thought the contract stated the buyer was to pay and order the inspection. As we were getting closer to closing, I had not received the termite inspection, so I decided to review the contract again and discovered it's a seller's expense instead of a buyer's expense. To get a clear inspection report, the home will need to be treated for termites, carpenter bees, and wood repairs need to be completed on the deck."*

Nancy - *"Ok. So, I assume that means that I am not closing today?"*

Andrew - *"I apologize wholeheartedly. No, we cannot close without a clear pest inspection report."*

Nancy - *"Ok, I understand. Do you have a company that can handle these inspection repair items?"*

Andrew - *"Yes, I have two companies that I will forward to you for consideration. I will forward the information to you as soon as we are off the call."*

Afterwards, Andrew contacted the buyer's agent to discuss the pest inspection report. The buyer's agent was left speechless upon hearing about the findings and was bewildered about why the inspection was completed the same day of closing. The conversation ended abruptly, leaving Andrew feeling uneasy about the situation.

After receiving the information from Andrew, the seller swiftly scheduled appointments with contractors for estimates. The total cost for repairing the wood damage was estimated to be $1,000, while the treatment for termites and carpenter bees added another $500. These repairs were completed swiftly within three days. In addition, the lender's underwriter demanded photographic evidence of the newly replaced wood on the deck and receipts for the treatment. Andrew promptly collected and forwarded the requested documents. Even though he was confident that the information supplied was accurate, the underwriter still had 48 hours to either give approval or deny the request, causing Andrew to have a nail-biting session.

There are more crucial details to this story that need to be uncovered. This particular real estate transaction occurred during a tumultuous period in financial history, where the stock market was in freefall, resulting in a steep rise in interest rates. This factor is particularly significant because the original closing date was June 10th and the buyer's interest rate lock expired on June 15th, leading to a sharp increase in their interest rate by several points.

The new interest rate that was imposed was too high for the buyer to afford the home. Consequently, they had to opt to buy down the interest rate to proceed with the transaction. This serves as a real-life example of the process of buying down an interest rate. In such situations, buyers can purchase discount points in order to lower their interest rates. Discount points are calculated as a percentage of the loan amount. For instance, if the loan amount is $100,000 and the cost to reduce the interest rate is 1%, then the cost of the discount point would be $1,000 (calculated as $100,000 x 1%). It's important to understand that purchasing does not equate to a direct reduction of 1% in the interest rate. The actual decrease in the interest rate will vary depending on the current cost of basis points and the buyer's profile. To obtain accurate information regarding the potential interest rate decrease, it is recommended to contact your lender and inquire about these details.

PHONE CALL
(With Andrew – Listing Agent and Charles Harris – Buyer's Agent)

Charles - *"Hello Andrew, how are you doing today?"*
Andrew - *"I am doing quite well, thank you. How may I assist you?"*
Charles - *"There have been several obstacles encountered in this transaction, however, my client is still interested in purchasing the townhouse. They are willing to pay an additional $1,500 in discount points to maintain their current interest rate. They are requesting that the seller bear the cost of this payment since the seller was responsible for the delay. I have forwarded the addendum to you for your client's*

signature."
Andrew - *"I see. Thank you for bringing this to my attention. I will discuss this with my client to see if they are willing to cover this cost. I will communicate their response as soon as I have an update."*

Andrew emailed Nancy (the seller) the addendum and briefly explained the new developments. After receiving the news, Nancy sent an email to Andrew and Cc'd his broker requesting a credit of $1,500 from the listing brokerage commission. This is part of her new closing cost expenses incurred because of the lock rate expiration. The reason for making the request was based on the listing agent's error.

The broker representing the listing agent approved the credit and forwarded a letter for this process to take place. Ultimately this was helpful in completing this transaction. Thus, the deal was successfully closed.

To obtain a real estate credit from the commission the broker in charge must submit a signed letter containing details:

- Property address

- Party (seller) receiving the credit

- Agent (listing) agent providing it

 The concept of "time is of the essence" is a fundamental aspect in real estate transactions. Time-sensitive dates, deadlines, and response timeliness are critical components in the success of any real estate transaction. Procrastination is not an option in this field as it can lead to adverse financial implications. Failing to create a well-defined timeline can result in a catastrophic outcome. In the context of this particular story, the buyers could have had adverse results if the stakeholders were not willing to give up something. On occasion an agency may need to step in and give up some of that hard earned commission to save the day.

As professionals in the field of real estate, it is our duty to ensure that our clients' contractual obligations are met with the utmost care and due diligence. Completing the necessary tasks involved in a transaction does not occur through mere chance or the wave of a wand. As exemplified in this story, the absence of a reliable system in place to guide the process can have adverse effects on all stakeholders involved.

When engaging in a real estate transaction, buyers and sellers rely on the expertise of their agents to manage deadlines and coordinate with industry professionals, much like the conductor of an orchestra. Just as the stock market rings the closing bell with a resounding "ding, ding, ding," there are important aspects to consider. In certain states, depending on the buyer's financing, the seller may be responsible for covering the cost of a termite inspection. It becomes the seller's duty, regardless of the state, to address any concerns identified in the inspection promptly.

THINK BEYOND THE STORY

- What was the cost of this real estate transaction? emotional, physical, or financial

- When do you think the listing agent should have ordered the home inspection?

- Did the buyer's agent use the right approach when asking the seller for a credit to extend their interest rate lock?

- Was there a chance to salvage the deal even if the broker balked at the $1,500 credit?

CLOSING POINTS

- Get to know your contract inside and out

- Procrastination can be costly in real estate transactions

- Buyers and sellers should be aware of deadlines and response times, and agents should stay in sync with contract obligations to ensure that tasks are completed in a timely manner

- When selling a home, the seller is usually responsible for correcting any issues identified in the termite inspection and providing a clear report with proof of treatment and a paid invoice if necessary

- A good practice is to have the termite inspection done at the same time as the home inspection to ensure that everything is done in a timely manner

12

DUE DILIGENCE

"Identifying red flags early in the process will save time later."
ReShawna Leaven

MOST NEW AGENTS TRAVEL a journey that mirrors a high-stakes basketball game, filled with challenges and obstacles that test their fortitude as a player. As they run into the real estate arena, they dribble through the unpredictable game of helping a seller or a buyer, aiming to score the elusive basket of success. To secure a spot as a starting player, the relentless hours of practicing a winning strategy is a daily drill. It's similar to executing a complex, yet perfectly timed play on the court, where every pass, every pivot, and every signal must be sharp and intentional. Remember, you can't rack up the scoreboard if you're not in sync with the game plan. This notion comes to life in this narrative that unfolds like a risky, high-pressure shot, teetering on the brink of a major loss or a spectacular win. The new agent's name is Bianca. Her tale is a poignant reminder that in the playoff game, the stakes are always high, and the cost of a misstep could cost you the game and the championship.

On a Tuesday afternoon, Bianca received a text message from an agent out of state.

TEXT MESSAGE
(With Kennedy Taylor and Bianca Lopez)

"Hi Bianca. This is Kennedy Taylor from Courtside Real Estate out in California. I have a referral for you. His name is James Williams."
[Kennedy sent at 10:15 AM]
"Hi Kennedy. Thank you for the referral. Can you email me over the details and your referral agreement? My email is B111@b111.com"
[Bianca sent at 9:30 AM]
"Sure, I have three home tours this morning. I will email you before 4 PM today." **[Kennedy sent at 10:15 AM]**
"Thank you Kennedy. I look forward to your email." **[Bianca sent at 10:30 AM]**

Receiving a referral from an agent out of state is a moment of great honor and excitement when you are new to the game. This is similar to being the top pick at the NBA draft. The chiming sound that precedes the commissioner's announcement at the NBA draft echoed in Bianca's head as she received the referral. Bianca received the email with the name, phone number and type of properties the client was looking to purchase.

In Bianca's haste, she did not elect to follow her typical business practice of a formal meeting (i.e., consultation) at the onset of this transaction. Instead, Bianca held her first meeting with James Williams on the phone. The potential buyer stated that he was an investor. He had a list of renters that needed to secure real estate but had challenged credit. He would purchase the property that the renter would like, then they would place a deposit of the first- and second-month's rent. Next, once they repaired their credit, they would get qualified for a loan and purchase the home from him within a year.

Bianca scoured listings and found several homes right away that checked all of James' boxes. Bianca gave James a call to set up a time to go on a home tour. James wondered if the tenants could join – after all, they'd be the ones calling it home. Bianca agreed but suggested keeping it cozy with just two extra people for everyone's safety. The home tour was like a real-life treasure hunt, with the last house on the tour turning out to be the pot of gold. The tenants were smitten; they called it their dream home. Without missing a beat, James asked Bianca to make an offer. He zipped through the paperwork electronically, sending over a copy of the earnest money deposit check and his proof of funds letter right away. Bianca bundled these items with the offer and sent them off and just like magic, the offer was accepted.

According to the contract, the earnest money deposit was to be held by the title company, so Bianca instructed her client to send the funds to the title company. However, as the closing date approached, it became apparent that the earnest money had not yet been turned in, despite James' repeated assurances to the contrary. She called the title company to see if funds had been received. The title company stated they still had not received the check by mail or wire transfer. She called James and he stated that he would send it by the end of the week. Bianca began to get worried.

Like a point guard checking the scoreboard, Bianca dialed up the title company to see if they had caught the financial pass – the earnest money. The response was like a missed shot; the title company hadn't received the check, neither swished through the mail nor slam-dunked via wire transfer. Switching gears, she called James, pressing like a coach in the final quarter. James, sounding like a player with a plan, promised to shoot the funds over by the end of the week. Bianca felt like she was on the sidelines, benched because of an upset stomach. The kind of discomfort that calls for TUMS and Pepto Bismol. Her thoughts were spinning, replaying the game plan over and over. She realized that she might have missed a key play: not securing the earnest money deposit check immediately at contract signing. In hindsight, she knew she should have had that check in her hands the same day.

In the days leading up to the closing, James stopped communicating with Bianca. Bianca called every day up until closing with no answer. She texted several times with no response. She left voicemails. She sent emails but no reply. On scheduled closing day, no answer, no check, no James. The listing agent (also the owner) stated that this was unacceptable and stated that he was going to take the earnest money for damages. However, there was no earnest money to be disbursed for damages from the title company.

In a last-ditch effort Bianca decided to reach out to James. To her surprise, he actually answered the phone. *"I'm so sorry for going silent,"* James said, his voice tinged with grief. *"I've been dealing with the loss of a family member to cancer and sorting out their affairs."* Bianca's heart softened for a moment, but she knew she had to stay focused. The release of the contract needed to be signed, and time was of the essence.

"James, I understand your situation, and I'm truly sorry for your loss," Bianca started, her tone a blend of empathy and urgency. *"But this silence has put me in a tough spot. I've been catching heat from the agent, who's not just anyone but a key player in my local industry."*

She took a deep breath, trying to steady her voice. *"Can we meet at the coffee shop where we connected before the home tour? We need to get these release papers signed. It's important for both of us to put this behind us."* James's apology came through the phone, sincere yet heavy with his own burdens. *"I'm sorry for the trouble this has caused. Let's meet and sort this out."*

At the coffee shop, the air was thick with unspoken tension as Bianca and James found a quiet corner. Bianca's demeanor was flat, almost mechanical, as if she had erected a wall around her emotions to stay professional. James, trying to cut through the awkwardness, offered to buy her a cup of coffee, but Bianca politely declined. She was there for business, not pleasantries. James, noting her resolute tone, didn't push further. Instead, she pulled out the documents, placed them on the table for James to sign so that this could bring an end to the ordeal. The clatter of coffee cups and the murmur of other patrons faded into the background as they focused on the task at hand, both eager to close this chapter.

When Bianca returned to her office to process the paperwork, she was told that two county police visited the office asking for her and had left their card for a callback. She returned the call and after the discussion was shocked at the discovery. An investigation was being carried out on Mr. James Williams and information had been unearthed that told a shocking story about his investment journey. James was neck-deep in a scam. He had played the role of a modern-day Robin Hood, but without virtue - swindling money from eager tenants and making a dash from state to state.

The tenants who had come on the home tour were without a place to stay and filed a complaint faster than you can say "real estate fraud", accusing James of making off with their hard-earned cash. Meanwhile, Bianca was in the clear with this complaint. These weren't her clients, and she had enough evidence to prove she wasn't anywhere near the cash they'd forked over. Talk about being in the wrong place at the wrong time!

However, Bianca was still in the hot seat. The earnest money, a vital part of the deal, was nowhere to be found. Adding to the pandemonium, she did not communicate this information to the listing agent - who was also playing double duty as the property owner. Then, just like a referee calling a foul, Brenden (the agent/owner) swooped in, filing a complaint with the real estate board quicker than a fast break. This move set Bianca's broker into a full-court press. He was forced to file a report as well. , because when it comes to earnest money deposits, every issue demands a timeout and a detailed play-by-play review.

Following the events described, Bianca was summoned to stand before the state board and an interview was conducted. The board of real estate held a hearing to investigate the matter. Here is a brief snapshot of the hearing:

THE FACILITATOR AND BIANCA LOPEZ

"Is Ms. Bianca Lopez in attendance for Case 1010-2005?" the

Facilitator inquired, scanning the room with a practiced gaze. *"Yes, I am present,"* Bianca responded, her voice steady but tinged with a hint of anxiety. *"Ms. Lopez, would you like to present your perspective on your case? The floor is yours,"* the Facilitator offered, gesturing towards her with an encouraging nod. Bianca stood, her voice clear and firm as she testified to the board members, her words interwoven with a strong conviction of her innocence. *"We appreciate your input on this matter,"* the Facilitator acknowledged the testimony with a note of formality in his tone. *"The board will deliberate and inform you of our decision via mail within 30 days."*

After a month had passed, the long-awaited correspondence from the board had arrived. Bianca received a certified letter from the real estate board that contained the results of her case. According to the real estate board, she was found guilty of the charges levied against her and was ordered to pay a $3,000 fine to keep her license active. Additionally, she was required to complete an additional 30 hours of real estate continuing education, on top of the standard education necessary for her current license renewal. While this fine was significant, there was a silver lining to the situation. The board could have recommended the suspension of her license, however, in this case things worked out for her livelihood.

The buzzer echoed the completion of the deal, a loss for Bianca. This experience served as a valuable lesson, a rookie's initiation into the unpredictable nature of the game. It was an eye-opener that could have marked the premature end of her career, but instead, it became the catalyst for her development. As the crowd of lessons learned and experiences gained applauded silently, Bianca emerged ready to face future games with a seasoned understanding of the rules. All agents should enter the game with this approach and use their playbook of gleaned strategies and procedures, ensuring that every transaction is conducted within well-defined limits and does not escalate beyond recoverable thresholds.

THINK BEYOND THE STORY

- What was the cost of this real estate transaction? emotional, physical, or financial?

- Do you think she received fair punishment from the board?

CLOSING POINTS

- If you are unsure about a transaction, ask your broker for assistance.

- Inform all parties early in the game.

- Don't be hasty with a real estate referral.

- You must always follow the same procedures with all clients

13

DYNAMIC DISCOVERY

"Real estate can be a wild ride."
ReShawna Leaven

CHILDREN AND ADULTS HAVE similar fondness of the amusement park. Navigating the layout by using the provided map system to wander through all that there is to see. It offers you – thrills one moment, being lost the next, and occasionally questioning why you made the choice to get on the roller coaster after eating pizza and ice cream. Sometimes real estate sales mirrors the exhilarating journey of a roller coaster, propelling you through peaks and valleys, subjecting you to the thrilling forces of gravity, guiding you through unexpected twists and turns, and ultimately bringing you to a satisfying conclusion which is like the sense of accomplishment felt when sealing a deal at the closing table.

This adventure begins at our story's amusement park called Dynamic Discovery Theme Park. Imagine yourself strapped securely onto a roller coaster, with the park crew signaling the green light for the ride to commence. As the ride starts to roll, you are elevated to a height of 300 feet, providing a bird's eye view of the entire theme park. The ride pauses momentarily at the highest point of the coaster, causing your heart to race because of the anticipation of what's to come.

Subsequently, the ride hurls forward at a staggering 100 mph, twisting and turning, looping, and flipping, before returning to the secure starting point. Despite your fears, you complete the ride successfully, your adrenaline now coursing through your veins, and you have thoughts of either taking this ride again or never wanting to return. Such is the nature of real estate transactions. Like an amusement park ride, some deals are calm and straightforward, while others are nail-biting, with that keeps you on edge.

ENTERING THE MAIN GATE

Prior to stepping into this story, a preliminary examination of the key elements of a foreclosure is imperative to grasp the basic foundation of this process. A foreclosure is a legal procedure initiated by banks, lenders, or servicers to recover outstanding mortgage payments from borrowers who have failed to fulfill their obligations within a specific period. Judicial and non-judicial foreclosures are the two different types of foreclosure processes, with each state following a distinct foreclosure process.

Upon completion of the foreclosure process, if the lending institution becomes the owner of the property, it is referred to as "Real Estate Owned" or "REO." Various methods are available for liquidating foreclosure properties, such as auctions, or through REO disposition companies. In the absence of an auction, the property may be listed by a listing agent specializing in real estate owned (REO) properties.

A common misconception surrounding foreclosure listings is that they are always sold at a price below their fair market value. In reality, the value of a home is heavily dependent on its condition, and as such, a foreclosure property's worth varies significantly. Such properties often appeal to individuals who are unafraid of undertaking renovation projects or investors who seek to flip properties for profit. However, the belief that such properties can be acquired for a mere fraction of their actual value is a misconception. REO disposition properties are sold at fair market value to avoid undervaluing the market and to maintain its stability.

Now, let us delve into the story of Andrea Coleman and partner Melinda Gray, who were clients of Melvin Spruill who encountered a host of dynamic challenges during a real estate transaction. With a clear goal, the couple had their sights on Raising Falls, a coveted neighborhood known for its diverse array of home styles from townhomes to sprawling suburban single-family homes. This was their main draw to this area. The well-regarded local high school was perfect for their twin daughters. Raising Falls was a unique community, unlike any other in the region. Residents tended to stay put, and only a limited number of homes were listed for sale each year. As such, the phrase "forever home" had become the cornerstone of this neighborhood.

Now, equipped with a "Our Dream Home" Pinterest board and a knack for DIY, Andrea soon faced the reality check of the present real estate market, which wasn't quite aligning with the idyllic visions of the mood boards.

THE CONCESSION AREA

Touring the few properties that became available in the well sought after neighborhood, they commented on the outdated layout in some of the kitchens and the vintage green appliances in another. After a period of waiting and searching online, they finally came across a home that checked all the boxes on their wish list. They quickly called their agent to find out availability so that he could set up a showing appointment. The home boasted four bedrooms, three and a half bathrooms, with a spacious 3250 square feet of living space. Melvin was able to schedule a showing the next day.

CONVERSATION – SHOWING APPOINTMENT
(With the Buyer's Agent and Buyers)

Andrea - *"So, what does "sold as-is" really mean? Are there any major issues with the property that we need to know about before making an offer?"*
Melvin - *"It means that the bank or the asset management company is*

not responsible for any repairs or damages that may exist in this property. It's up to the buyer to do their due diligence and get a home inspection to identify any issues. However, keep in mind that even if you do find any issues, the bank is not obligated to make any repairs or give you credit for them."

Andrea - With a mix of curiosity and trepidation. *"Got it. Well, is the bidding war more like a polite auction or a full-blown gladiator fight?"*

Melvin - *"According to the listing, they will accept bids from owner occupants only for the first 15 days. After that, they will consider offers from investors as well. We can submit an offer at any time, but it's important to keep in mind that the bank will be looking for the highest and best offer. We can work on putting together a strong offer that stands out among the competition."*

Melinda - *"Okay, that makes sense. I really like this house and I think it's worth the extra 5% premium. Let's work on putting together a strong offer and see if we can make this our forever home. What do you think Andrea?"*

ROLLER COASTER

Upon completion of the showing appointment, Melvin proceeded to draft an offer for the couple to carefully review and sign. Once the offer was accepted, escrow was initiated, signaling the beginning of an unpredictable journey. Andrea braced herself as she ventured into the daunting *Land of Expenses*. Her vision of a perfect home humorously collided with the stark reality of a seemingly endless cascade of fees and paperwork. She navigated the maze of utility activations, plumbing de-winterization, and a home inspection, each step punctuated by the "cha-ching" of closing costs. They wanted this ride to come to an end as they continued to uncover hidden buyer premiums and an excess of other closing fees during the loan process. It was exerting intense g-forces on her bank account, leaving them both financially and emotionally winded.

This theme park journey continued as they boarded the ferryboat to the *Land of Premiums,* where they were met with a barrage of transaction fees. A booming voice, like a game show host announcing a dubious prize, heralded their arrival into "The Land of Transaction Fees," where every step seemed to come with a price tag, much to Andrea's wallet's dismay. The premium fees were stacked with zeros at the end, including a technology fee, asset management fee, and other closing fees that the seller (the bank) had opted out of paying for the buyer. The couple felt the weight of these additional costs and realized that they would have to bear the brunt of these fees. To add to the already mounting expenses, the property only came with a **Limited Deed**, with no warranties of the property's condition or of the title. It was clear that navigating the real estate market required a deep understanding of the various costs and fees associated with buying a home of this type.

PHONE CALL
(With Melvin Buyer's Agent and Andrea – Buyer)

Andrea - *"I am not sure how much more our bank accounts will be able to stand with all the expected fees we are paying. I really want this house, but my account is hemorrhaging. I hope we have enough money for closing."*
Melvin - *"I know, foreclosures have a lot of fees. If you fall short, how much do you think you will need? I may be able to work something out, but I will have to speak to my broker first."*
Andrea - *"I think about $2,500 would cover it."*
Melvin - *"Ok. I will check and get back to you."*

Following the arduous journey through the <u>Land of Expenses</u> and the <u>Land of Premiums</u>, next the couple found themselves in the <u>Land of Credit</u>, where they were faced with the challenge of covering the remaining balance due for the closing costs and fees. Realizing that their available funds were insufficient, the buyer's agent, Melvin, came up with a solution - requesting a broker commission credit to be provided to the buyers at closing, in order to offset the negative balance due.

Melvin worked diligently with his broker to obtain the necessary letter and gather all required documents, which were then submitted to the closing company and to the couples lender for approval. Thankfully, after careful consideration, the broker credit was ultimately approved, providing some much-needed relief to the looming financial burden.

WATER RIDE IN A CAVE

After navigating through all the previous areas in the park, the buyers and Melvin found themselves at the last stop, the <u>Land of Title</u>. The journey through this land was like traveling through a dark cave until finally emerging into the sunlight after sliding down a slippery slope. However, the title company had some news for them - there would be a delay in the closing process because the ownership of the property was still in the name of the previous foreclosed owner. The title needed to be corrected with the lender's name officially on record before the closing could take place. This unexpected delay created some anxiety for Andrea and Melinda, who were eager to finalize the purchase and move into their new home.

PHONE CALL
(With Melvin Buyer's Agent and Andrea – Buyer)

Andrea - *"Hi Melvin. How's it going? We are ready for next week."*
Melvin - *"Hi Andrea. I am calling to give you a little bad news. The closing company informed me that closing will be delayed due to a cloud on title. The property ownership was not fully transferred to the lender. It is currently in the previous owner's name. So, we cannot close until this cloud on title has been cleared."*
Andrea - *"Are you freaking kidding me? I have already set up utilities and the movers are scheduled the day after closing."*
Melvin - *"I am so sorry. But, unfortunately without the correct ownership, the closing cannot take place until that happens."*
Andrea - *"Ok, Melvin. This is unsettling. Melinda is going to be upset. But, I still have time to cancel the movers without a penalty. Thanks again for the buyer credit for closing."*

Despite the one-week delay caused by the cloud on the title, the deal eventually closed, and the couple and their twins were able to move into their new abode.

Throughout the twists and turns, highs, and lows of this REO transaction, valuable lessons were learned. The dynamic nature of the process led to the discovery of many unforeseen occurrences. In the end, "REO" not only stood for "Real Estate Owned" but also "Really Expensive Odyssey," a fitting tribute to Andrea and Melinda's theme park journey in real estate. The significance of keeping clients informed of the intricacies of the transaction and the various processes involved cannot be overstated.

THINK BEYOND THE STORY

- What was the cost of this real estate transaction? emotional, physical, or financial?

- Should you sell a real estate owned home without knowing anything about the process?

CLOSING POINTS

- Advise your client on waiting to schedule their move until keys are in hand

- REO properties are always sold in as-is condition

- REO properties may have liens that are transferred to the buyer

- REO properties will likely have a transaction fee

- REO properties may not have utilities turned on

- Speak with a title company on the foreclosure process

- Instead of being reactive, be proactive.

14

'TWAS THE NIGHT BEFORE CLOSING

"As we plan to hang stockings by the chimney with care,
make sure your title is secured before you declare."
ReShawna Leaven

As the eve of closing beckons, a whirlwind of thoughts swirls in the minds of real estate agents, much like the classic anticipation in "'Twas the Night Before Christmas." This age-old poem lends itself to a whimsical twist, mirroring Bryan's journey as a listing agent, whose own story unfolds night after night with his prized listing. On this particular evening, Bryan cozied into his bed for a restful winter's slumber, the house he listed silent, devoid of any potential buyers. Documents neatly stacked by his bedside; he drifted off with dreams of flawless closing procedures spinning in his mind. So, let's dive into Bryan's tale, exploring the myriad of epiphanies and challenges he encountered while listing a condo, each revelation a steppingstone to the grand finale of closing day.

When we wake up on the page of this story, Bryan's listing is having a busy showing schedule. After several showing appointments, a pre-approved buyer expressed enough interest to submit an offer to purchase. Two offers were made, with one offering more favorable terms for the seller after accounting for expenses and fees. The contract was contingent on the buyer obtaining an FHA loan, which is a government-backed loan with certain guidelines and eligibility requirements that must be met for final approval.

The property, being a condo, must be on the FHA's list of approved condos in order for the transaction to move forward. The most crucial documents for a condo transaction are the condo association documents and the lender condo questionnaire. These documents contain vital information, such as the rules and regulations of the condo association, details about the master insurance policy, accounts receivable, and any special assessments or pending lawsuits.

Upon going under contract, the condo documents were requested. The association manager stated the documents would be completed within 14 days or less after the order, payment and interior inspection was received. This timeline was crucial to the success of the transaction. When the package was completed, Bryan received an email with the condo documents that contained a few surprises.

TWAS CONDO ASSOCIATION

Condo Inspection Violations

Items to be corrected prior to transfer of ownership or the new owner must sign off on acceptance of the violations.

- New windows installed. (Window design not approved by board. No record of installation)
- New patio door installed (Door not approved by the board. No record of installation)

By Condo Association Inspector

After receiving the condo association documents with violations, Bryan forwarded the documents to his client and explained the items that would need to be addressed for the buyer to move forward. (Condo violations are the responsibility of the current owner to address before passing ownership to another party unless parties agree to another remedy). His client agreed to get the approvals for the new windows and patio door installation. Bryan created an addendum for all parties to sign.

SEVEN DAYS LATER...

CONDO ASSOCIATION DOCUMENT

TWAS CONDO ASSOCIATION

Lender Condo Questionnaire

- Number of Units in the Project - 100
- Number of Delinquent Owners (30 days past due) - 20
- Number of Delinquent Owners (60 days past due) - 10
- Number of Owners - 33
- Number of Investors - 47
- Master Insurance Coverage - $1,500,000
- Contact: Project Manager: Janine Ward (555) 528-3000

A week later, the loan officer called Bryan to inform him that the property was not going to be approved with an FHA loan due to the condo association questionnaire. The two main reasons were the high delinquency rates and owners to investor ratios in the community. As a result, this contract was terminated, and the buyer received their earnest money back.

After the first contract was terminated, Bryan placed the condo back on the market with the following disclaimer in the listing: "Property has a high delinquency rate. FHA financing not approved. Conventional or cash buyers only." This was to inform potential buyers of the financing restrictions on the property.

Despite the challenges and setbacks, a new offer was finally received after 45 days and a minor price reduction of $5,000. The buyer was willing to finance a substantial portion of the purchase price with a conventional loan and put down a substantial down payment. The seller eagerly accepted the offer. Bryan then promptly sent the necessary paperwork, including the condo resale package and previous questionnaire from the other lender to the buyer. This was a momentous occasion, as it seemed that the road to a successful sale had been paved at last.

'Twas the week before closing, and all the tasks were done
The buyer and seller were excited to have won
But something new arose, that caused everyone to shudder
It kept them awake because their minds were filled with clutter

The road to closing this property was like a journey that Santa takes on Christmas night. Just when it seemed like the end was in sight, another obstacle appeared, it was like Santa Claus landing on the roof and not being able to fit down the chimney. This property had its own set of challenges that needed to be overcome before the road to closing could be completed.

Bryan received a call from the title company explaining that there was a condo lien on the property. Afterwards, he texted his client to see if she could discuss the matter further over the phone.

PHONE CALL
(With Bryan Bradley – Listing Agent and Ginnie Smaller – Seller)

Ginnie - *"I can't believe that bastard (sorry) sold me the property and didn't have the decency to pay the condo liens when we got our divorce."*
Bryan - *"You didn't sell with an agent or go through a title company?"*
Ginnie - *"No, he was being cheap and didn't feel it was needed. How much is the condo lien for?"*
Bryan - *"Well... it shows $29,000 owed from the lien and there will be additional fees from the new delinquent payments and interest. I am surprised that the association never mentioned it to you."*
Ginnie - *"No, they haven't.* (While Ginnie was talking, Bryan said to himself, *"I am sure that they must have mailed her a certified document between the divorce period and now."*) *They are so mis-managed and do a piss poor job which is one of the reasons why I am selling it.*
Bryan - *"The good thing is that this was caught early enough to get the payoff and there are enough proceeds from the sale."*

After a few days and an extensive amount of effort spent calling and emailing, the title company was finally able to secure the payoff amount for the condo liens. The total amount came to $41,528.30, as the file had been assigned to an attorney and was up for sale to a debt collection company as part of a debt sale. This was a significant achievement, as it cleared the way for the property to close.

To successfully navigate the complexities of owning or purchasing a condo, it is vital to be aware of and address any potential issues. This includes being aware of any title issues. Condo liens, which are title defects that occur when a lien is placed on a condominium for unpaid monthly condo fees. These defects can cause problems for the property owner, as they may result in title companies refusing to issue title insurance policies for properties that are subject to condo liens.

'Twas the night before closing when all through the house
Not a buyer was sleeping, consumed by their doubts
The contracts were signed, the paperwork stacked
In hopes that the keys soon would be an impact

The agents were fretting, their phones by their side
While visions of their commissions may not reside
The buyer lay restlessly, thoughts racing wild
With visions of defects that could be compiled

The seller, anxious, their future uncertain
Would the offer be fair, or would it be a burden?
The agents, in huddles, whispered and paced
Preparing their clients for this pivotal chase
The buyer, in bed, tossed and turned with unease
Reviewing inspections, each flaw they'd perceived

Foundation cracks haunted their restless dreams
While leaks in the roof caused silent screams
They wondered if this was the right investment
For the person they chose to be the contestant

The seller, too, worried about what's to come
Would the appraisal align with what they'd done?
Had they priced their home right, or were they mistaken?
Would the market deem their asking price forsaken?

They questioned if the timing was on their side,
Would they sell at a loss, their hopes cast aside?
The agents, caught in between the buyer and seller
Unbalanced emotions, their minds turning like a propeller

They reassured the buyer, calmed their dismay
Conveying that these doubts were just a delay
They comforted the seller, offering advice
Reminding them of the market's unpredictable dice

And the agents whistled, and shouted, and called them by name
"Now, INSPECTOR!
Now, TITLE AGENT!
Now, APPRAISER and LOAN OFFICER!
On, INSURANCE AGENT!
On, UNDERWRITER and CLOSING DEPARTMENT!
To the top of the porch! to the top of the wall!
Now dash away! dash away! dash away all!"

As morning approached, tension grew nearby
The closing awaited, a moment both feared
Buyer and seller arrived with trepidation
Their agents by their side, guiding their navigation

The room was abuzz, with papers to sign
Emotions ran high, like a pendulum's chime
But as the ink dried and the keys were exchanged
Relief washed over them; anxieties rearranged

The buyer, now owner, saw potential anew
With dreams of renovations and memories to accrue
The seller, moving forward, a weight off their chest
Ready for a fresh start, to embrace what comes next

The agents, their mission finally accomplished
Celebrating the closing, their efforts astonished
For in the realm of real estate's endless plight
They witnessed the anxiety transform to delight
With a sigh of relief and a bittersweet smile
They bid their clients farewell, having gone the extra mile

So, as the night settled and peace filled the air
Buyer, seller, agents, all relieved from their care
They reflected on the journey, the worries and stress
Knowing they conquered the anxiety, no less
And as they retreated to a well-deserved rest
They whispered, "Happy closing to all, and to all, the best!"

THINK BEYOND THE STORY

- What was the cost of this real estate transaction? emotional, physical, or financial?

- Should Bryan have asked the seller whether she was current on her condo fees?

- What would have happened if the seller did not have enough proceeds to cover the additional late fees?

CLOSING POINTS

- When the agent asks questions about a client's finances it's always a sensitive area. Building a rapport is important, so that they feel comfortable "spilling the beans' '.

- Order a title report as soon as the listing is signed

- Finding issues early allows the title company to research and correct issues

- Research FHA and VA condominium approved websites to ensure the condo is an approved condo. If the property is not approved, state this information in the listing to avoid unnecessary showings as well as inform the public of financing options.

- Inform your client that a Condo Questionnaire could derail the transaction if it contains any of the following issues - investor/owner ratio, delinquency rates, insurance coverage on the building, fidelity coverage on the building

- Ask the buyer's lender about their condominium lending requirements before accepting the offer

15

ODDS IN YOUR FAVOR

"There are many risk factors in a real estate transaction."
ReShawna Leaven

P URCHASING REAL ESTATE IS a risky endeavor, with every choice carrying potential consequences. It's like a high stakes game of roulette at the casino, with a wide range of variables to consider - from the red and black colors to the numbered slots and connecting lines. When you place your bet, you're crossing your fingers that the ball will land on your chosen area. If luck is on your side, you'll come out on top. But don't forget, the house always has an edge.

- *The agent is taking a risk with the transaction, hoping for a successful closing and a commission.*

- *The buyer is taking a risk by choosing a property that they hope will bring them joy and value in the future.*

- *The seller is taking a risk by selecting a listing agent and hoping they are the right person to sell their home for the best possible terms.*

The COVID-19 pandemic in 2020 sparked a frenzy of real estate buying, with a surge of new buyers motivated to jump into the market. A perfect storm of low interest rates, limited housing options, and a surplus of pre-approved buyers created the perfect conditions for a buying bonanza. This heightened demand had a ripple effect on prices, contingencies, and concessions. Agents had a challenge with explaining to buyers what was needed to seal the deal and the potential outcome of their real estate offer. This is when those persuasive skills had to come into play.

The fast-paced market left many homebuyers feeling frustrated and left out in the cold. Properties were being snapped up and placed under contract in the blink of an eye, leaving little time for other potential buyers to even view them. It was common for a buyer to see a home online, mark it as a favorite, and then find that the next day it was already a pending sale. In the end, the final sales price and terms often surpassed what a client might have ever hoped to offer.

In this narrative, the client gambled on a variety of properties, each with its own set of variables and risks. As the offers were submitted and the deals negotiated, it was as if the ball on the roulette wheel was bouncing wildly, veering from one address to the next and encountering a range of conditions along the way. However, each time an offer was submitted, it felt like a gamble that didn't pay off - like betting on ten and it landing on zero.

1ST 12 ON ROULETTE TABLE

Stephanie Davidson, a seasoned agent with Gambling Real Estate, received a promising inquiry from a pre-approved buyer looking to purchase a new home. Gila Robinson, a first-time homebuyer, was eager to take the plunge and had already secured FHA financing. Stephanie was eager to assist Gila and welcomed her as a new client. With several years of experience in the real estate industry, Stephanie knew the market well and warned Gila of the fierce competition she would face as a buyer. Despite the challenges ahead, Gila was determined to find her dream home and Stephanie was determined to help her every step of the way.

Stephanie scheduled tours at times that worked with Gila's busy schedule, and they embarked on the journey of finding a property that met Gila's criteria. She eagerly submitted offers on homes that caught her eye, "Oh, she had quite a few!" each one a new gamble in the competitive real estate market. As each offer was reviewed and signed, the tension mounted - would the seller accept her terms as written or present a counteroffer? The anticipation was palpable as they waited for the outcome.

Gila's nineteenth offer marked a turning point in her search for a new home. Desperate to secure a property, she was willing to forego a home inspection contingency and increase her purchase price by $15,000. The offer was carefully crafted and promptly delivered, but unfortunately, it met the same fate as the eighteen offers that came before it - rejection from the listing agent via email.

EMAIL (From Listing Agent to Buyer's Agent)

FROM: Susan Smith/ TO: Stephanie Davidson

SUBJECT: Re: 123 Main Street

Good Afternoon Stephanie,

Thank you for submitting your client's offer.

I'm sorry to inform you but your client's offer was not accepted. The sellers have selected another offer with better terms.

I wish you the best with finding a home for your client.

Thank you,
Susan Smith

Gila was thrown into a tornado of emotions when her latest offer was rejected. Not only did she have just 45 days left on her current lease, but her landlord was also selling the property, leaving her with no option to go month-to-month. On top of everything, the down payment assistance component of her loan was tied to a specific Census tract, limiting her options to certain areas based on population density and income levels. The market data showed that list-to-sold prices had surged due to buyers' motivations, making it even harder for Gila to find a new home.

2ND 12 ON ROULETTE TABLE

Gila was determined not to let the numerous rejections she had faced thus far defeat her. She had her heart set on homeownership and was determined to find a property that fit all of her needs and desires. She was determined to give it one last spin.

CONVERSATION - SHOWING APPOINTMENT
(While at a home that fit Gila's criteria)

Gila - *"Wow Stephanie! I really like this house. What do you think I should do with regards to this offer to make it work and get accepted?"*
Stephanie - *"I know you are exhausted with offers. I think that if you increase the sales price and have no contingencies you could possibly win this one. Keep in mind if you win, you are at risk because you have no contingencies, and this gives you no way out of the contract."*
Gila - *"Yes, I am exhausted! The last offer, I went $15,000 above the listed price and I waived a home inspection, and I didn't get it. What's a good offer price for this one?"*
Stephanie - *"I think the offer price has to be so obscene that the seller would be enticed to accept your offer over someone else's. Since property values are $410,000. I think $440,000 would be obscene enough (ha, ha). I know it's a stretch, but with the $25,000 that you have available, I would be willing to contribute $5,000 to make the deal work. A few days ago, I spoke to my broker to find another strategy, to assist you with your home purchase and he agreed to allow up to a $5,000 broker credit. I will just need a signed broker letter once the contract is accepted and submit it to all parties.*
Gila - *"Oh wow Stephanie. You would do that for me. I really appreciate it. What else do you think I have to do to get the offer?"*
Stephanie - *"Well, we are in a constant battle in this market. Since you are willing to go all in, so am I. I think you would need to waive*

these main contingencies (home inspection, financing, and appraisal contingency) in order to win. Let me explain the implications of each. If you decide to waive a home inspection, you won't be aware of any deficiencies with the home. If you decide to waive financing and the bank denies your loan, you will lose your earnest money deposit. If you decide to waive the appraisal contingency and the appraisal value comes in lower than the sales price, you won't be able to ask the seller for a price reduction and you will have to pay the difference.

Gila - *"I see the risk involved but I really need to secure something. Thanks for explaining it so that I can understand my options. I would like to move forward."*

Stephanie - *"Ok sounds good. I already started on a draft of the offer. I can have it ready for you in 30 minutes when I get back to my office and I will send it over."*

Stephanie eagerly returned to her office, fine-tuned the offer, and sent it to Gila for a quick e-signature. Her efforts were met with success as the offer was swiftly accepted, causing Stephanie to break out into a triumphant dance.

Her next step was to reach out to her broker for the commission credit letter, which was then promptly sent to the loan officer and title company for processing. The confirmation emails from both parties indicated that they had received the broker letter and were ready to move forward with the transaction. This was a major milestone in the journey towards homeownership for Stephanie's client, and she couldn't wait to see it all come to fruition.

Despite the absence of an appraisal contingency in the contract, Gila's loan still required an appraisal to proceed. Without hesitation, Gila paid for her appraisal through the online portal using her debit card and the loan officer promptly ordered the appraisal. Within a week, the appraiser visited the property, compiled the report, and submitted it to the bank. As soon as the loan officer's underwriting team completed their review of the appraisal, the report was available to be released to Gila and Stephanie.

EMAIL (From Loan Officer to Buyer's Agent)

FROM: Judy Lawson /TO: Stephanie Davidson, Gila Robinson
SUBJECT: Appraisal Report

<table>
<tr><td>

Good Afternoon Stephanie and Gila,

I received the appraisal back from the underwriter a few hours ago. Unfortunately, the appraisal came in lower than the sales price. Please create a sales addendum with the new sales price supporting the appraised value of $425,000 signed by the buyer and the seller. If the seller doesn't agree to lower the sales price, the buyer can get a release of contract and get her earnest money deposit back.
Attachments: Appraisal Report.pdf

Thank you,
Judy Lawson

</td></tr>
</table>

(In this email from the loan officer, the solutions were not based on the contract)

Listed Price	$410,000	The listed price is the price the seller agreed for the listing agent to market and place in the MLS (multiple listing service)
Sales Price	$440,000	The sales price is the price the buyer and seller agreed on. (a sales price could be the same, lower, or higher than the listed price)
Appraised Value	$425,000	The appraised value is the value of the properties condition based on similar/like properties that have sold in the given area of the subject property. (the appraised value could be higher, lower, or equal to the sales price)
Shortage	$15,000	The shortage is the difference between the sales price and the appraised value

TEXT MESSAGE
(With Buyer's Agent and Buyer)

Gila - *Hi Stephanie. Did you get Judy's email? I can't walk away from this deal. There are no contingencies. Just tell me what I have to do to*

move forward.
Stephanie - *Yes, I received it. I will give you a call shortly with my new strategy.*

Although Gila was fully aware of the contract's stipulation that the sales price couldn't be altered, Stephanie was determined to employ a roulette-like strategy: spinning the wheel to see if they could reduce Gila's out-of-pocket expenses. In real estate, strategies are often employed to salvage a deal at all costs. Following a discussion about the loan officer's email, Stephanie proposed a daring move: submitting an addendum to the seller, requesting a price reduction to $425,000. This addendum, much like a bet on the roulette wheel, held the potential to either be accepted, countered, or outright rejected by the seller. Gila concurred with Stephanie's recommendation and placed her signature on the addendum, thereby adjusting the sales price.

With eager anticipation, they awaited the seller's response, the seller surprisingly countered with $430,000. Despite the slight increase in price, Gila accepted and moved forward with the transaction. However, just two weeks before closing, Gila received an updated closing disclosure and was shocked to see that the funds required to close had significantly increased. She immediately contacted her loan officer, Judy, to inquire about the sudden change.

Gila also contacted her agent to discuss the sudden change. Stephanie, who had also received the disclosure, noticed that the $5,000 broker credit was not included in the document. She had sent the broker credit letter to the loan officer shortly after the contract was accepted. But upon further investigation, it was never added to the loan package by the loan officer. After a brief call to Judy, the mistake was remedied.

3RD 12 ON ROULETTE TABLE

Two days later, the underwriter rejected the use of the broker credit, leaving Gila short on funds needed to close the loan. Based on the guidelines of the program, Gila had reached the maximum allowable funds that she could receive (i.e., program contributions, concessions seller and/or broker credit) Let's review the special program notes:

UNDERWRITER PROGRAM NOTES FOR GILA'S LOAN:

- Type of Financing: FHA

- Down Payment Required: 3.5% of the sales price

- Sales Price: $430,000

- Down Payment Required: $15,050

- Appraised Value: $425,000 (lender will only lend on the appraised value or sales price whichever is less)

- Down payment assistance program will only give the required down payment. Since the property did not appraise for the final agreed upon sales price of $430,000, the program will only cover the down payment amount of the sales price. The buyer has to pay the shortage amount of $5,000 of her own funds or from gift funds.

- Final cash to close to be verified

- Employment verification needed

With just 72 hours before closing, Gila and Stephanie scrambled to come up with a solution to the unexpected obstacle. In order to secure the remaining funds needed for closing, Stephanie informed Gila that the only option available was to request gift funds from a family member, along with a gift letter. Gila reluctantly reached out to a relative for help in obtaining the necessary funds.

Following the unexpected events that occurred with her loan, Gila decided to file a complaint with Judy Lawson's manager and higher management. The complaints about Judy's work ethic and professionalism had been accumulating for the past two months, and as a result, she was promptly asked to resign from her position. Gila's loan was then transferred to another loan officer following Judy's departure.

Gila was finally able to secure the necessary gift funds, and a few days later, she closed on her new home with a sense of accomplishment and relief. After an intense and tumultuous journey, Gila finally landed on a winning number in the real estate game. Despite all the challenges and setbacks, she was able to navigate the process and emerge victorious. But she didn't come out unscathed - she learned some hard lessons about the inner workings of the real estate industry and how to navigate it effectively. Like spinning a roulette wheel, Gila and her agent were able to outmaneuver the odds and come out on top.

THINK BEYOND THE STORY

- What was the cost of this real estate transaction? emotional, physical, or financial?

- What should Stephanie have asked the loan officer about the loan program?

- What if the seller decided not to reduce the sales price?

CLOSING POINTS

- Be knowledgeable of the particular program that you are recommending for a client.

- Get a referral to a loan officer with experience in using a particular special program for home buyer assistance

- In a competitive real estate market, it may be necessary to consider waiving certain contingencies to increase the chances of a successful offer. As an agent, it is important to ask the buyer if they are willing to risk by waiving contingencies such as home inspection, financing, and appraisal in order to strengthen their offer.

- It is also crucial to remain in close communication with buyers, providing follow-up and clarification throughout the process.

- Having a competent team is essential for a successful transaction and can prevent issues (real estate agent, loan officer, title company)

- Make sure you inform your buyer client that a CMA (competitive market analysis) is just a tool to help you decide on the sales price you are willing to offer, but there is no guarantee that the property will appraise for that amount.

- All down payment and/or closing cost assistance programs that are approved by Housing and Urban Development (FHA) and may have different guidelines. In addition, the lender (bank or mortgage company) may have an overlay (guidelines that are created) that need to be followed to approve the loan.

16

NO ORDINARY MOVE

*"Each relationship that you build is a learning experience
as you move from one client to the next on a continuum."*
ReShawna Leaven

ON MOST OCCASIONS, REAL estate agents wear many hats and may undertake many roles. One of those roles is that of a counselor. In order to best serve their client, the agent usually takes an informal analysis of the client's personality, lifestyle, and background during the process. This involves establishing a deep connection with the client by initiating conversations about their needs, professional life, financial standing, and other relevant factors. In real time, this is usually a connection that is built over time in one's personal relationships with people, however, during a real estate transaction we don't have years to build this rapport. A real estate agent has to jump in at the deep end of the pool, diving to the bottom, holding your breath coming up to top quickly. This is comparable to an agent strengthening the bond with the client as the transaction progresses by establishing a quick rapport while nurturing the agent-client relationship.

This chapter begins with the seller, Leah Roberts, who was caught in the throes of a tumultuous divorce. At the outset, she engaged in illogical and unfounded discourse, and even rejected the outcome that her husband truly desired. Her husband, who was the "minister of finance" who solely managed their family affairs, suddenly departed to Alaska, and left her alone to sell their house. With a fresh chapter of life to write, she found herself without any tools to begin. Leah was now faced with the critical situation of managing all the household responsibilities, including listing their home for sale. She frequently yearned for a compassionate ear to hear her whoas. She quickly rekindled a relationship with Ava (who she called her 'family' real estate agent) by reaching out to her about listing the family home and also discussing the numerous challenges that she was facing.

Ava was surprised to hear from Leah and was empathetic about her situation. She had remembered the purchase of their new home and pulled up the file from her online archives. At the end of the phone call Ava scheduled a consultation to visit the property. During the visit, Ava scrutinized the home and provided Leah with pointers on improvements as they walked through the home. She promised to give a more detailed list for repairs and a decluttering schedule in a few days. At the top of the list were crucial documents like the power of attorney and mortgage information sheet that would be needed because Leah's spouse was not present.

Leah signed all of the listing documents and attached the power of attorney document and emailed them to Ava. Ava read all the documents in detail and electronically completed the listing. After submitting the listing documents to her broker, there was an issue that caused it to be declined. There was an issue with the power of attorney document. To proceed with the listing so that the contract could move forward, it was necessary to obtain a Specific Power of Attorney for 123 Power Way. Until this document was properly executed, all activities related to the listing had to be temporarily halted. Following the conversation with her broker, Ava instructed Leah on the type of power of attorney document and told her that she could get what was needed from the same attorney who drafted the other document. There was a sense of urgency to get this document in hand. So, Leah contacted the attorney and received this information right away. She sent it overnight to her husband. He signed it in front of a notary and overnighted it back to Leah. Leah took it over immediately to the real estate office and handed it to Ava to complete the paperwork.

Following the completion of minor repairs and a staging refresh, the property was primed and positioned on the market for sale. In a matter of over a week, Ava received multiple offers for her client's property. After she reviewed the offers, she presented the contracts to her client and advised her to select the offer that presented the most favorable terms. Once an offer was accepted, escrow was initiated and all the necessary steps and inspections on Ava's checklist were conducted seamlessly. With the successful removal of all contract contingencies, the property was one step closer to being officially sold. Finally, the day of closing arrived. Rachel Jolly, the buyer's agent, conducted a thorough walk-through with her clients to ensure that everything was in order before the settlement.

PHONE CALL
(With Ava – Listing Agent and Rachel Jolly – Buyer's Agent)

Rachel - *"Hi Ava. This is Rachel Jolly with Power of Attorney Realty. We just completed the walk through at 123 American Way and your client's personal belongings appear to be in the same place as when we completed the home inspection. What's going on?"*

Ava - *"Oh, Rachel. I apologize for the inconvenience. I wasn't aware of the walk-through being scheduled today. My client may have misunderstood the timeline for moving out and thought she had until the end of the day tomorrow to have all items removed. At this point, she will need a rent back. How do you think your client's will respond?"*

Rachel - (upset with a raised voice) *"Ahhh. Well... I don't think that they have much of a choice. Ava, this is not acceptable. We cannot close on the property with the seller's belongings still inside. The closing is tomorrow morning at 10 AM, and the house needs to be empty."*

Ava - *"Let me call you back after I speak with my client to see what's going on."*

After Ava's phone call with Rachel, she gazed towards the clock on the microwave in her kitchen, which displayed the time as 5:19 PM. Her mind began to race as she considered the sheer magnitude of the task that lay ahead for Leah. Despite her mounting concern, Ava refrained from voicing her inner thoughts, and instead remained focused on the phone conversation that she just had with Rachel. She knew that Leah would require not only boxes but also a moving truck, professional movers, and a storage unit to accomplish the move-out in time for tomorrow's closing. It was already well past 5 pm, and the evening was better suited for dinner and relaxation, rather than the arduous task of packing and moving. Nevertheless, Ava kept her composure and continued with the task of calling her client to see what was going on with her personal belongings.

PHONE CALL

(With Ava – Listing Agent and Leah – Seller)

Ava - *"Hi Leah. How is it going? Ahhhh, the buyer's agent just called and said all of your personal items have not been moved."*

Leah - "Yes, I have been under a lot of stress. My sister passed away and I had to go out of town to manage her personal affairs, but I am back now."

Ava - *"Oh, I am sorry to hear about your loss. (Pause) Closing is tomorrow morning. The only option that you have now is to close tomorrow with a rent back and get everything out this weekend. The buyers may be willing to let you stay and get everything together for a small daily fee and a small security deposit."*

Leah - *"Oh wow! It seems like everything is happening all at once."*

Ava - *"No problem. Let's focus on getting everything done in a timely manner. I can recommend some moving companies that can help you with packing, moving, and storage. You can also try contacting some charities that offer free moving services to people in need. Additionally, if you need any assistance with packing or moving, just let me know. I am happy to help in any way I can."*

Leah - *"Thank you, Ava. I really appreciate your kindness and understanding. It's been a tough time for me, and your support means a lot."*

Ava - *"Of course, Leah. You are not alone in this. We will get through it together. Do you have any questions or concerns about the rent back arrangement?"*

Leah - *"No, it sounds fair. I just need to make sure I can get everything out of the house by Sunday."*
Ava - *"I will contact the buyer's agent to see if they are in agreement right away."*
Leah - *"Ok. Thanks again."*

TEXT MESSAGE
(With Ava – Listing Agent and Rachel Jolly – Buyer's Agent)

"Hi Rachel, I just spoke with my client, and she is willing to do whatever it takes to get everything out, but she needs to rent back the property until the weekend to accomplish that. She apologizes for the misunderstanding and any inconvenience this has caused." **[sent by Ava at 7:02 PM]**
"Thank you, Ava. I appreciate you following up with your client so quickly. I will contact my clients to see if they are in agreement with that. I am glad we could come to a resolution so quickly. If we are all in agreement, I will complete the addendum and send it over and we will proceed with closing tomorrow." **[sent by Rachel at 7:06 PM]**
"Absolutely, Rachel. I apologize again for any inconvenience caused." **[sent by Ava at 7:10 PM]**
"No problem, Ava. Thank you for your cooperation. I look forward to a smooth closing tomorrow." **[sent by Rachel at 7:15 PM]**

After the property had closed, Ava quickly changed into comfortable attire that consisted of sneakers, jeans, and a t-shirt. She then proceeded to organize and coordinate the box truck and helpers to assist with the move. Leah had also reached out to her friend, Sean, who came by to help with packing. They worked tirelessly, packing boxes, breaking down beds, and organizing everything until it was all ready for the movers. The process took the entire day, but in the end, everything was successfully packed and ready to be transported to the storage unit. As the night drew to a close, they celebrated the successful sale of the house with pizza, soda, and a sense of exhaustion. For Ava it was another valuable lesson learned and another deal successfully closed.

Sellers may have to relocate due to various life events, such as job changes, marriages, the arrival of a new family member, or divorce.

As real estate agents, we listen to our clients' relocation goals and devise a strategy to accomplish them while reducing their stress as much as possible. This profession is more than just financial rewards derived from commissions. There is a sense of satisfaction that comes from assisting clients in selling their homes and moving on to a new chapter in their lives, whether it's a local or an international relocation. However, sometimes the responsibilities can be challenging, involving both emotional and physical labor. The question we must ask ourselves is: "Are we willing to do what is necessary?"

As a real estate agent, it is common to face situations that require a hands-on approach. Whether it's helping clients pack and move their personal belongings, cleaning up a property to make it market-ready, or even assisting with minor repairs and renovations, the job often demands more than just negotiation and paperwork. In these situations, it's essential to roll up your sleeves and put in some elbow grease to get the job done. Ultimately, a willingness to go the extra mile can be the difference between a successful transaction and a missed opportunity for both the agent and the client.

THINK BEYOND THE STORY

- What was the cost of this real estate transaction? emotional, physical, or financial?

- How will you make sure your clients are ready to move and insured that they have moved?

- How can you set clear expectations for a seller?

CLOSING POINTS

- Develop a seller package with a detailed timeline and responsibilities.

- Provide reminders for when personal belongings must be removed.

- Conduct regular on-site visits based on timeline and move-out day.

- It is crucial for clients to obtain legal document requirements early for loan approval.

- Don't be afraid to roll up your sleeves when things are not complete.

- As real estate agents, we do not practice law and the clients are to seek the advice of a licensed law professional for specific documents.

17

THE GIFT

*"Always brainstorm as many alternative solutions
as possible to keep a deal from falling apart."*
ReShawna Leaven

THE REAL ESTATE JOURNEY can be similar to a rollercoaster ride with its twists and turns. As a real estate agent, you are tasked with guiding homebuyers through these twists and turns. It is imperative to possess a deep understanding of the intricacies of the buyer's experience and the potential obstacles that may arise at any given moment, as real estate experiences come with surprises - some delightful, while others are not so pleasant. The agent always wants to receive the accolades in the end for the great work and guidance that was given during the transaction. However, sometimes certain situations may override the hard work put in that is not seen "with the naked eye." In this case, when some areas of the deal go sour it may cause an upset buyer(s) to become bitter with the entire transaction even at the end (when it closes) or if there is a negative outcome. Then your name is "mud."

Housing is a necessity, and in recognition of this fact, several states across the country have established housing assistance programs to aid homebuyers in fulfilling their dream of homeownership. According to the National Association of Builders recent data reported that, *"Housing's combined contribution to GDP generally averages 15-18% and occurs in two basic ways: Residential investment (averaging roughly 3-5% of GDP), which includes construction of new single-family and multifamily structures, residential remodeling, production of manufactured homes, and brokers' fees."* The housing industry is one of the top essential businesses in the United States. It provides shelter that we all need for survival. The Housing and Urban Development Administration along with lenders have allocated funds to help low-income homebuyers with down payments and closing costs, allowing a vast number of buyers to realize their dream of homeownership, which would otherwise be unattainable without such programs. If the buyer satisfies the program's requirements, they are eligible to participate in the program.

Let's take this turbulent ride with agent Zoey Cambell as he embarks on a journey with his client, a first-time home buyer who is using one of these programs. The "G-forces" in this story will keep you on the edge of your seat. This journey begins during the underwriting period for these clients.

PHONE CALL

(With Loan Officer and Vivienne – Buyer)

Loan officer - *"Vivienne, the down payment assistance program denied your loan."*

Vivienne - *"What do mean? I don't understand, I thought Mark, and I were approved?"*

Loan officer - *"Yes, you were in the part of the process that we call underwriting. Let me explain. Your loan had to go through two underwriters, one with our company and the second with the local housing authority. You are fully approved for your FHA loan from 123 Mortgage. However, the local housing authority (first time home buyer program) has their own guidelines with regards to your student loan repayment plan. After their underwriter reviewed the completed file, they denied the funding based on the student loan (income-based payment plan) that you have. With this information, they could not use* *the income-based payment plan, which was a lower payment. They had to use 1% of the student loan debt to calculate the estimated monthly payment. The estimated student loan payment amount affected your ratios. Unfortunately, we are at the mercy of their policies. The only option now is to get a gift from a relative for your down payment or get out of your contract."*

Vivienne - *"Wow! I can't believe this is happening. We really need to move. I will need to talk to my husband, and I will also let Zoey know the updates with regards to our file."*

After the troubling phone call, with the loan officer. Vivienne called her agent to discuss the latest issue.

PHONE CALL
(With Vivienne – Buyer and Zoey Campbell – Buyer's Agent)

Zoey - *"This is Zoey Campbell."*
Vivienne - *"Hi Zoey. It's Vivienne."*
Zoey - *"How can I help you today?"*
Vivienne - *"Well, I was fine until about 30 minutes ago. The loan officer called and said that we no longer qualify for the down payment assistance program because they changed some of the guidelines since we applied for the loan. Now my debt ratios are too high because of my student loan payment plan."*
Zoey - *"This is heartbreaking news to hear. I am sorry the housing program changed the guidelines on the program. The only option right now would be to see if you can get a gift for the downpayment from a relative. Do you have a relative that would be generous enough to give you a gift?"*
Vivienne - *"Mark and I will make a list of relatives and start calling to tell them our plight."*
Zoey - *"What's Plan B if you cannot get the gift funds?"*
Vivienne - *"That's not an option. We have to get the gift because I am not walking away from our $5,000 earnest money deposit. It took us a long time to save up to buy a home. I will find the money."*
Zoey - *"I understand. Well... make your list and check it twice.*

Remember the gift can only be received by one person. It cannot be split between multiple people giving the funds to you. It will also need to be verified and sourced. That means we will need to see that person's bank statement to see where it came from. They will have to be comfortable with that. I will call the loan officer now to get some more parameters on how this should be sourced and the final numbers so that you know how much money to request."

Vivienne - *"Thank you for the insight. That helps me narrow down the list even further."*

The call ended, and Zoey couldn't help but think about the looming uncertainty of whether his clients had a relative who could supply the gift funds and if that could be secured in time. The gravity of the situation left him pondering about this plight. He thought to himself, *"all they could do was rely on luck and faith to see them through."* Zoey called the loan officer to work out the numbers so that his clients knew how much to request.

It was required to review the closing disclosure to see the requirement around need for the gift funds. This was imperative. Only through careful examination of the closing disclosure will they be able to ascertain the final amount needed is correct.

CONTRACT DETAILS

Sales Price: **$350,000**

Financing Type: **FHA**

Down Payment: **3.5% of the sales price**

Buyer Total Closing Cost Amount: **4% of the sales price**

Earnest Money Deposit (EMD): **$5,000**

Buyer Available Funds: **$3,000**

Seller Subsidy (Closing cost assistance): **3%**

TOTAL AMOUNT DUE AT CLOSING

Down Payment | ($350,000 x 3.5%)	$12,250
Closing Cost and Including Impounds	$14,000
Total	$28,250

FORMULA TO CALCULATE TOTAL GIFT AMOUNT

Total amount due at closing	$28,250
Earnest Money Deposit Credit	- $5,000
Total remaining needed	$23,250
Buyer available funds in checking	- $3,000
Total remaining needed	$20,250
Seller Subsidy (Credit towards closing)	-10,500
Total remaining needed	$9,750
Total Gift Funds Amount Needed	$9,750

The loan officer was able to email Vivienne and her husband a final number needed to assist with their plight. Vivienne and Mark went over their list and pondered over the last two names. They decided to call Vivienne's uncle Raymond (her mother's brother) to ask for the gift funds. He was a retired Colonel and owned investment properties, so he understood the importance of home ownership.

CONFERENCE PHONE CALL

(With Vivienne & Mark – Buyers / Raymond – Vivienne's Uncle)

Vivienne - *"Hi Uncle Raymond. It's Vivienne, how are you?"*
Uncle Raymond - *"Hey, ViVi! How are you, baby doll?"*
Vivienne - *"I am fine. I enjoyed seeing you and all the family at your 70th birthday celebration last month. I wish I could see you guys more, but Mark's new position has taken us away from our hometown."*
Uncle Raymond - *"How do you like the area so far?"*
Vivienne - *"We love it! It's a growing and thriving area with lots of opportunities. Actually, Mark and I have run into an opportunity to make our first home purchase, but we have run into a snag. We need some funds to close, and I thought about how you understand the importance of homeownership. I have Mark here listening in and I can put him on "speaker."*
Mark - *"Hi, Uncle Raymond! Nice hearing your voice. Would you be willing to give us gift funds to close on our new home? We have talked to the real estate agent and loan officer, and we need $9,750.00. The first-time homebuyer program we had changed some of their guidelines and we do not qualify for it anymore. So, they suggested that we ask a relative for gift funds. We don't take this amount lightly and we would appreciate your generosity."*
Uncle Raymond - *"Well... That's a large amount. You know... (he went on talking for about 20 minutes about how much houses cost when he purchased his first house). Then he said, I would be glad to assist my niece and nephew with their first home purchase. Just send the information to my email so that I can get started with the process. I may need to move some funds from one of my accounts."*
Vivienne - *"Ohhh, thank you Uncle Raymond! This means so much to us. I will forward the email from the loan officer with all the information. We can talk tomorrow morning and I will give you all the details after you have read the instructions, and thanks again. We love you!"*
Mark - *"Thank you, Uncle Raymond. Talk to you soon.*

Mr. Smith (Vivienne's uncle, the gift donor) was able to follow the instructions by providing the gift letter and deposit of $9,750.00 with Vivienne's assistance. This paved the way for Vivienne and Mark's imminent closing. The underwriter verified the source of funds and other documentation, ensuring that all the requirements were met, and ultimately granted the stamp of approval for the "clear to close."

The phrase that all people in this industry like to hear from the underwriter is, *"it's clear to close."* This statement holds immense significance and underscores the critical role of lenders in ensuring that all the requisite formalities are fulfilled before granting their seal of approval.

To ensure a smoother transaction for his clients, one may say that Zoey could have kept a close eye on the lender's requirements, thus eliminating the likelihood of any last-minute surprises or delays. However, if we analyze this transaction with a microscope the latter was an issue that was not in control of any of the stakeholders in the case. They were not in control of the guidelines being changed.

Real estate will surprise you in ways you never expected.

<u>BOOM</u> that happened!
<u>NOW</u> that happened!
<u>WOW</u> that happened!

Even the most skilled and experienced loan officers encounter surprises when reviewing a buyer's files. This is why the underwriting process is so rigorous - every detail is scrutinized, and there is little room for error. It is a grueling tug-of-war between loan officers and underwriters, each vying for control over the loan's outcome.

Loan officers strive to provide accurate information and ensure that everything is in order. However, underwriters hold the final "stamp of approval" in the matter, and their word is law. Therefore, loan officers must tread carefully, navigating the complicated terrain of regulations and protocols while trying to keep the buyer's best interests in mind and keep them happy.

The underwriting process involves a re-verification and resubmission of documents, leaving no stone unturned in the quest for approval. Loan officers are ever-vigilant, constantly double-checking their work, but even the most diligent efforts can be undone by the strict demands of the underwriters.

Vivienne and Mark found themselves in an utterly perplexing situation in their quest to purchase a home. Faced with this daunting challenge that no one wants to have to do, they brainstormed a list of potential family members who might be able to help them. Luckly, Vivienne's uncle was able to come to their rescue. After much anxiety, the deal closed. Another victory for Zoey, as he was able to guide his clients through the complexities of the process and save the day once again!

THINK BEYOND THE STORY

- What was the cost of this real estate transaction? emotional, physical, or financial?

- How could Zoey have prepared his clients for this scenario and others?

- What do you think about guidelines changing as this one did in midstream?

CLOSING POINTS

- Don't limit yourself to a simple buyer questionnaire, provide your clients with details and different scenarios based on your experience and this book!

- You may want to ask the lender how they handle gift letters when you are under contract.

- Provide your buyers with information on how gift letters and funds work.

- Each loan type has allowable gift fund amounts. You should familiarize yourself with the loan gift amounts and keep up to date with that (Conventional, FHA, USDA, VA)

18

NOT YET

"Patience is a virtue that you can control, on the other hand
temperament is a part of your nature -
both are needed in real estate."
ReShawna Leaven

WHAT IS ONE OF the most crucial components to achieving a successful real estate transaction? One of the components of achieving a successful real estate transaction requires displaying patience and maintaining an appropriate temperament. Adopting an appropriate attitude, results in a less complex, complicated relationship along the continuum of the deal. As a real estate agent, it can be hard to restrain emotions during tense times. Regardless of the actions taken, the clients' perception of their experience with the agent during this moment in time of the home buying or selling process is what truly matters. Thus, it is significant to make that experience the best that it can be. Howard Crimson, the buyer's agent in this story, serves as an inspiration for demonstrating the essential qualities of perseverance and patience that are necessary to ensure a successful real estate transaction.

Howard had prior experience navigating through hot selling seasons, but the one he encountered while working with William and Pauline Overly presented unprecedented challenges. The Overly's relocated from a region in the country where the buying and selling market maintained a neutral stance most of the time. However, in their relocation to the eastern region of the country, the market had scarce resale inventory, leaving them with limited options. To secure a home for his clients before their looming deadline, Howard embarked on extensive research of new home communities.

WILLIAM AND PAULINE'S HOME BUYING WISHLIST

Type of Home	*Single family home (open to a townhome if large enough with an office)*
# of Bedrooms & Bathrooms	*4 bedrooms with 2.5 bathrooms*
Square Footage	*At least 2,500 square feet*
Additional Notes	*Open floor plan and modern design with 2 car garage*
Timeline	*Must be in a home no later than June (6 months from now)*

Howard took The Overly's wish list and began emailing and calling several new home communities.

After speaking with the new homesite representatives, he created a list to share with his clients.

- Floorplans - base price and included features

- Upgraded options

- Available lots

- Community features

- Construction timelines

- Area amenities

- Shopping and entertainment

After compiling a thorough list featuring an array of floor plans,

Howard presented his clients with a selection of options to evaluate their level of interest. In response, the clients promptly conveyed their top three choices via email.

During this particular instance, the county was faced with a backlog of approving home sites, conducting inspections, and granting occupancy permits, resulting in construction delays for various builders in the area. Consequently, the only viable option presented by the builders was to add potential homebuyers to a waiting list. The Overly's thus added themselves to the waiting list of some of the new home communities that they favored, knowing that they would have to exercise patience while they awaited a favorable outcome.

Waiting is easy if you know the outcome
But the outcome was unknown
Unknown outcomes bring anxiety
And anxiety causes panic

In this scenario, the situation is reminiscent of children repeatedly inquiring, *"Are we there yet?"* However, in this case, the query pertains to the release of home sites posing the question, "Are the homesites ready yet?" The passage of several weeks without any positive developments left the Overly family in a state of uncertainty. Adding to their anxiety was the onset of the holiday season, resulting in the closure of offices and limited communication with the community.

Howard's life was a complex web of competing priorities, demanding his attention and energy. His real estate career alone presented numerous responsibilities and obligations, requiring him to navigate complex transactions while ensuring the satisfaction of his client base. On top of this, he also had to juggle his family commitments, adding to the already overwhelming demands on his time and resources.

On one fateful day, while in route to dropping his daughter off at school, Howard found himself grappling with a pressing concern. He thought to himself, "How am I going to find a suitable home for this family within their deadline? The resale market is rapidly diminishing, and time is running out." However, he refused to succumb to despair and instead began to think innovatively. Eventually, he thought of a plan that may expedite his clients' position on the waiting list and secure a lot for building within their desired timeline. This was crucial, since securing the right lot is often the first critical step in building a dream home. He had sold several homes in Acres Landing, which was one of their desired neighborhoods. He had created a good working relationship with the site representative and was known for preparing them for the new home buying process.

PHONE CALL
(With Howard – Buyer's Agent and William & Pauline – Buyers)

Howard - *"Hi, Pauline. How are you?"*
Pauline - *"Hi Howard. I am well. Any news?"*
Howard - *"No, but is William around so you both can hear my idea?"*
William chimed in - *"Yes, I am here."*
Howard - *"Great! I have an idea if you are both up for it. Why don't we go to that community that you like with the golf course to see if you can be bumped up on the waiting list or to see if there are any new developments or fallouts. We can go next week on Monday."*
Pauline - *"That's a great idea!"*
William - *"What time?"*
Howard - *"I was thinking of meeting up at 10:30 am. They open at 11:00 am just in case there are others with the same idea, so we will be first."*
William - *"Perfect. Sounds like a plan. I like the fact that you are thinking outside the box for us. We appreciate it. See you on Monday."*
Howard - *"Great. There are no guarantees' but it's worth a shot."*

Monday morning had finally arrived, and the day was met with clear skies, setting the stage for a good Spring Day. At precisely 11:00 am, the Overly's and Howard entered the model home, where the home site assistant received them. Although the sales manager was running late, they did not have to wait long before they heard the sound of the security chime from the door opening around 11:05am. A towering man speaking on the phone stepped into the site office (usually the garage space). *"Hi, Howard. How are things going out there in the jungle? Sorry for being a few minutes late. I was on the phone with corporate. They don't understand what's going on here. I'm the one with boots on the ground. I have clients running through this model like cars in a Grand Prix race. They are ready to buy, but I don't have anything available."* He apologized for the delay and informed the Overly's that the lots had not been released yet, and there were over 75 individuals already on the waiting list. Undeterred, the assistant assured them that he would add their names to the list and get back to them soon. Howard chimed in, *"Oh, but we are already on the list."* Frank sat down to the computer to check out some things on the waiting list. He offered everyone a cold drink and asked them to sit down in the glass enclosed space of the garage office layout.

CONVERSATION - NOT YET LANDING
(With Sales Manager, Buyer's Agent and Buyers)

Howard- *"Frank, I was wondering if I could get my lovely clients into a home today."*

Frank - *"Let's see what I can do. Let's look at the waiting list to see where you are on the list. Oh, you are number 6 on the list. That's good! In the meantime, while I wait for my manager to call and give me an update, let's take a look at the next building to be released and price out a new home. Some of those numbers could change a bit, but not much."*

Howard - The agent and his clients were looking at the map of the community. He pointed to the next available lots in the townhouse building set to be released and asked, *"Do you like where these lots are in the community?"*

Pauline - *"Yes, I like this location. How about you William?"*

William - *"Yes, that works for me. What needs to happen now?"*

Frank - *"Which lot are you interested in?"*

Pauline - *"We're interested in Lot 28."*

Frank - *"Ok, Lot 28 has a $5,000 premium on it which is good. The other*

lots have a $10,000 premium which would be added to the price. Do you know which floor plan you like?"
William - *"We like the Hillman floor plan."*
Frank - *"Ok, Let's price it out so you will know ahead of time how much your new home will cost with all the options and upgrades."*

The Overly's, along with Howard and Frank, began to go through the options and engage in a detailed cost analysis. They aimed to stay with their pre-approved budget while factoring in the various upgrades from their wish list. However, while in the midst of this task, Frank received a significant phone call from his manager. The news was music to the ears of the Overly's and Howard: the lots had been released, and to their delight, lot 28 was included in the list. This was an incredible milestone for Howard's clients, who had been awaiting this moment for what seemed like an eternity. At last, their home choice journey could officially begin.

The construction of the new home spanned over a period of five long months. As the project drew towards its conclusion, one of the final steps before closing was to conduct a new home orientation with the project manager. The primary aim of this orientation was to allow the buyers to survey the completed home, familiarize themselves with its functionality, and identify any imperfections that needed to be rectified before the closing. Howard was there with them every step of the way. He accompanied them to the design center to explain the importance of design and express making choices that would bring value to their home in the future. He kept them abreast with the expectations of buying a luxury town home and things to focus on during their new home orientation.

Once the buyers identified the deficiencies, they were added to a builder punch list and signed by both the project manager and the buyers. Typically, the new home orientation would take place a week before the closing, with the final walkthrough scheduled on the day of closing to confirm that all the corrections had been made and that the home was ready for delivery. In this case, although the new home orientation was successfully conducted in this manner, it was still unclear to Mr. and Mrs. Overly whether the closing would occur as scheduled the following week. There was something else holding up the process.

SATISFIED CONDITIONS

LENDER CONDITIONS	SATISFIED
The appraisal was in and supported the sales price	YES
The homeowner's insurance supported the loan type and coverage amount	YES
The buyer's verification of employment was completed and satisfied	YES
The buyer's funds to close had been verified and sent to the title company	YES

What other factors might be hindering the closure of this home? Three days before the closing date, the lender had yet to receive the final condition required for the loan: the certificate of occupancy. This vital document, also referred to as an occupancy permit, verifies that the home meets all habitability standards set by the county inspector. Unfortunately, the county was facing a backlog and could not provide an estimated completion date for the certificate of occupancy, further delaying the closing process.

PHONE CALL
(With Frank – Sales Manager and Howard – Buyer's Agent)

Howard - *"Is there any way around this occupancy certificate, Frank?"*
Frank - *"No, unfortunately not. The lender needs this in order to fund the loan. The county is backed up and the county building inspector is scheduled to come out within the next few days."*

Although William and Pauline were dissatisfied with the unexpected delay, they had no choice but to remain patient and wait for the county and building supervisor to grant them the certificate of occupancy. The wait lasted for twelve days. During the waiting period, unfortunately the couple had to move into an extended stay hotel since their lease had expired. Furthermore, the change in the closing date forced them to rent three storage units and board their two dogs in a kennel, which added to the already substantial costs of their relocation. But with resolve and patience they finally closed.

In a real estate transaction, one must remain adaptable since certain outcomes lie beyond the control of the immediate stakeholders. One should always account for variable change. It is vital to acknowledge the outcome of the situation and refrain from allowing emotions to cloud one's judgment. It is imperative to keep clients informed of possible delays and assist them in planning a way to adapt (i.e., moving process, sustainable housing during transitions). The ability to endure challenging situations with fortitude and patience is a key component of achieving success. Displaying "BAI" or Buyer Agent Intelligence, which entails utilizing one's accumulated knowledge and experiences to resolve issues logically and objectively without being influenced by emotions, is critical.

THINK BEYOND THE STORY

- What was the cost of this real estate transaction? emotional, physical, or financial?

- What do you think about the agent thinking outside the box?

- Do you think they would have asked to be released from their buyer agency agreement out of frustration of no results?

CLOSING POINTS

- Understand the new home sales process

- Being proactive in the new home sales process can assist buyers

- Inform your clients that they should not schedule their movers until an occupancy permit is granted as the closing will not take place until the lender receives this document.

- This component was not displayed in this story, however, keep in mind that if a buyer is going to get an inspection performed by a third-party inspection company, the builder must get a copy of the home inspector's license, insurance to give to the builder. The builder may also have additional requirements for a third-party person to be on their premises. Recommendations are to get this approved at least 3 weeks in advance.

19

SUMMER RAIN

*"Umbrellas aren't just for rain - in real estate,
they're essential for weathering the storm
of unexpected surprises."*
ReShawna Leaven

A S THE OLD ADAGE goes, *"April Showers Bring May Flowers"*, notwithstanding its splendor, Mother Nature can exhibit a wide spectrum of weather patterns ranging from a serene breeze to a fierce thunderstorm. Geographic regions experience distinct temperature vortexes and currents across various seasons. In the same manner real estate bears a resemblance to the weather in terms of its cycles. It undergoes buying, selling, and neutral seasons. An imbalance of any of these factors can significantly impact the outcome. This narrative unfolds during the peak summer selling season when an agent encounters an event during a prolonged spell of rainy weather. It was quite memorable.

The property, despite being listed for a substantial period, had garnered a meager number of showings. It was an REO (Real Estate Owned) being sold by a local agent who had an account with bank owned properties. Consequently, after analyzing the market conditions and to try to generate a sale, the asset manager granted approval for a $25,000 reduction in price. This revision brought the listing price down to $375,000, thereby sparking interest among prospective buyers. The surge in demand led to several scheduled showing appointments, indicating a promising outcome for the property.

The day after the price reduction, the city found itself under siege by a sky full of ominous cumulonimbus clouds. For nearly five hours, these brooding clouds hovered with the looming threat of a hurricane. Elliott Gibson, our intrepid listing agent from 99 Problems Realty, watched anxiously as his listing at 999 Bar Street sat right in the storm's path. Originally predicted to be a tropical storm, it had thankfully been downgraded to heavy rain and potential flooding. As the sky darkened to a menacing gray, it appeared to be a prelude to chaos brewing above.

As if the storm wasn't enough, the local weather service threw in a curveball - there was a tornado warning within a 30-mile radius. That afternoon there was a relentless downpour, complete with a side serving of hail and the occasional ballet of falling trees. It left its mark, and the aftermath was a landscape littered with damage, leading to a surge in insurance claims throughout the area.

The first showing a couple of days after the storm had been scheduled for 2:00 pm at 999 Bar Street with several others to follow. The first agent to show the property with her clients was Grace Baker. When she reached the basement with her clients, they made a huge discovery. She immediately made a call to Elliott. He was unavailable to answer, so Grace left him a voicemail.

VOICEMAIL (From (555) 123-5555 (26 seconds)

"Hi Elliott! This is Grace Baker from XYZ Realty. Please call me back as soon as possible. There is an emergency at your listing. I can be reached at 555-123-5555. Thank you."

Elliott returned Grace Baker's call after his appointment within the hour.

Elliott - *"Hi Grace. Sorry I missed your call. I was at another appointment. Tell me what seems to be the emergency?"*
Grace - *"Hi, Elliott. Thank you for returning my phone call. There is a pool of water in the basement at 999 Bar Street. You could actually swim in it. It's up to my knees. There has been a lot of rain in the area, and I suppose it has seeped in somehow and flooded the basement there. Probably a defective sump pump."*
Elliott - *"Wow! A pool in the basement? I don't remember listing that feature! Thank you for telling me. I need to hurry over to assess the problem. Thank you so much. I apologize for the issue in the basement. I was out of town and had not had time to go by the house and check on things after the storm. If I had known, I surely would have canceled your showing for today. Sorry for the inconvenience."*

This was Elliott's first REO listing, and he needed guidance. Luckily, it had an unfinished basement and did not need drywall repairs or carpet installation. Elliott asked some of his colleagues for recommendations for mold remediation and other services. Elliott created a list of items that needed to be assessed for damages.

Checklist for 999 Bar Street

1. Cancel all showings and place the home temporarily off the market.

2. Visit and take photos

3. Call plumbing and mold remediation companies

4. Make appointments with contractors to get estimates for repairs

5. Create a summary of what happened and send it to the asset manager of the REO company along with the estimates.

It was determined that the sump pump stopped working, so a new sump pump was installed with a backup battery, as well as mold treatment. Fortunately, it was less costly because the basement was unfinished and only the insulation that covered the walls needed to be replaced. The contractors had the job completed in two weeks.

EMAIL (From Listing Agent to Asset Manager)

FROM: Elliott Gibson/TO: Kimberly Bradshaw
SUBJECT: (Asset Manager Approval Needed) Report for 999 Bar Street

Hi Kimberly,

There was a bad storm and the sump pump stopped working due to a power outage. I have attached photos and estimates to repair the home. Property showings have been suspended due to the current damage of the home.

Please find the photos of the damage and estimates from several plumbing and mold remediation companies.

Elliott Gibson

Attachments

- Photos

- Estimate 1, 2, 3 - Plumber

- Estimate 1, 2, 3 - Mold Remediation

EMAIL (From Asset Manager to Listing Agent)

FROM: Kimberly Bradshaw/ TO: Elliott Gibson
SUBJECT: Re: (Asset Manager Approval Needed) Report for 999 Bar Street

Hi Elliott,

Thank you for acting so quickly on this. I approved the work. From estimate (1) of the plumbing company and estimate (3) from the mold remediation company. Let me know if there are any additional damages associated with this property. Enjoy your week.

Kimberly Bradshaw
Asset Manager

All labor had to be documented with photos (timestamps) along with the invoices of the completed work. The collective cost of the services rendered by the vendors, amounted to a staggering sum of $2,500. Elliott had to use his funds (real estate business) to pay upfront for the cost associated with this peril. He submitted a reimbursement invoice to the asset manager and got reimbursed a month later.

After this two week repair the house was placed back on the market, however, the selling season was going into the winter months which can be a slow time in the real estate market. In addition, this was a particularly challenging period, given that there was a glut of inventory on the market. At the time, the prevailing conditions presented a daunting challenge, necessitating a significant amount of effort and perseverance to ensure that the sale was eventually executed. It took six months to sell.

The presence of a sump pump in a basement is an absolute necessity, as it effectively pumps water away from the structure, thus mitigating any potential water damage that could occur. However, for the pump to function optimally, it requires a constant supply of electricity. In cases where the power supply has been terminated or is disrupted by a storm, the sump pump is rendered ineffective, leading to potential damage to the property. It is a good idea to install a backup battery to avoid any negative consequences that may result from a malfunctioning sump pump. It is noteworthy that the cost of repairs necessitated by a faulty sump pump is not typically covered under a standard homeowners' insurance policy.

Now this story adds another hat that real estate agents have where among all the other hats, meteorologist. We must know and understand what "Mother Nature" could have in store for our properties. The outside elements can cause damage to real estate, from a fallen tree or heavy snow on a deck. In this case, there was a flood in the basement from a faulty sump pump. There are many lessons to be learned from this story. The main lesson is to be proactive with listings. One scenario would be to visit your vacant listing periodically, especially after a storm, to check for any changes (i.e., check to make sure the property is secure, animal intrusions, water damage, etc.).

THINK BEYOND THE STORY

- What was the cost of this real estate transaction? emotional, physical, or financial

- What are some things that Elliott could have improved on in this scenario?

CLOSING POINTS

- During an initial meeting with the seller, ask if they have had any issues with their sump pump in their basement

- A backup battery should always be present in a sump pump

- Inform clients of potential problems during severe weather

- After severe weather, always check the listing (vacant)

20

BUYER'S REMORSE

*"The possibilities of something going awry
in a transaction are endless."*
ReShawna Leaven

M AKING A PURCHASE WITHOUT a trial run is similar to purchasing a car without taking it for a spin. While online specifications may appear satisfactory, the in-person experience can fail to meet expectations of comfort and individuality. This narrative revolves around a mentor who assists a mentee in addressing a client's feelings of post-purchase regret.

In the realm of real estate, a mentor is a seasoned professional who aids a novice agent in navigating the intricacies of the profession on a daily basis. Acting as a reliable resource, they offer invaluable guidance and support to the mentee, and serve as a backup to the supervising broker for non-brokerage related matters. By providing clarity and direction on questions such as "Should I?" alleviates the need for the broker to address every single query.

George assumed the role of mentor to James, a recent addition to his real estate agency, who had embarked on a personal transaction to purchase a home with his girlfriend.

James, fresh out of real estate classes and acing his exam with more colors than a peacock, found his way into the world of real estate thanks to a tip-off from a colleague. This colleague had a buddy at ABC Real Estate, and James, seizing the opportunity, contacted George, the agency's recruiting wizard. George, thrilled to have James on board, didn't hesitate to welcome him to the fold. James, ever the planner, had already earmarked his first deal: buying a house with his girlfriend, Amy. Armed with a new real estate license and bubbling with enthusiasm, James sailed through the necessary paperwork and orientation like a pro. But, sensing he still had much to learn, he roped in George as his mentor, who agreed to take him on.

The home hunt began with James and Amy diving into the sea of listings. Their eyes sparkled at two properties, prompting James to arrange a tour. Those houses were just the appetizer, though, as they craved more options. The following weekend, another tempting listing popped up, but Amy, tied up at work, couldn't make it. Not wanting to miss out, she nudged James to check it out solo and, if it felt right, to jump on it with an offer. Trusting his instincts, James drafted the contract and, voila, the sellers gave it a thumbs up!

Next, James navigated the paperwork maze like a pro test-driving a new car, smoothly shifting gears as he passed each document to the rightful receiver: the loan officer, the title company (complete with a check in hand) and organizing the home inspection. It was like fine-tuning the engine of his dream car — every piece had to click perfectly into place. In this real estate road trip, James was firmly behind the wheel, ready to steer his way through the twists and turns of his first transaction.

Following the successful negotiation of a contract, James contacted George to seek counsel on a newly emerging dilemma involving this personal transaction.

PHONE CALL
(With George – Mentor and James – Mentee)

James - *"My girlfriend no longer wants the house. She didn't see it until yesterday at the inspection and doesn't like the floorplan or wall colors."*
George - *"Now James, I know that you are new at this, and you are trying to understand all the components of this process, but you have entered into a legally binding contract with the seller. This means that you must comply with the terms of the contract. You need to wait for the home inspection report from the inspector. Then, submit the report and home inspection contingency removal addendum to the seller of your requested items for repair or replacement. If the seller does not comply with fixing the home inspection items, you will be able to submit a release of contract since you have a home inspection contingency in place."*
James - *"Ok. I will send the inspection items to the listing agent and see where it goes from there."*
George - *"Ok. Let me know how it goes. I am here for you."*

Eager to tackle each point raised in the home inspection report, James sent a comprehensive list of thirty issues to the listing agent. However, the seller balked at the terms outlined in the home inspection contingency removal addendum. Seeing that further bargaining would be a dead end, James decided to initiate the release of the contract and request a refund of the earnest money deposit. Sadly (which was what they wanted) this led to the termination of the contract.

Consider an alternative scenario where the seller agrees to all the items on the home inspection contingency and submits the addendum with unaltered terms. In such a situation, the contract would remain valid, and the only plausible manner to exit would be via homeowners' association documents in the case of an HOA or if financing were denied.

This story drives home a crucial lesson, similar to test-driving a car before buying it - it's essential to have all the key decision-makers present when showing a home. Just as someone wouldn't buy a car without all drivers giving it a spin, in real estate, the absence of a key player can dramatically sway opinions. This shift often steers the initial excitement of "I love it" to a later gear of "I don't like it," a trend commonly seen in the industry, much like a car buyer changing their mind after a test drive.

THINK BEYOND THE STORY

- What was the cost of this real estate transaction? emotional, physical, or financial?

- What other ways could the buyer have terminated the contract?

CLOSING POINTS

- Make sure all decision makers are present at the showing.

- A new agent should use their mentor as a reliable resource.

21

UNDER THE MICROSCOPE

*"Properties and ownership interests are analyzed
to the tenth power under the microscope lens."*
ReShawna Leaven

ENGAGING IN A REAL estate transaction can be a journey filled with unexpected surprises. It is not common for clients to withhold pertinent information that may significantly impact the transaction, whether intentionally or unintentionally. In this particular scenario, one of the parties had "ownership interest" in another property. This story highlights the importance of full disclosure of all things important that could be connected during a real estate transaction.

Our journey begins with Paulina Goodwin, an agent assisting first time home buyers, Sean, and Trisha Flowers, through their home purchase. The Flowers had utilized an online mortgage search engine that advertised an appealing interest rate coupled with a first-time home buyer program to secure their mortgage loan pre-approval. Upon receiving their pre-approval letter, they forwarded it to Paulina to initiate their home buying process.

After viewing numerous homes in their desired area over the course of three weeks, Sean and Trisha finally found a home that met their specific needs and desires. To assist the buyers with crafting a competitive offer, Paulina prepared a comparative market analysis utilizing recent sales data in the area.

Paulina sent an email to her clients Sean and Trisha to highlight her recommendations for their offer.

EMAIL (From Buyer's Agent to Buyers)

FROM: Paulina Goodwin /TO: Sean and Trisha Flowers
SUBJECT: Recommendations for 567 New Home Road

Hi Sean and Trisha,

Based on the recent sales in the neighborhood, here are my recommendations for an offer below:

- Sales Price: $350,000

- Earnest Money Deposit: $3,500

- Closing Cost Assistance: 3% of the sales price

- Closing Date: 45 days from contract acceptance

- Home Inspection, Financing Contingency and Appraisal Contingency

I have attached the recent sales for your review as well in the attached PDF. Let me know if you are ok with the terms or would like me to make any changes and I will send you the offer to electronically sign.

Sincerely,
Paulina Goodwin
<<Comparables pdf>>

Paulina's clients promptly replied agreeing to the terms that she outlined in her email. After receiving their acceptance, she prepared their offer and sent it over for review and signatures. After they signed the offer, she forwarded it to the listing agent who presented it to the sellers.

Following the review of their offer, the sellers on New Home Road agreed to the terms and signed for acceptance. This pivotal moment marks a significant milestone in the home buying process, as this is the time that buyers and sellers arrive at a mutually beneficial agreement.

PHONE CALL
(With Paulina - Buyer's Agent and Trisha Flowers – Buyer)

Paulina - *"Happy Tuesday Trisha!"*
Trisha - *"Hi Paulina. I hope you have good news for us."*
Paulina - *"Yes, I do! The sellers have accepted your offer with no changes. We are now under contract."*
Trisha - *"That is wonderful. I will let Sean know right away. What are the next steps?*
Paulina - *"The first step is to send in the earnest money deposit. Next, we will schedule and attend the home inspection. I will send you a checklist with step-by-step instructions."*
Trisha - *"Ok great."*

The home inspection was conducted with diligence, and the results proved to be satisfactory, indicating that the property was in good condition. Next, the appraisal was conducted to determine the value of the property. The appraised value supported the sales price and further cemented the deal. In the meantime, the buyers were tasked with securing adequate homeowners' insurance. This protects the lender and buyer from perils.

In the subsequent weeks, Sean and Trisha dedicated themselves to collecting all necessary documents and submitted them diligently to their lender to enable a smooth and efficient closing process. However, two weeks before the anticipated closing date, the lender transmitted the buyers' file to the underwriting department for processing. During this phase, an unexpected discovery was made that presented a challenge.

PHONE CALL
(With Paulina - Buyer's Agent and Andrew – Loan Officer)

Andrew - "Hi. Mrs. Flowers. How are you?"

Trisha - "I am well. Andrew, how are you?"

Andrew - "Great, I found out some information today from the underwriter that I would like to ask you about. We found another home loan on your husband's credit report?"

Trisha - "What!? Another house on his credit report? No, I am not aware of that."

Andrew - "He is the co-signer on a property. This makes him have ownership interest and will not allow him to be a first-time home buyer. You will not be able to qualify for the first-time homebuyer program. In addition to that, this will change your debt-to-income ratios."

Trisha - "What? I can't believe this. He is the co-signer for a mortgage. Where is the home and who is the other person on the loan?"

Andrew - "Ma'am I can't tell you that."

Trisha - "Please Andrew. It's public knowledge. It will take me a while to find it, but it would be easy if you could just tell me now. I need to understand the whole story. I feel my blood pressure going up."

Andrew - "The name that came up was Irene Jameson. The home was purchased about a year ago in 2015 in Tennessee." (As Andrew stated the facts, Trisha went into a trance state of mind. She was not completely naive to the fact that her husband did have a previous relationship with a woman named Irene. She continued to ponder over the situation at hand). Andrew presented Trisha with several alternatives to purchase the home, and after a brief discussion, they concluded the call.

While sitting on the deck of their apartment, Trisha lit up a cigarette and opened a bottle of red wine to calm her nerves. By the time she was on the last eight-ounce glass, she heard keys rumbling at the door.

IF WALLS COULD TALK CONVERSATION
(With Sean and Trisha about the new developments)

Sean - *"Hey babe."*
Trisha - *"Hey (she said in a tired voice)"*
Sean - *"What's wrong Trisha?"*
Trisha - *"I'm disappointed. I found out today that I am living with a liar."*
Sean - *"Trisha, what are you talking about?"*
Trisha - *"I found out today that you are the co-signer on a home with Irene and this purchase occurred since we've been married. She's the reason why we almost broke off our engagement. I can't believe that this is going to keep us from buying our dream home."*
Sean - *"No, I ended it."*
Trisha - *"You must take me for Boo Boo The Fool. You have a mortgage with this woman. Mortgages are 30 years long. That's like marriage."*
Sean - *"So what do you want to do?"*
Trisha - *"Well, the loan officer said we can't get the house through that program, because you brought a house with that girl. So, when you went on all those Tennessee work trips, you were seeing her, I guess. Andrew said that we would need $15,000 to buy the home from our own funds which is money we don't have, and we can't ask for it from a family member. I need to let Paulina know what's going on. This is just too much..."* (He was looking dumbfounded about how his wife found out about his extra loan)

Trisha called Paulina the next morning with the bad news. Paulina was surprised and empathetic about the whole situation. She sent the necessary documentation to get the buyers released from the sales contract and get their earnest money back since they were still in their financing contingency period and entitled to receive the funds back. The transaction was officially released, and the buyers received their earnest money back. Regrettably, the clients were forced to confront the reality of their marriage, which ultimately led to their separation.

Despite the difficulties, Paulina remained a supportive presence throughout the process and worked tirelessly with Trisha to find a new property that was within her budget that would fulfill her needs and aspirations. After an extensive search and careful consideration, the home was found, and Trisha was able to close on a property that she could truly call her own. With Paulina's unwavering support and guidance, Trisha was able to embark on a new chapter in her life with confidence and optimism for the future.

THINK BEYOND THE STORY

- What was the cost of this real estate transaction? emotional, physical, or financial?

- What would have happened if the financing contingency had been removed from the sales contract?

CLOSING POINTS

- Always ask your clients if they have any ownership interest in any state.

- Advise your client that "what is done in the dark always comes to light?" with credit, income etc.

- Real estate is an emotional rollercoaster for clients, be prepared to help them with the loops and turns that they will face.

22

EXPLORATION

"My mother always said -
" I have eyes in the back of my head."
ReShawna Leaven

EMBARKING ON A HOUSE tour with a real estate agent can often feel like setting sail on uncharted waters. Much like a seasoned captain navigating through the unpredictable seas, a skilled agent must steer clients through the intricate and often surprising journey of finding a new home. The story of Mia Edwards, a real estate agent, and her clients on a sunny Saturday afternoon perfectly encapsulates this adventure. Just like a ship venturing into the unknown, Mia and her clients—Justine, Ralph, and their young daughter Josephine—begin their exploration, unaware of the twists and turns their journey will take.

It's a sunny Saturday afternoon in a well sought after neighborhood and Mia Edwards and her clients finally arrive at the last house of their tour of homes. Approaching the lockbox, she inserts her real estate agent card, and the lockbox opens. With keys in hand, Mia opens the door and invites her clients inside. Justine, Ralph, and their adorable four-year-old daughter Josephine. They begin to eagerly explore the spaces in the home. Mia guides them through each room pointing out specific features.

As Justine, Ralph, and Mia discussed the kitchen's features, Josephine frolicked in the living room, twirling, and blowing bubbles with glee. Suddenly, Justine looked around after discussing the features in the kitchen and called out to her daughter Josephine, beckoning her to join them in the kitchen. Reluctantly, Josephine followed her mother, and the group began ascending the stairs to explore the rest of the townhome.

They viewed each bedroom and they finally arrived at the loft area in the primary suite. Justine called out again for Josephine as they toured the fourth level, but this time there was no response. *"JOSEPHINE* where are you?"* Justine called out in a firm motherly tone that echoed through the vacant home. When she did not get an answer, she and her husband became concerned. *"Why isn't she answering Ralph?*

Mia's eyes darted around the room and glanced through the window of the primary suite where she saw Josephine twirling outside in the front yard with her bubbles. *"Oh no, Justine,"* Mia exclaimed. *"She's outside!"*

Mia's urgent words propelled Justine into immediate action. Her heart began to race with panic, and she sprinted down four flights of stairs like an olympian in the 100-meter race. Navigating the steps was challenging because she was in her sixth month of pregnancy. Upon reaching the bottom, she burst through the front door to find Josephine, happily twirling but startled at her mother's appearance. In a frightening turn, Josephine darted towards the busy street.

Chaos ensued as Justine, Ralph, and Mia all ran after her. Justine, driven by a mother's instinct, caught Josephine just in time, barely two minutes before a flurry of dump trucks roared down the street. The close call was a stark reminder of the ever-present dangers and the preciousness of their family's safety.

When everyone was back in the house safe and sound, Mia realized how important her job was, not just in selling houses but in keeping her clients and their families safe. This experience brought light to being careful during showings and being ready for anything that can happen. After this, Mia made a special "children's kit" with fun things for kids to do (toys and books). She began to change her showing strategies when parents needed to bring their children. On those occasions she would watch the children and sit with them and the "children's kit" while the parents viewed the other floors. This added another layer and service to her business.

The home tour on the next day illustrated this new approach. Greeted by an enthusiastic Josephine, Mia invited her to play a special role as her "Mini-Assistant," turning the home tour into an exciting adventure. The parents, watching their daughter's enjoyment, found their anxiety alleviated by the cheerful atmosphere Mia had cultivated. Mia and Josephine made a good connection. Mia playfully assigned Josephine tasks (flashlight inspector) that left a lasting impression on the family. This family finally settled on a new home and their bond with Mia remained strong, leading to future referrals.

This series of events served as a stark reminder for Mia of the demanding nature of her profession. It reinforced the importance of her dedication to her clients' safety and happiness. Reflecting on the incident, the thought of what could have happened without their quick response continued to haunt her, a reminder of the fine balance between safety and danger in her line of work.

"Today, I was a negotiator, a problem-solver, and, unexpectedly, a child-rescuer. Who would've thought?" she continued; her voice tinged with humor. *"One minute you're discussing property lines, and the next, you're orchestrating a search party like Indiana Jones. It's like being in a 1970s soap opera where you never know what the next episode brings."*

THINK BEYOND THE STORY

- What was the cost of this real estate transaction? emotional, physical, or financial

- What kinds of conversation and rapport can you build with a parent about home tours when they have children?

- What would you have done in this situation? Do you have the skills needed to keep your eyes on children?

CLOSING POINTS

- Be informative about the process of home tours

- Make sure to lock the door behind you. (Stay in close proximity to the door)

- It's ok to ask parents if they can get a relative to watch small children during a home tour

- Create a "kids kit" when you have to show houses with children

- Showing a house with small children present requires keeping an eye on them at all times.

23

SOLD TOO FAST

L IFE OFTEN MIRRORS THOSE high-octane car commercials that dazzle us on our screens. Picture this: in a mere thirty seconds, an advertisement whisks you away with its sensory smorgasbord - eye-catching imagery, showcasing a sleek moving machine with a tantalizing soundscape in the background. This sleek machine usually moves effortlessly through the heartbeat of a bustling metropolitan street (with no other cars) flanked by sky-piercing towers and breathtaking panoramic views. Or, imagine a winding mountain road, with the vast ocean stretching into the distance, all under the captivating spell of the sunset in the distance. These commercials are not just selling a car; they're selling a dream. Whether it's the thrill of living on the razor's edge or the cozy embrace of a comfortable journey, the vision promises joy with every turn of the key, painting a picture of the good life, one drive at a time.

Imagine this same vision of exhilaration in the air, your heart beating fast, as you embark on the journey of selling a home in just 24 hours after being listed. Each step in this race to the end is like preparing for an auto race, yet the finish line – the sale – remains a mystery as you come around the bend on the last lap and the sharpness of the curve gives you a sign of caution (am I making the right decision), but you continue to go full speed ahead. This unpredictability is the heartbeat of real estate. A swift sale, a dream for many, can evoke a storm of emotions, mirroring the thrill and apprehension of rounding such a sharp bend.

It's an exciting moment, but it can also be overwhelming, plunging both the seller and their agent into a flurry of activity. However, this situation can showcase the advantages of having a strong partnership between a buyer's agent and an engaged selling agent. We start this adventure with the agent in her office, going through multiple offers that have come in for her client's new listing. This opening scene sets the stage for the often unpredictable world of real estate.

On a Tuesday morning, Tracy received the final offers for her listing, bringing the unanticipated listing phase to a quick close. Tracy swiftly set to work preparing a comprehensive presentation and invited her client to her office to showcase the offers. Randy walked into Tracy's office and was hit by a buzz of activity. Phones were ringing non-stop, and agents were busy moving around, looking focused and excited. The room was full of energy, with the smell of fresh coffee in the air and the sound of printers busy at work. In the middle of all this, Tracy's desk was like a calm spot. She sat there, looking calm and collected, very different from the busy scene around her.

As Randy arrived at the office, Tracy greeted her with a warm smile and ushered her into one of the conference rooms, ready to dive into the details of the various offers. Drawing upon her extensive knowledge and experience, Tracy reviewed each offer with Randy, highlighting the pros and cons of each and providing invaluable insights into the potential impact of each.

Through her thoughtful analysis and expert guidance, Tracy enabled Randy to make a fully informed decision, with a deep understanding of the financial implications of each offer. With the seller's net sheet at the forefront of their discussion, Tracy's recommendations were informed and insightful, reflecting her unwavering commitment to securing the best possible outcome for her client.

After their initial greetings...

Tracy - *"Hi Randy! Come in and have a seat. You can close the door behind you. I have water here if you would like a bottle. I have several offers, but one in particular stands out in the crowd. This offer has terms to close quickly. In three weeks! The market's always fluctuating. A few years back, I experienced a similar trend, and it taught me the importance of timing and adaptability in this business. It's not just about selling; it's about understanding and navigating through these waves."*

Randy - *"Wow. This process is so overwhelming. Do you think we priced it too low?"*

Tracy - *"No, we priced it at market value based on the neighborhood comparables. If you choose this offer, you can send a counteroffer with a "later" closing date, so that you will have enough time to pack. What do you think about that?"*

Randy - *"No, I don't need to send a counteroffer. I am ok with the closing date. I have been scouting out places to move and I have found a suitable rental property. My house just sold quicker than I expected."*

The seller's net sheet is the amount of funds the seller has left before deducting any other unpaid mortgages, real estate brokerage fees, city/county fees and other closing costs from the seller's side of the transaction.

Randy - (Randy decided to take the offer with the three-week closing). *"I'll go with offer #3."*

Tracy - *"Ok. Randy. This one closes in a few weeks.* [Even though the timeline for this transaction was discussed earlier when they were reviewing offers, she wanted to reassure and confirm again so her client fully understood the process.] *I know it seems daunting, Randy. This is a solid offer and a good choice. I just want to make sure you are comfortable with the timeline."*

Tracy set aside the other offers and placed offer #3 in front of Randy.

She reviewed each page of the contract and instructed her client where to initial, sign, and date.

Tracy - *"Ok, that's the last signature."*
Randy - *"Great! What are the next steps?"*
Tracy - *"I have a booklet that I will leave with you to review that goes over everything step by step. After you leave the office, I'll scan and send the contract to the buyer's agent, title company, loan officer and change the status in the system. I will also blind copy you on all email correspondence moving forward, so you are aware of what's going on. You don't need to reply to these emails. They're for your reference only."*
Randy - *"Great. Thank you so much for everything."*
Tracy - *"You're welcome."*

As Tracy and Randy concluded their meeting, satisfied with the ratified contract, they exchanged heartfelt goodbyes. With the seller having accepted the original offer without any changes. The contract was now fully ratified, representing a significant milestone in the transaction.

Tracy promptly made her way to the copy room in her office, where she utilized the state-of-the-art multifunction printer to scan the contract. With the scanned copy now available in her email, Tracy implemented her best practice of renaming documents before sending them out, ensuring that she would have a clear and concise reference to the property. The renamed PDF was now known as "RatifiedContract_123EasySt," instead of (107fefgfyf290.pdf) enabling Tracy to easily locate and retrieve it in the future.

Now, Randy returned home with thoughts of where she lived for so many years. As the reality of the sale sank in, a myriad of emotions raced through Randy's head. Her eyes, reflecting a storm of memories, sparkled with both relief and a hint of sadness. The corners of her mouth twitched upwards in a bittersweet smile as she looked around the room that had been her sanctuary for years.

With all necessary documents in order, the transaction proceeded smoothly, culminating in an emotional settlement for Randy. Shedding a few tears of joy, Randy embraced her agent tightly, expressing her gratitude for a job well done. Despite the split settlement, with the buyer and seller closing at different times, the process was executed with the utmost professionalism and efficiency, a testament to Tracy's unwavering commitment to excellence.

Seller and agent's conversation after closing.

Randy - *"I appreciate everything you've done during the sale of my home. You are truly a blessing." she said in a quivering voice.*

Tracy - *"You are very welcome, Randy. It was a pleasure."*

Randy - *"This is the first home that I purchased on my own after my divorce. The divorce left me in a financial debacle but I was able to secure this property. I am sad to let it go. I'm just so emotional." (sobbing)*

Tracy - *"I understand. The saying goes, home is where the heart is. It's where we gather with family and friends and find solitude. It's our security and shelter. This reminds me of a tough situation I faced a couple of years ago. It was challenging, but it taught me to stay focused and solution-oriented, no matter what."*

Randy - *"I appreciate your kind words. It's hard to move on to something new, but it's time."*

Tracy - *"Your new life awaits".* (As she opened the door from the title company) *Every successful sale, like yours, reaffirms why I do this. It's not just about closing deals; it's about making real connections and helping people start their next chapter. That's what keeps me going."*

Randy - *"Yes."* (She walked through the door with her head in the air and a smile on her face).

Tracy - (with a thoughtful expression) *"You know, Randy, this journey we've been on together, really makes me think. In real estate, just like in life, sometimes the unexpected paths lead to the most fulfilling destinations. We started with a plan, but it was our ability to adapt and embrace the unexpected that really brought us here."*

A WEEK AFTER CLOSING

Tracy received an email from her client.

FROM: Randy Ellis/ TO: Tracy
SUBJECT: Thank you

I want to truly thank you for your assistance with selling my home. You made it easy and I'm grateful that I had you. Many of my friends wanted me to go with another agent, but I knew that you were the best fit for me. When someone needs an agent, I will be sure to refer you. Thanks again for helping me with my new journey.

Thank you,
Randy

SAMPLE EMAIL TO FUTURE SELLER(S)

This will be an emotional ride. Some of my past client's experience selling a home with an array of emotional responses from tears of relief to tears of joy. Keep in mind as you take this journey, you will go through many emotional feelings. I am here to assist you through this process within the realm of this transaction. Know that you are in good hands with me and my team to get you to your next destination.

Being empathetic and supportive is key. Agents need to really understand their clients' stories. Knowing what the client is going through helps agents be more sensitive to their needs, especially when there are challenges.

THINK BEYOND THE STORY

- What was the cost of this real estate transaction? emotional, physical, or financial

- Could this have been a different experience for the seller if she had chosen a different offer?

- What if the seller changed her mind to sell after she signed the offer?

CLOSING POINTS

- During a listing presentation give the seller information so that they can make an informed decision

- A good timeline is helpful

- Create a flow chart as you present the offers to the client

  - If you choose this offer, it's a longer process and this is what will happen...

  - If you choose this offer, it's a shorter process, and this is what will happen...

- Set clear expectations for the seller relocation process

  - When do you need to pack and move?

- Provide a checklist of what's next during their transaction

  - Weekly reminder of what's next

24

LENDER LANE

*"You need to scrutinize any pre-approval
letter for its validity."*
ReShawna Leaven

MANY POTENTIAL HOMEBUYERS SEEKING to purchase a home may perceive a pre-approval letter as an assurance of smooth sailing. However, it is essential to note that this is not a case of being bestowed with an inexhaustible supply of wealth similar to that of Mr. Warbucks, with unlimited access to funds. As agents, we should evaluate pre-approval letters, like that of a highway Civil Engineer. They design and oversee the construction of highways, requiring precision to ensure proper alignment, grading, and adherence to safety standards. Alas, some of our buyers get hypnotized by the siren song of loan officers. These smooth-talkers spin tales of a mythical EASY STREET - a place where mortgages grow on trees and interest rates frolic in the lowlands. Our role? To be the voice of reason, guiding our clients through the real estate jungle with a mix of wisdom, wit, and a sprinkle of humor, ensuring that their journey to homeownership is successful.

Acquiring a pre-approval letter is merely the tip of the iceberg when it comes to securing funds for a home purchase. One must consider the accessibility of funding and the complex regulations associated with loan types. For example, a specialized loan program tailored for first-time home buyers may have levels of approval guidelines (one set of guidelines from the lender and one set from the specialized program). Home buyers are so excited when they receive a letter with these words on it: *Congratulations! This pre-approval letter states that you are eligible for a mortgage loan of $400,000 (These are similar words found on a pre-approval letter).* However, it is imperative to recognize that these words alone do not guarantee financial security. The buyer's overall stability and creditworthiness must undergo rigorous validation to ensure a successful and sustainable investment.

During the mortgage process, various factors must be closely examined. This includes the potential financial "skeletons" hidden in the closet of the buyer (credit report, employment history, ownership of other properties, etc.). These hidden issues can unexpectedly surface at any time, sometimes even amidst the celebration of a pre-approval.

It is only the underwriter's seal of approval that truly matters. One can think of an underwriter as a highly skilled private detective who looks at each page with a magnifying glass and investigates and analyzes the buyer's financial profile, determining the level of risk involved for the lender. If the underwriter deems the buyer to be a high-risk investment, the lender may request additional information for reconsideration or outright deny the loan.

Let us accompany Bob Yancey and his buyers down **"Lenders Lane,"** which felt more like a busy highway with numerous potential exits, each leading to a unique financial destination. Bob was thrilled to discover a loan officer who offered an enticing first-time home buyer program, complete with exceptional terms. Despite never having worked with this particular loan officer or company before, Bob was confident in the loan officer's assurances.

With eager anticipation, the Jansen's, Bob's clients, promptly submitted their documentation for pre-approval including driver's licenses, paystubs, W2s, and tax returns. After only a brief waiting period, the pre-approval was delivered via email to Bob and the buyers, setting them on a path down the highway to find their ideal home.

EXIT - NO HOME PARKWAY

The tireless search for the perfect home was an exhausting cycle of touring properties, submitting offers, and receiving constant rejections, all due to the persistently low inventory. This real estate market felt similar to being lost on an endless country road with no homes or buildings in sight, just endless fields of corn and evergreen trees stretching as far as the eye could see.

Weeks turned into months, and the search felt never-ending until finally, after three months, they were able to find a home and get an accepted offer, bringing an end to the seemingly endless journey on *No Home Parkway*.

EXIT - VIOLATION ALLEY

As per the sales contract instructions, the listing agent had the homeowner's association documents sent to the buyer's home for review. However, a problem arose when the HOA mailed the documents during a time when the buyers were out of the country.

Even though the buyers were away during the delivery of the HOA documents, this did not halt the review period. In this case, the time needed to review the HOA package (for budget, rules, violations) had been lost. After the buyers returned, they immediately delved into the documents and made an alarming discovery. The documents revealed several violations on the home, leading the buyers down the treacherous path of *Violation Alley*.

Covenant violation

- Storm door on front of home - Not approved

- Deck installed - Not approved

PHONE CALL

(With Bob -Buyer's Agent and Theresa Clark – Listing Agent)

Bob - *"Hi Theresa. How's your day going?"*
Theresa - *"Hi Bob. I am a little congested, but I'm getting through it with some allergy medicine."*
Bob - *"I am sorry that you are under the weather. The reason that I called is to let you know that there are several violations on the home that my clients would like fixed in order to move forward."*
Theresa - *"Thanks Bob... (Cough, cough) Unfortunately, it's past your client's deadline to request that the seller fix the violations, though I will still speak with my clients to see if they are willing to fix the violations."*

Bob and Theresa shared a few additional words and ended their phone call.

After speaking with her clients, Theresa graciously informed Bob that her clients were willing to make accommodations for the buyers, despite the deadline for correcting HOA violation items having already passed.

EXIT - HIGH RISE BRIDGE

As the underwriting process began, the buyers felt as though they were traveling across a large body of water over a bridge with a high peak. The anxiety continued as each item was checked off the list: the verification of employment, application, and HOA information. Despite the loan officer's assurances that there would be no hiccups, the fear of unexpected obstacles lead to the sign *"Road Work Ahead."*

As the financing contingency deadline approached, the pressure continued to mount. The listing agent requested the removal of the contingency, prompting Bob to send the Financing Contingency Removal Addendum to his clients for signature. Once signed, the document was forwarded to Theresa (the listing agent) for the seller's signatures.

At this crucial stage of the sales process, there were no additional opportunities for the buyer to withdraw from the contract without incurring penalties. The buyers were firmly trapped in the credit ramp, with no choice but to ride out the rest of the process and hope for the best.

EMAIL (From Loan Officer to Buyer and Buyer's Agent)

FROM: Marc Boone/TO: JHanson@buyer.com, Bob@youragent.com
SUBJECT: Loan status: Julian Hansen

<table>
<tr><td>

We regret to inform you after reviewing the credit file of borrower Julian Hansen that there is a delinquent student loan that has been in default for over four months 30 x 4 = 120 days. We are using a new system that protects the lender from borrower defaults, which is why the original credit report did not have the item listed. In the new system, the student loan is stated as being delinquent.

Marc Boone

</td></tr>
</table>

EMAIL (From Buyer's Agent to Loan Officer)

FROM: Bob@youragent.com/ TO: Marc Boone
SUBJECT: Possible Solution - Jansen

<table>
<tr><td>

Can the loan be done in just one of the borrower's names?

Bob Yancey

</td></tr>
</table>

EMAIL (From Loan Officer to Buyer's Agent)

FROM: Marc Boone/TO: Bob@youragent.com
SUBJECT: Re: Possible Solution - Jansen

<blockquote>
No, we ran the ratios and other scenarios and it's not possible without both incomes.

Marc Boone
</blockquote>

Bob had explored every avenue to salvage the deal, but to no avail. He made the difficult call to Theresa, breaking the news that his client's loan application had been denied. As a result, they had to forfeit their earnest money deposit of $4,000, as they had removed their financing contingency when signing the addendum. Despite their best efforts, the buyers were unable to secure the necessary funding to close the deal, leaving them with a heavy financial loss and no home to call their own.

Unfortunately, the seller faced the daunting task of starting the whole selling process from scratch. In the midst of tough market conditions, it was a taxing four-month journey before the house was successfully sold and closed with a different buyer.

Furthermore, an ill-fated deal with disappointed buyers does not assist in real estate referrals for the agent. It's worth noting that just one lost deal could potentially have negative reviews, loss of future business and no referrals. Not every real estate transaction can be a joyous celebration. It's the ones that challenge your professionalism and integrity that should be a teachable moment. When a deal goes sour, it's a snapshot of your experience level at the time. In this narrative, it all unfolded with the clients going down a major thoroughfare with the agent that consisted of numerous exits, and the exit that everyone aspired to reach was the final destination (a new home) of a completed sale. However, this can and did abruptly come to a **DEAD END**.

THINK BEYOND THE STORY

- What was the cost of this real estate transaction? emotional, physical, or financial

- Do you think things could have turned out differently if they had used Bob's recommended lender?

CLOSING POINTS

- Interview loan officers and ask agents for recommendations

- Be sure to get recommendations from lenders and to check their reputation for closing ratio

- Prepare a checklist of questions to ask your loan officer

- Follow up weekly to determine the status

- Ask more questions to avoid future issues

25

THE SUPERHERO

*"Asking more open-ended questions will
provide insight from the client."*
ReShawna Leaven

S TARR LOVE, A STEADFAST real estate agent, dedicated five years of unwavering service to her current real estate firm since obtaining her license. Over the course of her career, Starr had successfully closed numerous transactions, earning a reputation that resonated with a good working relationship among her colleagues in the industry. Her commitment to excellence had not only resulted in a substantial client base but had also led to repeat business and referrals from satisfied friends and neighbors. During the Spring market, Starr received one such referral from one of her friends. In her initial consultation with the new customers (the Fordson family), they clearly communicated their housing aspirations, expressing the desire for a detached single-family dwelling, because they were they grew up there were ranch style homes and that's what they loved, a spacious yard, three bedrooms, two and a half bathrooms, and a den.

A search for a suitable abode can make a real estate agent feel like they need to put on a superhero cape, drink an energy drink and leap into action. Each client's quest for the perfect home sometimes presents a unique challenge, demanding the agent's superhuman abilities to navigate through a myriad of preferences and specifications. But armed with market knowledge and a keen eye for detail, the agent embarks on a mission to match dreams with available properties, striving to be the superhero of each client's story. The agent's phone becomes a hotline, ready to respond to distress calls and urgent inquiries, ready to swoop in and save the day by scheduling viewings and negotiating deals. Transforming uncertainties into opportunities. They use the superpower of persuasion and expertise to guide clients through the levels of paperwork and decisions, providing reassurance and support at every turn. At times, it feels like a crusade against time and competition, but the thrill of finding the perfect home for them makes every effort worthwhile, reinforcing the agent's belief in the superhero within.

In our modern era, the daunting question that plagued Starr Love's wits was how to effectively scour the real estate market to find the Fordson's a home with those features, in the area they desired within their budget. The listing prices of homes that possessed the upgrades that they were looking at were all above board. Their budget and visual interest was more aligned with a home with luxury features. Starr began to think about some of her past transactions, where she was able to persuade her clients to have an open mind to other home types that would give them more options. A change to a luxury townhouse would give them more features and upgrades, as opposed to the ranch style they had described. As Starr scoured homes online, those ranch style homes had dated finishes and would need to be upgraded to today's new sought after open floor plan with ungraded flooring and bathrooms that don't have "hospital green" tile (often seen on HGTV home make over shows).

- Will the duo triumph in their pursuit of their ideal home?

- Will Starr Love procure a dwelling that matches the couple's requirements before the expiration of their buyer agency agreement?

- Can they be persuaded to change their location or home type?

Following a challenging period of exhaustive searching, involving more than forty properties, Claire and William arrived at a crucial juncture. They determined that it was imperative to broaden their quest for a suitable residence. They were persuaded to view luxury townhomes since the single-family homes they viewed were outdated and most would need budgets of $60,000 to $80,000 in renovations and upgrades to bring them to their standards.

CONVERSATION - NEW HOME COMMUNITY
(With Starr Love – Buyer's Agent and William and Claire – Buyers)

Claire - *"I am tired of looking. This townhome has great features! This would be great for us."*

William - *"Ok if this is truly what you want. I know you said that you really had your heart set on a single family."*

Starr - *"Listen, this is a new construction community, and you won't have any competition with other contracts. You will just need to make a decision on a lot and all of the features that you desire and wait for it to be built. That's just the condensed version, because of course there are all the other intricacies in the middle of the transaction like: financing, design center choices, pre-drywall walk through and so on. I know it's a big decision. But don't wait too long. The market can change with the wind."*

Claire - *"William and I will think about it some more and get back to you later today."*

Starr - *"Ok, Claire. Sounds like a plan. In the meantime, I will get all the details from the sales agent about lot availability, options, pricing, financing, incentives (what they are enticing the customer with) and if they have any standing inventory."*

Claire and William called Starr a few hours later and decided to go write and offer on the luxury townhome they had viewed earlier that day. They met back at the new construction site the next week to write an offer. They chose an end unit, three level (above ground), three bedrooms, three and a half-bath with a rec room/office on the bottom floor. The property was equipped with modern finishes, including stainless steel appliances, quartz countertops, dual sinks in the hall bathroom, on-suite in the primary bedroom, comfort level toilets in two bathrooms of choice and smart home wiring. The builder also offered financing incentives (if the Fordson's decided to use their preferred lender). They accepted that offer because they were able to use this closing cost incentive to buy down their interest rate.

In conclusion, the pivotal role of conducting an insightful consultation with clients at the outset of the home-buying process cannot be overstated. The absence of such a crucial step may introduce complications and impede the overall purchasing experience. It's essential to acknowledge that, despite trying to collect as many details as possible about a client's desires during the consultation, it is not the end all of the process. Unforeseen variables such as housing stock availability and many other variables may necessitate adjustments. Therefore, a key message to convey during the initial consultation is the importance of flexibility. Agents should emphasize the need for adaptability, recognizing that the dynamic nature of the real estate market may require changes in the course of the journey. Building a strong relationship with the buyer(s) becomes paramount in gauging their willingness to be flexible. Establishing trust is fundamental, as clients need to feel that their agent is wholeheartedly working in their best interest, ensuring a smoother and more successful home-buying experience.

It is clear that Starr earned the nobility and a reputation as a superhero in the eyes of her clients. She employed skills and expertise to provide her clients with a high level of service. By persuading them to consider other options she was able to assist them in getting what's called "part of the American dream" home ownership. This is sort of a philanthropic effort that all agents in the industry participate in every time they work with a client. We are all superheroes!

THINK BEYOND THE STORY

- What was the cost of this real estate transaction? emotional, physical, or financial?

- What do you think about Starr's style of working with her clients?

CLOSING POINTS

- A buyer consultation is strongly recommended. It ensures your client knows what to expect

- Build a rapport with your clients so that they will trust your judgment. when you make a suggestion to change something in the middle of the course.

26

THE STATEMENT PIECE

"One action can cause a domino effect of consequences."
ReShawna Leaven

J UST AS A SINGLE reckless decision can have far-reaching
consequences like in the movie Risky Business (1983), the same is
true in the world of real estate. One hasty choice, such as overpaying for
a property or failing to thoroughly inspect a home before purchasing,
can lead to a series of negative outcomes that can significantly impact
a person's financial situation. This type of poor decision in real
estate can be a tipping point that causes a ripple effect of negative
consequences.

As real estate agents, we are often faced with the challenge of helping
our clients navigate the decisions that can arise during the home
buying process. It is our responsibility to assist them in avoiding
impulsive choices that may hinder the transaction. This can be
particularly challenging when buyers are excited about the home
buying process. They are often excited about buying new furnishings
and decorative items. We may be asked to return to the property
multiple times to measure for new appliances or furniture. As a
society, we are surrounded by temptations, and it is up to us to make
careful, thoughtful decisions in order to avoid potential roadblocks
and setbacks. This introduction leads us into the story of Janice and

George who wanted to find their dream home.

After dating and residing in an apartment for over five years, Janice and George resolved to make the transition to homeownership. In their pursuit of the perfect property, they conducted extensive research online. They also interviewed three real estate agents before ultimately selecting Niles Harper. Usually, the beginning stages of the home buying process includes a home buyer consultation. A buyer consultation serves as a vital foundation for the home buying experience, establishing the roles and responsibilities of both the client and the agent, and providing a clear understanding of expectations on both sides. Without it, a transaction is likely to be marked by confusion and uncertainty.

Niles had spent his entire career at a small boutique real estate firm that did not prioritize training on how to conduct consultations. This lack of guidance left him ill-equipped to provide his clients with a clear roadmap for navigating the complex and often-unpredictable process of buying a home. Without a clear vision of their destination and the path to get there, on occasion both Niles and his clients were often at risk of veering off course.

However, Niles did focus on an important component that was needed to start the home search and be a prepared buyer that was being pre-approved with a lending institution. Niles would ensure that his clients were pre-approved with one of his preferred lenders. After receiving their pre-approval letter, he would provide them a list of homes that met their search criteria. Once his clients had identified their favorite properties, he would schedule appointments and accompany them on tours of the homes.

While not conducting a full buyer consultation can be considered putting the "cart before the horse" approach it is not an uncommon practice for most real estate agents, it is not necessarily the most efficient or reliable method but it is practiced often. Many real estate agents are anxious and don't want to lose the customer so they fast forward without building a relationship at the onset. While there is nothing inherently wrong with this process, it may not always yield the best results.

Janice and George were able to find a suitable home and all the boxes were checked except one. A week before the scheduled settlement of their new home, Janice visited a popular furniture store with the intention of merely window shopping for new bedroom furniture. However, as she perused the showroom, she became intrigued by a stunning four poster mahogany bed adorned with carved pineapples, and ultimately allowed herself to be convinced by the salesperson's persuasive tactics to make the purchase. Unaware of the potential repercussions of her impulsive decision, Janice secured credit from the finance department and moved forward with the bedroom set purchase. Little did she know that this extravagant statement piece would complicate the closing of her home and threaten to derail the entire process.

IF WALLS COULD TALK CONVERSATION
(With Janice and George)

Janice -*"Honey, guess what?"*
George - *"What?"*
Janice - *"I found a beautiful new bed for our new home!"*
(George does not reply and was simply staring at Janice in disbelief)
Janice -*"Did you hear me? I said I got a new bed."*
George -*"I heard you the first time. I'm just wondering why you would purchase a bed while we are in the midst of buying a home, and without even consulting me".*
Janice -*"I know you'll love it. Just look at this picture (shows him the picture on her phone)."*
George -*"It looks nice, but I'm worried about the cost. We're already stretched to our limits with expenses."*
Janice -*"Don't worry, we'll be fine trust me."*
George -*"Okay, we'll see."*

George was the conservative person in the relationship and the minister of finance in the household. A few days later, the loan officer called to confirm George's fears.

PHONE CALL
(With Larry – Loan Officer and George)

Larry - *"Hi George, it's Larry."*
George - *"Hi Larry, how are you?"*
Larry - *"I'm doing well, but there's an issue that's come up. There's a new credit inquiry on Janice's credit report."*
George - *"Oh no, how much is it for?"*
Larry - *"$2,690."*
George - *"What? $2,690! I can't believe this. I know that she made a purchase the other day. How will this affect the purchase of our new home?"*
Larry - *(the loan officer sighs and states)* *"I'm afraid that Janice's credit score dropped and the increased debt changed your combined debt-to-income ratio. This means you don't qualify for the loan program we had originally recommended. I've looked into alternative loan programs, but unfortunately, I haven't been able to find one that meets both your needs at this time."*
George - *"Wow, this is really bad news."*

As George ended his conversation with Larry, he heard the front door open, and Janice walked in. He said, *"We need to talk."* This was going to be one of the most difficult and significant conversations of their relationship. He explained to her that the decision to purchase the bedroom furniture was risky and as result created a ripple effect that ultimately jeopardized their ability to purchase their dream home. This had been a problem from the onset of the relationship. Janice was always impulse shopping and hiding bags in the closet.

It was a triple loss.

- They lost their home.

- They lost their earnest money deposit ($10,000)

- The couple lost their relationship.

As a result of her impulsive decision to purchase the furniture, Janice had to move her new extravagant statement piece to the basement of her mother's house. One can never control the actions of others, however, sometimes clients need "hand holding" (like when we hold a young child's hand to cross the street, to guide them to a safe place).

It is crucial for real estate agents to keep their clients informed of any potential issues or roadblocks that could derail the transaction. This means providing them with timely and accurate information on a consistent basis throughout the process, rather than waiting until the last minute to address any problems or concerns. By proactively communicating with clients and keeping them in the loop, agents can help to ensure that the transaction progresses smoothly even though this does not alleviate all unexpected setbacks it can ease the setbacks when they arise. This is especially important in today's fast-paced and competitive market, where the success of a real estate transaction can hinge on a variety of factors, both in and out of an agent's control.

THINK BEYOND THE STORY

- What was the cost of this real estate transaction? emotional, physical, or financial?

- How could her agent have assisted better?

- How could the agent improve with the next client?

CLOSING POINTS

- Making large purchases of furniture or appliances can be tempting for many homebuyers. However, it is generally not advisable to make any major purchases while in the process of buying a home. This is because making a significant purchase can affect a buyer's debt-to-income ratio, which is a key factor that lenders consider when evaluating a mortgage application. If a buyer's debt-to-income ratio increases significantly, it could result in being denied a mortgage. This can put the entire home purchase in jeopardy, as the buyer may not have the necessary funds to complete the transaction. It is generally best to wait until after the home purchase has been complete before making "any" purchases.

- Buyers should not take on any new lines of credit, such as credit cards, personal loans, or car loans.

- Assist your buyers with steps to the lending process.

- Keep the client informed about the final stages of the underwriting process.

- Utilize storytelling to illustrate the reasoning behind your recommendations.

- Share a relevant anecdote to help the client better understand your perspective.

- Experience does not necessarily equate to having knowledge of the processes needed to make for a smooth transaction.

27

CONTINGENCY CONUNDRUM

"Not all transactions end happily ever after."
ReShawna Leaven

D URING A REAL ESTATE transaction, everyone involved is dedicated and focused on the process, much like recipients savoring a bouquet of flowers. The exchange of property ownership becomes a momentous event, especially when the transaction unfolds seamlessly. Imagine the journey of real estate similar to the lifecycle of a bouquet of flowers. Initially, the bouquet arrives vibrant and full, symbolizing the commencement of the process. As the transaction progresses, the bouquet blooms, representing the signing of contracts and advancement. Yet, challenges, similar to wilted petals, emphasize the need for swift resolutions to maintain transaction momentum. Just as the recipient of a bouquet trying to use the strategy of cutting the stems and lower leaves, changing the water every other day, and avoiding direct sunlight to preserve the beauty. In the same manner, a successful real estate deal depends on using strategies to resolve issues before an opportunity fades away.

As in the case of a beautiful bouquet of roses having a lifespan, a real estate transaction also operates on a strict timeline. However, the unpredictable nature of some sales can result in numerous twists and turns, which can cause anxiety and frustration for all parties involved.

This tale aptly demonstrates why "time is of the essence" is important.

Logan Taylor's clients dedicated several months to scouring the housing market, and after an extensive search, they finally discovered a property worthy of an offer. With Logan's expertise and guidance, they carefully analyzed recent sales data, discussed a recommended offer price, reviewed, and signed offer documents, and submitted their proposal. Logan's hard work paid off when the offer was accepted, and the clients found themselves on the path to homeownership. Now, it was time for escrow!

The inspection process began with a thorough home inspection followed by a termite inspection, and the appraisal was next. In many cases, the appraisal report can be a nerve-wracking event, as it can trigger a renegotiation of the sales price if the property's value is lower than the sales price. Fortunately, this was not the case in this transaction, and the final appraisal report came in slightly above the sales price, providing much-needed relief for all parties involved. The only remaining task was to satisfy the lender's underwriting conditions, which Logan and his clients tackled with the same diligence and expertise they had displayed throughout the entire process.

Logan's clients conducted extensive research on reputable lenders and ultimately chose Rose Petal Bank, a banking institution that they had a relationship with for several years and that had garnered positive reviews online. It is essential for homebuyers to select a trustworthy lender when purchasing or refinancing a home, and Rose Petal Bank met their stringent criteria for excellence in the lending industry.

The financing contingency represented the last hurdle in this sale, with the deadline for its resolution was fast approaching. The listing agent made an urgent request to Logan for the removal of the financing contingency, accompanied by a loan commitment letter, to be delivered via email. Failure to comply with the deadline would have given the seller the option to proceed with the contract or terminate it altogether.

Logan advised his clients that by removing the contingency, their earnest money deposit would become vulnerable in the event that the sale did not reach fruition. (TAKE A PEEK INTO THIS CONVERSATION)

PHONE CALL
(With Logan – Buyer's Agent & Richard and Tracy – Buyers)

Logan - *"Hi Tracy. This is Logan. How are you? Is your Richard around?"*

Tracy - *"Hi Logan. I am great. Yes, Richard is here, I will change to "speaker phone" so that we can conference."*

Logan - *"Ok great. I have something to share with you both. The listing agent has sent a gentle reminder that the financing contingency be removed as the deadline is two days away. Your lender still has not finalized your loan commitment. If you both remove the financing contingency, this poses a risk."*

Tracy - *"What kind of risk?"*

Logan - *"Well, Rose Petal Bank has not issued a loan commitment letter, yet which means you are not fully approved for the loan."*

Richard - *"I thought we were already approved when we got the letter from the loan officer."*

Logan - *"No, not quite. A pre-approval is an initial step in the mortgage process where a lender assesses a borrower's creditworthiness to determine the maximum loan amount they can receive. It is not a guarantee of a mortgage loan and is subject to change based on changes in the borrower's financial situation or the market. A mortgage commitment is a formal offer from a lender to a borrower that guarantees a specific loan amount, interest rate, and terms for a specific property. It is issued after a thorough underwriting process and the home appraisal has been completed successfully. It then signals that the borrower's mortgage application has been approved. The borrower is usually required to sign the loan commitment, and the mortgage process moves towards closing."*

Richard – *"Oh, I see. Thanks for explaining it in detail."*

Logan - *"Let me present the available options, although they may not be the most favorable ones. Option #1 entails removing the contingency* *without a loan commitment letter, risking the earnest money deposit if financing falls through. Alternatively, the second option involves obtaining a release of contract, leading to the return of your earnest money deposit, and starting anew in your home search, which I assume is not your preferred choice."*

Richard - *"No, no. We don't want to start over. I am confident that we will close with Rose Petal Bank. We can go ahead and proceed without the loan commitment letter."*

ANOTHER PETAL HAS FALLEN...

Following the telephone conversation, Logan promptly forwarded the financing contingency removal addendum to his clients for their signature, which was then followed by the sellers' endorsement, paving the way to move forward with the remaining items in the transaction.

After an additional week had passed, Logan received disconcerting news: new developments had become known that led to the underwriting department denying his clients' loan application. The issue arose due to the discovery of an undocumented student loan that had to be added to their debt-to-income ratios, causing them to no longer meet the requirements for the loan. This resulted in recalculating the income to debt ratio which rendered them ineligible for the loan for which they had previously qualified.

PHONE CALL
(With Logan – Buyer's Agent & Mary – Listing Agent)

Mary - *Hi, Logan. This is Mary calling about the Blackwater property. How are you?*

Logan - *"Hi Mary. This is not a good day for me. I've been trying to think of some strategies to help this family with the issue at hand. Their loan was denied by the underwriter for reasons that I cannot share, though I think it's possible for them to still close on the home."*

Mary - *"I'm so sorry to hear that. I'd like to see if your clients can get a loan done with my in-house lender to keep this deal alive. Do you think they would be open to that? If not, they will lose their earnest money*

deposit, because they have removed the financing contingency."
Logan - *"Sure, I think that they will be open to any possibilities right now. Can you email me the information, so that I can discuss this with them. If they agree I will make sure that they make a connection with your lender as soon as possible?"*
Mary - *"Yes, I will send it over right now. Also, the seller will need to reduce the closing cost that they were going to give the buyers by $3,000 because of the delay of closing. They will now have to pay two mortgages for this delay. Since this transaction is closing later, they now have a mortgage on their new home and this home too."*

After his discussion with the listing agent, Logan presented Tracy and Richard with a practical solution to rescue the deal. He advised them to use the listing agent's preferred lender. This lender offered loan programs with less rigid mortgage loan guidelines and higher debt-to-income ratio allowances. Additionally, he explained how their original offer of closing costs from the seller would need to be reduced. He proposed a clever resolution to offset the difference with a credit of some of his commission for the $3,000 needed in closing costs, which involved broker approval.

ANOTHER PETAL HAS FALLEN...

The buyers took the only option available and used the listing agent's recommended lender to secure a loan. The new lender was able to approve them for financing with the additional student loan payment. Logan sought guidance and expertise from his broker for the reduced seller credit. The reduced seller credit amount was solved with a broker credit letter for $3,000. The broker wrote a broker letter and sent it to the lender and title company. In real estate, the real estate commission belongs to the broker and requires permission to be released to pay another party in the transaction. In this story, after the broker approved the request, the funds were offered to the buyers at closing as a credit on the closing statement, and the title company deducted the amount from the total broker commission of $12,000, resulting in a commission check of only $9,000. This strategy allowed the buyers to move forward with the purchase of the home and prevented Logan from losing his commission.

The successful conclusion of this transaction can be likened to a magical moment, reminiscent of a scene from a movie where the scenes throughout the movie are chaotic and at the end everything falls perfectly into place. It truly was a miracle, considering that many real estate deals do not have a successful conclusion. When a deal falls through, it often results in the property being relisted, requiring the listing agent to spend additional marketing dollars to find a new buyer, starting the negotiation process all over again, and leaving the sellers feeling anxious and disappointed. In this case, all parties involved worked collaboratively and creatively to find a solution that allowed the deal to be saved. Hopefully, both sides learned from this experience and will apply those lessons to future transactions.

Tracy and Richard, Logan's clients, made the decision to use their bank for their mortgage lending needs rather than selecting a lender from Logan's recommended lender list. Although larger banking institutions are well-equipped for banking services, they may not have the specialized capabilities required for specific mortgage lending programs. It is crucial to not only provide a list of preferred lenders but also to explain why they are being recommended. Telling a story can provide further confirmation as to why a particular lender is being suggested. Selecting the wrong lender can result in significant monetary loss and a waste of time. As a real estate professional, compensation for services rendered is only received upon the successful completion of the transaction. Therefore, financing is undoubtedly the most crucial aspect of any real estate transaction.

THINK BEYOND THE STORY

- What was the cost of this real estate transaction? emotional, physical, or financial?

- What would the results have been if the seller had been hasty and released the contract?

CLOSING POINTS

- An agent needs to build a strong relationship with the client to make them feel comfortable about "spilling the tea."

- Before removing the financing contingency, it's essential to verify all significant conditions with the lender to prevent any potential issues or complications that may arise.

- Building strong relationships with lenders who possess expertise in their field and offer excellent customer service is essential in this business

- Nurturing a positive co-agent relationship makes things run smooth and alleviate anxiety

28

THE DERBY

*"Real estate resembles a race to the finish line,
similar to the Kentucky Derby."*
ReShawna Leaven

THE PULSE OF A "derby," refers to a fiercely intense and competitive race of three-year-old horses. This grand event has an unexpected parallel to the world of real estate transactions. Here, the sprawling tracks of the housing market hosts a different kind of race – one that can be compared to the race of a derby. One where the lending institutions take on the mantle of "jockeys," urging their steeds, the loan officers, forward in a frenetic dash towards the coveted finish line. In this charged atmosphere, the real estate agents emerge as the guiding force, like skilled trainers, navigating the complexities of the course, providing essential insight, and acting as the crucial link between buyers and sellers. Each stride, each maneuver, mirrors the strategic push and pull within this high-stakes arena. Just as a seasoned jockey harnesses their potential, a proficient loan officer diligently hones their expertise like a horse going through a rigorous training regimen. The journey from novice to virtuoso echoes the rigorous hours of preparation of these stakeholders to get to the finish line, fostering trust and reliability in catering to the diverse needs of potential homebuyers. Get ready for an exhilarating sprint filled with many hurdles that this client had to overcome before reaching the finish line.

Judy Goodie was standing gracefully in a stunning black dress adorned with white polka dots, a black "bowler" hat and red pumps. She exuded an air of a refined attendee at a Preakness event. Her fashion sense was impeccable, a true embodiment of sophistication. Her art of style will translate into possessing the expertise and abilities needed to successfully navigate the intricate landscape of this real estate deal. She operated in the realm of "first impressions are lasting impressions".

TEXT MESSAGE
(Before Buyer Consultation)

"I'll be running a little late." **[Henry sent at 10:15 AM]**
"Okay that's fine. I am at my office. Ask the receptionist to buzz you in and I will come to the lobby and get you." **[Judy sent at 10:18 AM]**
"Thank you for understanding." **[Henry sent at 10:20 AM]**
"See you soon." **[Judy sent at 10:21 AM]**

JUDY GOODIE'S OFFICE

Judy extended a warm greeting to her prospective client, Henry White. She apprised him of the diverse loan program options available, explained the home buying process, and expounded upon her pivotal role as a resolute buyer's agent.

Judy - Having concluded her comprehensive presentation, Judy posed a direct statement to Henry, *"How do you feel about moving forward with my style of doing business? I would like to represent you as your real estate agent."*
Henry - *"Yes, Judy. I want you to be my agent. I already knew it was a good match before our meeting after my research of your services. I could feel it. This meeting was just the clarification I needed to confirm that."*
Judy - *"That's great to hear, Henry. I will need your driver's license so that I can make a copy. While I am doing that here is the buyer agreement and other documents needed to get started. The initial and signature sections are highlighted for you. If you agree please complete*

those areas. Henry reached in his back pocket, got out his wallet and handed Judy his driver's license.

Judy - *"Thank you, I'll be right back."* When she returned with his identification, she noticed that he had finished signing all the necessary paperwork. Judy reassured him by saying, *"Thank you for signing all the documents. I will scan and forward a copy of what you have signed so far and after my broker signs it, I will send you the completed documents."*

Henry - *"Okay sounds good."*

Judy - *"Do you want me to use jbhenry@email.com for all your real estate transactions and e-signatures or another email address moving forward?"*

Henry - *"Yes, please use jbhenry@email.com."*

As the meeting drew to a close, Judy courteously accompanied Henry on his way back to the main lobby entrance, extending a warm farewell and ensuring that all of his questions had been satisfactorily addressed.

PLACE IN THE DERBY
MOVING UP TO 15TH PLACE

Making a debut at a less than impressive 15th position, he was in the loan pre-approval process. Henry contacted Judy with the exciting news about securing a pre-approval for his home purchase through 102 Mortgage. He expressed his unwavering commitment to the company, citing their unparalleled responsiveness being the decisive factor of choice over other competitors.

PHONE CALL
(With Judy Goodie – Buyer's Agent and Henry White – Buyer)

Henry - *"Hi Judy. I have news to share. Do you have a few minutes?*

Judy - *"Hi Henry. Sure, what's your news?*

Henry - *"I am pre-approved for $425,000 with a USDA loan."*

Judy - *"That's wonderful news, Henry."*

Henry - *"Thank you. Do you think we can look at homes on Thursday? There are three homes that fit the USDA approval zone."*

Judy - *"Sure. I have a 2 p.m. available on Thursday. Would that time work for you?"*
Henry - *"That works. I am taking Thursday off. I have a doctor's appointment at 8:30 a.m."*
Judy - *"Sounds good. Can you email me the addresses so that I can check availability for showing? I will schedule the appointments and let you know the first place to meet me for our home tour."*
Henry - *"Ok. I will email you the list in a few minutes."*

PLACE IN THE DERBY
MOVING UP TO 12TH PLACE

Continuing the race at respectable 12th position, Henry is at the pivotal stage of viewing properties. After evaluating three properties on his tour, he made a decision to submit an offer for the last property viewed. Judy prepared the offer, reviewed it for accuracy, and promptly forwarded it to Henry for his approval. Following Henry's review and approval, Judy submitted the offer to the listing agent for the seller's consideration.

EMAIL (From Listing Agent to Buyer's Agent)

FROM: Tracie Jefferson (Listing Agent)/TO: Judy Goodie (Buyer's Agent)
SUBJECT: Re: Offer - 789 Seller Way

Hi Judy,

The seller accepts your client's offer with no changes. We are now under contract. Please let me know when you will schedule the home inspection, so that I can coordinate that with my client.

Please find the attached ratified contract.

Tracie Jefferson

Attachment - RatifiedContract_789 SellerWay.pdf

EMAIL (Buyer's Agent to Listing Agent)

FROM: Judy Goodie (Buyer's Agent)/TO: Tracie Jefferson (Listing Agent)
SUBJECT: Thank you (Create a new thread with a new subject line)

Hi Tracie,

Thank you so much Tracie. I have let my client know the good news.

The home inspection has been scheduled for Wednesday at 10:00 am.

I look forward to a smooth transaction.

Judy Goodie

PLACE IN THE DERBY

MOVING UP TO 10TH PLACE

While being 10th during the race may be considered lackluster, in the high-stakes world of real estate, all parties involved are looking at this position as gaining speed to emerge victorious and get to the finish line. The segways into moving along with a completed appraisal. The house appraisal value came in at a whopping $7,500 above the initial offer price. With all inspections seamlessly concluded there was no cause for major concern. This was like placing a bet to "win" and your horse coming in first place.

As the team moved forward in the race, all necessary steps had been executed to ensure a seamless and unbroken stride towards a successful completion. As Judy planned her week of real estate activities, she decided to make a Monday call to Henry's loan officer for a comprehensive status update. When she did not get an answer, she decided to create a concise text message, conveying the urgency of communication.

TEXT MESSAGE
(With Braden and Judy)

"Hi Braden. This is Judy Goodie. I am checking the status of Mr. White's file for 789 Seller Way. Can you give me an update?" **[Judy sent at 1:19 pm]**
"Hi Judy. The file is in underwriting. I will give you an update as soon as I get it." **[Braden sent at 1:31 pm]**
"Thank you." **[Judy sent at 1:33 pm]**
"The underwriter needs more clarification on a few items with Henry's file. The underwriter has reached out to him directly." **[Braden sent at 4:02 pm]**
"Thank you for the follow up." **[Judy sent at 4:25 pm]**

For a week, Judy and Henry's loan officer exchanged texts, but there was no progress beyond "the loan is in processing."

Another week went by and the listing agent checked in to see if there was any update on the loan. Unfortunately, the status remained the same with the same message: *"the file was still being reviewed."* The underwriting process is widely regarded as the most stressful part of the homebuying journey for buyers.

PHONE CALL
(With Henry – Buyer and Judy Goodie – Buyer's agent)

Judy - *"It's all or nothing if you do not supply the underwriter with satisfactory supporting documents for your loan file."*

Henry - *"I have gathered everything that they have asked from me and then more. I am not sure what else they need to get the loan done. I am over it."*

Judy - *"I am sorry about your frustration with this process Henry. It may be a new guideline that's holding up the process. The listing agent also requested that the financing contingency be removed, or the seller will void the contract and move on with another buyer."*

Henry - *"What do you think I should do at this point?"*

Judy - *"It's up to you. If you remove the contingency and can't close due to financing, the earnest money of $10,000 being held in escrow will go to the seller and they could also take you to court."*

Henry - *"I see. Well… I still love the house. With this market, I don't think that I will find anything else like that within my budget. What do we have to do to release the contingency?"*

Judy - *"There is a financing contingency removal addendum that has to be signed."*

Henry - *"Ok, please send it and I will sign. I will call Brendan again to see what's going on."*

Judy and Henry said their good-byes. She sent the addendum to Henry for electronic signature and forwarded the contingency removal to the listing agent.

TEXT MESSAGE
(With Judy and Braden)

"Good Morning, Judy. I do not have good news to share with you. The

underwriter rejected the submitted loan conditions that Henry sent. He also does not have enough reserves to cover the closing in addition to limited funds for closing." **[Braden sent at 10:09 am]**
"Good Morning, Brendan. This is VERY upsetting news. A phone call would have been better than a text message. Though, I appreciate the information and insight either way. So, is there anything that can be done at this point?" **[Judy sent at 10:20 am]**
"Unfortunately, not." **[Braden sent at 10:22 am]**

Henry's home purchase was being financed with a USDA loan, which is a government-backed loan provided by the United States Department of Agriculture. This loan program enables buyers to purchase homes in rural or low-density areas, based on eligibility maps and income restrictions. However, the loan conditions were rejected by the USDA's underwriting department, leaving Judy and Henry in a tight spot. With the loan being denied, they had to quickly find another viable option to fund the purchase.

PLACE IN THE DERBY
MOVING UP TO 5TH PLACE

This part of the transaction was like, the race taking place in the pouring rain and the horses galloping in the mud. Judy put on her best "derby fascinator" and strategized a means of how to get her client into the house of his dreams. On occasion, buyers are often aware of their credit shortcomings, even if they do not express them to their agent. Although the race was not yet over, this downpour was posing a challenge.

Review rejected documentation

- Conduct a thorough review of the rejected documentation

- Verify the source of funds for the required 2 months of reserves

- Check the length of employment, including any gaps in employment

Evaluate alternative loan programs

- Conventional loan: Requires a 5% down payment, which is eligible but Henry doesn't have enough funds

- FHA loan: Requires a 3.5% down payment, and Henry is eligible

- VA loan: Requires a 0% down payment, but Henry is not eligible

Judy's mind galloped and galloped until she found a solution for her client. After tapping into her extensive network of lenders, she finally struck gold with Game On Mortgage. The best bet for Henry was an FHA loan. But it wasn't a simple trot to the finish line. First, Henry had to nod in agreement, then they needed the seller's thumbs-up, and only after that could they kick-start the new loan process. The plot thickened when they realized the property's appraisal report had to be released from his previous lender's appraiser. Like passing the baton in a relay race, the lender's appraiser needed to transfer the appraisal to the new lender. Judy laid out the roadmap for Henry, who eagerly jumped on board with the loan application. Next, Judy swung into action, contacting the listing agent to negotiate a 21-day extension through a sales contract addendum, which the seller graciously accepted. But the hurdle wasn't cleared yet - a funding gap loomed large, and Henry couldn't turn to anyone for a financial gift. In a twist worthy of a caper movie, Henry decided to sell his car, a creative maneuver that secured the funds needed to seal the deal on his dream home.

PLACE IN THE DERBY
COMING IN 2ND PLACE (CLOSING)

The race was finally ending. During a crucial call with Yemane Dubois (Henry's new loan officer) and Judy Goodie, excellent news filled the air. Yemane confirmed that all the necessary approvals had been secured, and the lender was ready to move ahead with the closing. With elation in her voice, Judy received the coveted "clear to close" confirmation, and they were one step closer to the finish line.

PHONE CALL
(With Yemane Dubois – Loan officer and Judy Goodie – Buyer's agent)

Yemane - *"Hi Judy. We're CLEAR TO CLOSE!"*
Judy - *"This is great news! You have made my week. This was a tough one that we all learned a lot from."*
Yemane - *"They are not all going to be easy. But I am glad we were able to step in and help your client get to the finish line."*

They ended the call and Judy completed the next steps with Henry.

- WALK THRU - Completed successfully.

- CLOSING - Completed successfully.

The race to secure a home loan for a client can be a grueling test of endurance and stamina. It's crucial to thoroughly vet both the lender and the client for any potential issues before signing and delivering an offer. When a horse enters a race, they need to be in peak physical condition, in comparison, a client's financial spreadsheet and documents.

The lending process can be like the serpentine shape of a horse tract with its complex financial activities. There's paperwork to be submitted, verifications to be made, and resubmissions of documents, all culminating in the waiting game for the final approval. If all goes well, then the closing occurs as scheduled. However, when mishaps happen, it can be likened to a horse going off track and the jockey being thrown.

THINK BEYOND THE STORY

- What was the cost of this real estate transaction? emotional, physical, or financial

- How will you validate a loan officer and company with which you have never worked?

CLOSING POINTS

- Verify if the buyer has student loans

- Verify if the buyer has a local bank and where the funds for earnest money will come from

- Always have other options for your buyer's financing to be sure the buyer is truly qualified

- It's helpful to have a few loan officers on hand to be able to review loan options and new updates

29

DEDUCTIBLE

"Allocating funds for business is essential for its growth."
ReShawna Leaven

MANY INDIVIDUALS OUTSIDE THE real estate industry are unaware that those of us who pursue real estate as a profession essentially become entrepreneurs. Contrary to common belief, our work extends beyond most 9-to-5 office jobs. Our routine involves proactive efforts such as following up with client correspondence, coordinating listing processes, contacting closing officers, new home sales representatives and the list goes on. All of this on most occasions with delayed compensation. We purchase gasoline, signs, coffee, lunch, marketing materials, and so much more without an upfront deposit. This profession operates with the culmination of our hard work being rewarded with a substantial check at the conclusion of the transaction, reflecting the dedication, effort, and perseverance invested throughout the entire process.

We squirrel away funds to conduct business from month to month to ride around on home tours, market open houses, purchase signs, pay real estate office fees and more. This is the part of the trade where the earned commissions also incurs expenses. Therefore, it is imperative to carefully devise a plan and diligently monitor the financial affairs of one's business very closely. This approach will enable you to gauge the ebbs and flows of your business, discern its overall trajectory, and determine the rate of return for the systems that are contributing to the success of your enterprise.

Real estate entails numerous costs, including licensing fees, realtor dues, and expenses related to daily business operations, among others. The challenge arises when the income of the business owner, (i.e., the agent), reaches its maximum capacity, and funds become limited.

- Marketing: A significant portion, reflecting the importance of advertising and client outreach in real estate.

- Transportation: Costs for traveling to properties, meetings, and networking events.

- Office Rent: The expense for maintaining a professional workspace.

- Licensing Fees: Necessary expenses for staying legally compliant.

- Continuing Education: Investment in professional development and staying current in the industry.

- Miscellaneous: Other expenses that arise in the course of business.

In this business, obtaining and maintaining a license entails a number of costs, but we'll delve into those details later. In this narrative, we witness the unfortunate financial blunders that Lauren Goldvein fell victim to as a result of poor money management.

During the tumultuous period of the 2008 mortgage crisis, the real estate market underwent a significant transformation. Without any established blueprints or rule books, agents quickly realized that adaptation was key to remaining competitive to avoid being replaced by more ambitious rivals. Some real estate professionals made connections with the pendulum swing of an REO market.

This niche area of real estate possesses REO (Real Estate Owned) properties which are foreclosures owned by the bank which require agents around the country to market and sell these properties. It requires an agent to possess the skill level to properly allocate expenses. It's imperative to conduct due diligence and ensure that expenses are properly categorized and managed according to industry standards. If the agent is not a good money manager it can be a recipe for disaster, leading to confusion and omissions that can have negative consequences.

In the REO world, property management companies play a critical role, overseeing assets and enlisting the services of experienced REO agents who report directly to the investor or REO manager in charge. Real estate agents, on the other hand, are tasked with performing broker priced opinions, preserving the property, marketing and selling it, managing vendors, securing the asset, rekeying, getting the home market-ready, determining its value, and selling it as quickly as possible.

Most companies have a compliance score that measures an asset's performance against local market trends and the performance of other REO agents within the company. If the matrix does not align with the market, then restructuring is necessary to liquidate the asset.

Lauren managed to forge a relationship with an asset management company that specialized in servicing REO (real estate owned) properties. She quickly learned how to complete broker price opinions (BPOs). She completed enough of these to create a stable income that was equivalent some months to that of a commission check. She felt this experience gave her the foundation to service distressed properties.

As an agent tasked with representing REOs for the bank, Lauren's responsibilities were extensive and multifaceted. In addition to weekly reports and photographs, she had to manage monthly expense reports, oversee contracts and contractors, conduct on-site visits, provide reimbursements for upfront expenses, and stay updated on market developments, among other duties.

EXPENSES FOR DECEMBER 2008

Lawn Care	10 properties	$250
Electricity	12 properties	$350
Gas	10 properties	$200
Water	12 properties	$200
Rekey	2 properties	$400
Trash out	2 properties	$1,000
Winterization	12 properties	$1,750

The cumulative total of expenses for the month before (November) soared past the $2,200 mark, encompassing not only the standard costs of lawn care and utilities but much more. Now, December's expenses exceeded November's expenses.

As the real estate market experienced a slowdown, properties remained on the market for an average of 60 to 70 days before receiving an offer. Although Lauren had some successful closings in her other business endeavors, the REO business continued to drain her savings as she struggled to keep it afloat. This predicament poses the question: *"How much money is needed in order to sustain the properties until payment for the invoices was received?"*

During the first week of January, the temperatures plummeted to unprecedented lows, creating a frigid and unforgiving environment. It was the kind of weather that caused tears to freeze instantly on your cheeks. As Lauren toiled away at her office, working on paperwork for her bank-owned listings, she received a troubling call from a homeowner living beneath one of her listed properties.

PHONE CALL

(With Homeowner in Unit#B and Lauren Goldvein – Listing Agent)

Homeowner - *"Can I speak with Lauren Goldvein?"*

Lauren - *"Hi, this is Lauren Goldvein."*

Homeowner - *"This is Ms. Baker who lives in the unit below the condo you have listed for sale."*

Lauren - *"Yes, how can I help you?"*

Homeowner - *"There is a major leak coming from my ceiling. The condo association's manager came today to see where the water was coming from and it's coming from the unit you are selling. When can you get over here to look at this mess? My place is being destroyed minute by minute from leaking water."*

Lauren - *"I am sorry to hear that your condo is getting damaged. I will be right over to assess the damages."*

Lauren hurried over to the condo to assess the damages with her own eyes and was met by the homeowner below her unit at Waterfall Village. She took photos and video of the damage so that she could upload them to the asset management company's portal. She extended her apologies again to Ms. Baker and she went upstairs to visit her listing. There was no visible damage in the listing unit.

Later that afternoon, she created an email to send to her asset manager to explain the details. The following day, she received a reply email from the association manager. As Lauren read the email, her stomach started churning like someone was making ice cream.

EMAIL (From Association Manager to Listing Agent)

FROM: Wesley Stevens (Association Manager of Waterfall Village)/TO: Lauren Goldvein (Listing Agent), Sarah Reinhart (Listing Broker)
SUBJECT: Status of Insurance Investigation

Good Afternoon Ms. Goldvein,

We regret to inform you that after the insurance company investigated the source of the damages from your listing, it was determined that the cause of the damages was due to the temperature of the unit being too low (no heat turned on in your listing) for over 30 days during frigid temperatures. The deductible is $5,000. The funds for the deductible are due prior to the work being started.

I have attached the insurance claim information.

Best Regards,

Wesley Stevens

Association Manager of Waterfall Village

Attachment: Insurance adjuster information.pdf

After speaking with her asset manager, he stated that she was responsible for the fee because the heat was not turned on. This was part of her responsibility as the listing agent. Luckily, she was a good agent, and they liked the way she conducted business because they could have stripped the current REO listings that she was managing if they had felt that she was not being responsible. She was grateful and apologized for her mistake and stated she would take care of the insurance deductible as soon as possible.

As she pondered having to pay yet another debt from her drained account, she inquired about E&O insurance covering the cost for the insurance deductible. However, in Lauren's case, the policy only covered specific types of errors, and her negligence was not among them. Consequently, she was forced to bear the cost of the insurance claim deductible.

On the following Tuesday, Lauren headed to her bank and obtained a certified check for $5,000, which was made payable to Waterfall Village Association. She then delivered the check to the association manager at the management office, thereby fulfilling her financial obligations.

The incident at Waterfall Village was both a rock-bottom and a pivotal moment for Lauren. Initially, it brought a surge of self-doubt, questioning her competence in the field. Yet, this event became a catalyst for change. Lauren transformed her perspective, seeing not failures, but valuable lessons in each misstep. This experience enriched her personal and professional journey.

Simultaneously, the Waterfall Village event shattered a prevalent myth among real estate agents about Errors and Omissions Insurance. Lauren discovered that such insurance doesn't provide a safety net for all errors, a revelation that highlighted the necessity of financial readiness for unforeseen liabilities. This insight was a significant learning curve. One that would influence her approach to real estate for years to come.

Reflecting on her initial beliefs about Errors and Omissions Insurance, Lauren couldn't help but chuckle. "I used to think E&O Insurance was like a superhero cape," she quipped. *"Just put it on, and suddenly you're invincible to mistakes. Well, Waterfall Village was my kryptonite moment. Turns out, the cape doesn't make you fly, it just breaks your fall a bit softer. Lesson learned: always pack a parachute – or in real estate terms, it provides a safety net during unexpected situations."*

THINK BEYOND THE STORY

- What was the cost of this real estate transaction? emotional, physical, or financial?

- What if Lauren did not have the $5,000 to pay the deductible?

- What type of insurance would cover an issue like this?

CLOSING POINTS

- In low temperatures, always keep the heat on at minimum levels at any home

- Check vacant properties

- Utilities need to be on in a listing

- Provide your client with information about the dangers of low temperatures and how they can result in damages that they are responsible for if they are at fault

- When clients are away or out of town, check their properties for them

- If you own a condo, make sure you understand your liability if something is determined to be your fault due to negligence

30

UNITED WE STAND

*"Our unity forms an unyielding fortress;
our division, a crumbling facade."*
ReShawna Leaven

THE POPULAR PHRASE "UNITED we stand, divided we fall" - has remained a profound truth for centuries. This is especially applicable in the fiercely competitive world of real estate, where maintaining a collective spirit and shunning grievances to achieve success. However, in the ongoing narrative of this business, a listing agent and buyer's agent may plunge into a tumultuous conflict, jeopardizing a highly promising transaction. During this conflict they may not even take into consideration the undeniable magnitude of the property of type (high end) for which they will both reap a large reward at the end. In this example, unity takes a back seat, and the discord in a transaction such as this resembles a dog and cat fight jeopardizing not only the transaction but also the very essence of collective prosperity that defines success in this business. This story mirrors some of the characteristics mentioned here.

In the midst of one of the most cut-throat seller's markets in history, Jackson, who loved selling properties in the suburbs of popular metropolitan areas, was tasked with the challenge of listing a property in a neighborhood where his listing was the only home available for sale. In an economic environment characterized by low interest rates and scarce inventory, it was not surprising that the property generated intense interest and competition. Within a few short days of its listing, four offers had already been submitted, each of them promising and alluring. However, one offer stood out as the clear winner, so compelling and enticing that one could hardly resist the offer. As Jackson read through this offer, he double-checked every line to ensure its accuracy. This offer was nothing short of irresistible. It consisted of: VA financing, no home inspection contingency, no closing cost assistance, and a 28-day closing. It represented the absolute best offer Jackson had received. With an appraisal gap of $40,000 and a purchase price of $790,000, it was a gem of an offer amidst the sea of competing offers received.

All VA financed transactions feature an escape clause, which provides the buyer with the option to walk away from the transaction if the property's appraised value falls below the contract price. In such an event, the buyer is entitled a refund of their earnest money deposit.

STEPS IN THIS CONTRACT

- The property was originally listed for $750,000. The accepted offer was $790,000 with VA financing, and an appraisal gap of $40,000. An appraisal gap is a term that refers to the amount the buyer agrees to pay in the event of a shortage of value between the sales price and the appraised value. Lenders only provide financing based on the appraised amount.

- There were no contingencies, except for the financing, in the offer.

- Following the acceptance of the contract, the title company received the necessary documents, and the lender ordered an appraisal.

- The loan officer informed the buyer's agent that the appraiser was going to invoke the Tidewater Initiative. The buyer's agent and listing agent had 48 hours to submit new sales documentation to support the contract sales price.

- Both the listing and buyer's agent submitted comparable properties to the appraiser to support the sales price of $790,000. (there was no guarantee that the value would be increased to support the sales price from this documentation). The appraiser reviewed the newly submitted data and finalized the report. The appraised value was $740,000, which was $10,000 less than the original list price.

Appraisal Gap Analysis

Line Items	Pricing	Explanation
Listed Price	$750,000	Price listed in MLS
Sales Price	$790,000	Price offer for home
Appraisal Gap	$40,000	Amount needed if appraisal comes in low
Appraised Value	$740,000	VA Appraised Value (This value remains with the home for 180 days)

At the onset of the transaction, there was a sense of harmony and unity between the agents. They communicated with each other in a jovial and cordial manner, fostering an open and friendly atmosphere. However, as negotiations progressed over the next two weeks, tensions between Jackson White, the listing agent, and Madison Clark, the buyer's agent, began to rise. Future conversations between the two were marked by an air of displeasure and dissatisfaction, as they struggled to overcome the challenges that arose in the transaction.

As the transaction progressed, a new development emerged that required urgent communication. The buyer's agent, Madison Clark, reached out to the listing agent, Jackson White, to relay this important news.

PHONE CALL
(With Listing Agent and Buyer's Agent)

Jackson - *"Hi, Madison. How can I help you?"* (His voice carried a strong, quick tone, but he tried to mask it with professionalism).
Madison - *"Hi, Jackson. The lender mentioned the appraiser is invoking the Tidewater Initiative for our VA loan. I'm worried it signals a low appraisal."*
Jackson - (Jackson thinking to himself, the Tidewater Initiative often meant a potentially low appraisal, but thankfully, the buyers were prepared to cover up to $40,000 if it fell short). *"Understood, Madison. No worries, I've dealt with the Tidewater Initiative before. It's a VA procedure to review appraisals before finalizing them, especially if they're likely to be low."*
Madison - *"Got it, thanks, Jackson. Just wanted to keep you in the loop."*
Jackson - *"Appreciate it. Enjoy your afternoon. I'll touch base with the appraiser and see if we can navigate this."* (He ended the call with a more cordial tone, reflecting a mix of professional assurance and friendliness in his voice).

EMAIL (From Loan Officer to Listing and Buyer's Agents)

FROM: 123 Mortgage Co./TO: Madison and Jackson
SUBJECT: Appraisal for 987 Good Luck Way

> Thank you for submitting comparables to the appraiser. While the comparables were good and similar to the property. The appraiser is not justifying an increase in the appraised value at this time. Unfortunately, the appraised value remains at $740,000.
>
> Benjamin James
> 123 Mortgage Co.

After receiving the loan officer's email, Madison promptly requested a reduction of the sales price to match the appraised value. Jackson couldn't help but think sarcastically, *"Ah, not so fast! Your clients* *agreed to cover a $40,000 shortfall in case of a low appraisal."* Now, it was crucial for Jackson to discuss these latest developments with his clients.

PHONE CALL
(With Jackon – Listing Agent and Sellers)

Sellers - *"We are not willing to lower the price. If they don't want to pay the difference, we will put the house back on the market. They will have to search for a new place to live. We are not in a desperate situation. We don't have to sell at a low price. It's the principle of the dang thang."*
Jackson - *"I wholeheartedly agree with you. I am sure their agent advised them of the likely possibility of a low appraisal. They made this decision when they offered terms above list price.*
Sellers - *Well... we need some time to think about our bottom-line. Give us a few hours.*

Around 7:30 PM - a few hours later after the sellers had time to discuss and make a final decision, they sent a text message to Jackson

TEXT MESSAGE
(Between Jackson and Sellers)

"My wife and I decided to counter with a price of $780,000." ***[Seller at 7:40 PM]***
"Ok, I will proceed by creating an addendum with the new purchase price." ***[Jackson at 7:52 PM]***

After the text message from Jackson's clients, he sent an email to the buyer's agent with their response.

EMAIL (From Jackson to Madison)

FROM: Jackson /TO: Madison
SUBJECT: Re: Reduced Sales Price for 987 Good Luck Way

Hi Madison,

After careful consideration, my clients have decided to counter your clients adjusted sales price to $780,000. I have attached the addendum for your clients. We would like a response by the close of business tomorrow.

Thank you,

Jackson

987 Good Luck Way_Addendum.pdf

EMAIL (From Madsion to Jackson)

FROM: Jackson / TO: Madison
SUBJECT: Re: Re: Reduced Sales Price for 987 Good Luck Way

Hi Jackson,

I will talk with my clients and get back to you tomorrow.

Thank you,

Madison

While he was in the parking lot of a local coffee shop, Jackson received a call from the buyer's agent. Glancing at his smartphone, he muttered to himself, *"I wonder what she wants now,"* before answering the call.

Jackson - *"Hi Madison, I hope you have good news for me."*
Madison - *"Hi Jackson, well... I have another inquiry. I am calling to get a good number for your broker, so I can send this documentation over*

so that our brokers can have a conversation about this transaction."
Jackson - *"Oh really? Speak to my broker. Why do we need to get the brokers involved?"*
Madison - (with a hesitant tone) *She sighed. "Well, there's a bit of a mix-up. The square footage listed for the property seems off, and my broker suggested resolving this at the broker level."*
Jackson - *"I see. That's important for accuracy and valuation. I wasn't aware of this issue, but I'm glad you brought it up. Here's the broker's number: 555-555-5555. I'll also give my broker a heads-up about this issue."*

Upon receiving notice of the impending call, Jackson quickly contacted his broker to provide an update. In an effort to ensure the accuracy of the property listing, Jackson had arranged for a professional floor plan measurer to measure the property. However, when the square footage data was entered into the MLS system, it became apparent that the basement square footage did not match the recorded measurements. Due to a limitation in the newly upgraded MLS system, it was not possible to change the square footage data accurately. Consequently, Jackson made the decision to include all of the home's square footage on the top two levels, which encompassed the basement square footage, with the exception of just 10 sq ft.

PHONE CALL
(With Jackson and his broker after greeting and small talk)

Jackson - *"Yes, I was using the measurements from the floorplan company. The square footage from the tax record was not correct and when I changed it in the MLS, the system added the square footage incorrectly. It's highly unlikely that a basement would be 10 sq ft. The new system did not allow me to make the appropriate updates."*
Broker - *"I will back you up 100%. You are one of my best agents. This is foolishness."*
Jackson - *"They have asked for a price reduction and the lender has enacted the Tidewater Initiative on the appraisal."*
Broker - *Ok, let's see how it goes. Let me know their response. I'll wait for*

the broker to contact me. Thanks for giving me a heads up."

Jackson's broker spoke with Madison's broker about the square footage issue. After their conversation, it was determined that there was no need for the broker to reprimand the agent for any breach of conduct or professionalism.

It had always been Jackson's priority to keep all parties informed of any positive or negative developments in the transaction. His broker had come to rely on Jackson's proven track record of maintaining high standards of character and business practices, particularly during challenging situations such as the one they were currently facing.

EMAIL (From Madison to Jackson)

FROM: Madison/ TO: Jackson
SUBJECT: Addendum for 987 Good Luck Way

Hi Jackson,

My clients have decided to move forward and have accepted the new sales price of $780,000.

I have attached the addendum and have forwarded it to the lender.

Thank you,

Madison

987 Good Luck Way (2) Addendum.pdf

The sale closed two weeks later, though it was marred by drama from the buyer's agent. The success of any real estate deal often hinges on the agents' emotional balance or lack of. This situation was like lemonade made without sugar - it left a bitter aftertaste for everyone involved. Agents are expected to resolve most issues independently, resorting to involving their broker only when absolutely necessary.

At the onset of this transaction, the collective attitudes and persona of all the stakeholders was filled with excitement and a jovial spirit. However, as soon as a challenging detour came along in the road the ability to communicate amicably diminished. When communicating in this business, the tone of voice, whether in a phone call or a text message, can significantly influence the dynamics of how one may think about moving forward with the other party. In the absence of visual cues such as body language, the manner in which words are expressed and the professionalism can come across as harsh and unprofessional. Ensuring that all communication is respectful and considerate is not just a professional obligation but also a fundamental aspect of successful deal-making.

THINK BEYOND THE STORY

- What was the cost of this real estate transaction? emotional, physical, or financial?

- Do you think that Madison suggested to her clients to submit the offer by using the appraisal gap strategy in order to win the offer?

- Do you think that Madison was being spiteful by going after the square footage?

- Did the sellers have to lower the sales price to the appraised value?

CLOSING POINTS

- Don't respond with emotion. Take time to respond based on facts and logically.

- When entering data check it twice times or more for clarity (sometimes these mistakes can be costly to your clients)

- It's important to understand about financing and how to protect your clients.

- The VA Tidewater Initiative is a unique process in the appraisal of properties for Veterans Affairs (VA) loans. When an appraiser believes that a property's value might not meet the estimated purchase price, this initiative kicks in.

  - Here's how it works:

    - Opportunity to provide aditional information: Once the Tidewater Initiative is invoked, the lender (and often the real estate agent) is notified. They are then given a brief window, typically 48 hours, to provide additional information to support the contract price.

This might include recent comparable sales or other relevant market data that the appraiser may have missed.

- Review of additional data: The appraiser reviews this new information and considers if it affects the property's valuation. This step is crucial as it allows for a more informed and potentially higher appraisal value, which is beneficial to the buyer.

- Final appraisal report: After reviewing the additional data, the appraiser completes the appraisal report with the final estimated value of the property.

31

LURKING IN THE DARK

*"In the woven fabric of courthouse files, a hidden essence
resides within the gaps of missing paperwork, spinning a
tale of shadows that come to life amidst the known and the
mysterious."*
ReShawna Leaven

T HERE ARE MANY ELEMENTS in this sphere of business we call
real estate that have a complexity that has to be dealt with in each
transaction. One of those complex items is the title to a property. The
integrity of the real property title can be compromised by unresolved
record-keeping issues and somethings oversights in local courthouse
bookkeeping. While no supernatural presence may be lurking within
the property, sometimes it's like opening a closet and finding skeleton
bones.

The ramifications of human error can be quite significant, potentially
resulting in substantial financial losses for the property owner. The
following account serves as a poignant reminder of this reality, as the
owner was confronted with issues on the title of the home she was
selling. This narrative evokes the imagery of things that represent "All
Hallows Eve;" skeletons in the closet and dark rooms with things
walking around that lurk in the dark.

The area below gives a little education on the title research process.
Upon the exchange of ownership or documentation filed by a title
company or attorney's office, certain prerequisites must be fulfilled

to facilitate a successful closing or sale, contingent on the procedures employed by the relevant state.

Let's first explore how the title to a property is researched and title insurance is issued.

Step 1	The title company orders an abstractor to compile a comprehensive chain of titles. This document lists all previous property owners, any liens levied against the property, and any other judgments concerning the owners.
Step 2	Next, the title company scrutinizes the abstract to ascertain its accuracy and ensure that it corresponds to the current contract and obligations of the seller. In the event of any discrepancies between the title work and the contract, a "cloud on title" is created. Such a cloud must be resolved before the title company can provide lender's title insurance for the lender and owner's title insurance for the buyer.
Step 3	The final step is initiated once the cloud on title has been cleared, and title insurance has been issued. It is at this point that the closing may take place.

When a real estate transaction is concluded, a transfer fee is typically paid to the county and/or city. The amount of these fees is determined based on the particular locality. These fees are an expense used to cover the processing associated with recording the title. The manner in which records are maintained may vary between states, however, there are fundamental similarities that exist among them. Having now gained an understanding of the intricacies of the title process, we will proceed to delve into the tale of "There is Something Lurking in the Dark."

As Samatha took a sip from her coffee mug with the words **"GET IT DONE,"** she sat at her desk, gazing out of the window. The digital numbers on the clock glaring 10:30 am, and yet she was already on her third cup of coffee. *"Today is shaping up to be one of those days..."* she thought to herself as she set her cup down on the desk. Little did she realize the extent of the drama that would soon unfold with one of the transactions she had in escrow.

Samantha gazed at her computer screen where she became engrossed in the details of her client's real estate transaction. She was startled at the ring of her cell phone during the silent mood in the room. She swiftly answered the call with a professional tone, responding to the call with, *"Hello Samantha Wells speaking."* On the other end of the line was Elizabeth Barker, representing ABC Title, delivering news that would send a chill down Samantha's spine.

PHONE CALL

(With Samantha – Listing Agent and Elizabeth – Title Agent)

Elizabeth - *"Hello Samantha. Elizabeth Barker from ABC Title here. There is a title issue that needs to be resolved on one of your client's homes before we can close."* (Dismayed and confused as Samantha has never had a transaction with a seller having an issue with title)

Samantha - *"Oh wow. What kind of issue?"*

Elizabeth - *"Well, there is an unreleased deed of trust from the prior owners of the home. We have already tried reaching out to the previous title company, but they are no longer in business. We also tried making contact with the lienholder and left a message."*

Samantha - *"Oh, wow! I never had this happen before. Is there a solution to this?"*

Elizabeth - *"There is a solution. Do you know if your client purchased owner's title insurance?*

Samantha - *"I am not sure. I will have to ask."*

Elizabeth - *"Ok let me know as soon as possible. I will have to inform the buyer's agent of the title issue which could cause a delayed closing."*

Samantha - *"Sure. Thank you for calling."*

WHAT'S LURKING - THE ZOMBIE LOAN

After sipping the last drop of her coffee, Samantha sat down with her mug and decided to take a much-needed break. With a deep breath of fresh air, she embarked on a 15-minute walk to clear her head and ease the stress that had built up inside. As she strolled along a path, many thoughts crossed her mind. She began to get an upset stomach and wondered how she was going to explain the title issue to her client. She knew that a clear and concise explanation was essential, and so she took out a notepad to jot down some key points and details that she would need to convey. With a sense of calm determination, she continued her walk, her mind continued to race with thoughts of how to navigate this sticky situation.

NOTES FROM PHONE CALL

- *Previous title company is not an option*

- *HUD-1 statement (needed)*

- *Previous paperwork when home purchased (needed)*

PHONE CALL
(With Samantha – Listing Agent and Yolanda – Seller)

Ring, ring.

Yolanda - *"Hello?"*

Samantha - *"Hi Yolanda. It's Samantha. How are you?"*

Yolanda- *"Hi Samantha. I am well and you?"*

Samantha - *"Well, there is an issue with the title of your home. The title company called me to let me know that there is an unreleased deed of trust from the prior owner on the title. Do you know if you purchased owner's title insurance when you bought your condo?"*

Yolanda - *"I will have to check. What if I didn't purchase owner's title insurance?"*

Samantha - *"Well the title company that closed the deal is no longer in business, and Elizabeth at ABC Title could not get in touch with the lienholder. We need to try and make a connection with them. The only other solution would be to pay the lien balance."*

Yolanda - *"What! Oh really? May I ask how much it is? If it's small enough. I might be able to swing that."*

Samantha - *"Not sure if that will work. It's $75,000."*

Yolanda - *"Oh h$@! no. I can't and won't do that. I will move back in the house before I pay for that. Let me get off the phone and look through my paperwork. I swear this condo has caused me more trouble than it's worth. I will be glad to get rid of it."*

Samantha - *"I understand completely. Let me know what you find. The closing statement or owner's title policy are the documents that are needed. When you find the closing papers, can you send me the documents and I will review them."*

WHAT'S LURKING? - FRIGHTENING DISCOVERY

The shuffle of the papers and moving of boxes. Unwrapping boxes, re-wrapping boxes. Only to be left with the disappointment of not finding the required documents. Yolanda (the seller) was sure that she had the closing paperwork with her other important files but somehow, they were missing. She asked Samantha if it was another solution for locating the documents. Samantha requested that she contact the real estate office where she purchased the home to see if they could provide the closing documents that she needed since the title company was no longer in business. With a 15-minute phone call to the real estate brokerage that assisted Yolanda, the receptionist was able to send an email with her requested documents. After receiving the documents, Yolanda was anxious and forwarded the documents to the title company.

EMAIL (From Title Representative to Seller)

FROM: Elizabeth Barker (Title Representative)/TO: Yolanda Hathaway (Seller)
SUBJECT: Re: Offer - 777 Lurking Lane

Good Afternoon Yolanda,

Thank you for sending over the HUD-1 from your closing when you purchased the home. However, after careful review of the document. It looks like you elected NOT to purchase an owner's title insurance policy when you bought your condo. Since, this is the case. You do not have the protection to file a claim with the title insurance to remove this unpaid lien.

We were able to contact the lienholder to find out the status and if there was a balance. They said that it had not been paid. So, in order to move forward, we will have to add the additional cost of $75,000 to your closing fees. I am sorry that this was not able to work out in your favor. Let me know if you have any additional questions or concerns.

Elizabeth Barker

Processor

ABC Title

The title company created the final closing documents with the final numbers and sent it to Samantha for review. Samantha received the email and reviewed the HUD-1 statement (now called the ALTA statement) with breakdown numbers. She was shocked to discover that her client would only receive $5,000 in seller proceeds after all closing fees (settlement charges, current loan, brokerage commissions and the unreleased deed of trust amount)

PHONE CALL

(With Samantha – Listing Agent and Yolanda – Seller)

Samantha - *"Hi Yolanda, it's Samantha. I hope I'm not catching you at an inconvenient time. I've just received the final closing documents from the title company and wanted to go over them with you."*

Yolanda - *"Hi Samantha, no, it's a suitable time. I've been anxiously waiting for an answer. How does everything look?"*

Samantha - *"Well, Yolanda, I've gone through the HUD-1 statement, and after accounting for all the closing fees, the current loan balance, brokerage commissions, and the unreleased deed of trust amount, it looks like you will be receiving around $5,000."*

Yolanda - *(There is a long pause of silence) $5,000! Is that all? I don't want to sell my house and only get $5000. That's ridiculous.*

Samantha - *"Well... you have a contractual obligation to sell to the buyer. I wouldn't want anything bad to happen. In this situation, if you do not close, you will be in breach of the contract and the buyer could sue you for specific performance."*

Yolanda - *"Oh really! They could sue me. This is just TOO much. This is a nightmare."*

Samantha - *"I am so sorry. Sometimes we don't know what can be lurking in the dark. I discuss purchasing title insurance with many of my buyers and sometimes they opt not to make the purchase because they think everything is going to be ok, but we never know what can be lurking in the dark. I don't want you to be sued for specific performance. Oh, my!"*

Yolanda - *"Well... I just need a moment to digest this information. This is all just a bit overwhelming. I will text you later."*
Samantha - *"Of course, Yolanda. I understand, we can talk later."*

Something really lurked in the darkness in this story. Trying to find a solution was a key element. Even when you do all the right things to win in real estate, sometimes when you enter a sphere and area of the transaction that returns information that is detrimental to the transaction it does not always have a happy ending. In this case there was not much that Samantha could do.

THINK BEYOND THE STORY

- What was the cost of this real estate transaction? emotional, physical, or financial?

- Would an owner be able to simply cancel the contract and stay in the home?

CLOSING POINTS

- Ask the seller if they have owner's title insurance when you are at the listing appointment

- Find out if there are any potential liens on the property

- During your initial seller consultation explain the problems that can arise when transferring title if things were not properly documented

- Identify if there were major renovations or projects completed and see if they were permitted

- If a copy of the owner's title policy is not available, a copy of the closing statement will state whether the current owner of the property purchased the policy. The closing statement will have the name of the insurance company, type of policy (either standard or enhanced) and one-time premium fee paid at closing.

32

THE OUTCOME

*"Each day is part of your journey in discovering
who you will become."*
ReShawna Leaven

PICTURE THIS: After several months of tumultuous and volatile income levels, Mason Brown was in a crossroads. He had three closings in the Spring market (April) which could give rise to a false sense of security, only to be followed by two months of radio silence, leaving him scrambling to secure new business. The harsh reality is that a total of 61 days had passed with no income to speak of, leaving him to wonder where his next sale would come from. He had some prospective clients (buyers and sellers) but not all prospects' deals come to fruition. Consequently, he needed to take this reality into account in his business planning and vision for the year, calculating the likelihood of deals that will ultimately close versus those that may not. Only the closings that materialize can be counted as income.

Mason should have used this criteria on a spreadsheet (client base: what's going well; what can/needs to be done to move forward) as a learning tool to grow his business. He could have used the strategy of looking at each one on the spreadsheet and brainstorming scenarios of what happened and what he could have done to improve the process the next time. One suggestion would be thinking of strategies to keep them "alive" for future business, such as, connecting with their family and friends for future business.

EXAMPLE OF FIRST AND SECOND QUARTER CLOSINGS

Months	Client Base	Solutions
JANUARY 30 DAYS 4 - Closings	2 - Buyers Closed 2 - Listings Closed	N/A
FEBRUARY 31 DAYS No Closings	Buyer - Mr. Jones needs to pay off some bills	Create an action plan and send it to Mr. Jones
	Seller - Ms. Harper Estate - Needed to complete some home repairs	Send seller list of home repair items and a list of repair companies
MARCH 30 DAYS No Closings	Sellers - Harper Family waiting for probate, needed to make repairs	**Follow up with client on a more ongoing basis**
APRIL 31 DAYS No Closings	No new prospects	Held some open houses for people in his office
		Needed to network with real estate industry professionals
		Could have attended community activities
MAY 31 DAYS 3 - Closings	3 - Buyers Closed The buyers that closed in May were new construction sales written 10 months ago.	N/A
JUNE 31 DAYS No Closings	Buyer - Waiting for new section to open in new community	Continue to follow up with the new home site for new developments

This man's state of mind had grown increasingly uneasy and
unsettling, leading to sleepless nights and a complete loss of appetite.
The very idea of food had lost its appeal, as he went without sustenance
for days on end. When hunger finally did strike, he would often choose
the least nutritious options, turning to greasy fast-food staples like
hamburgers, fries, or buffalo wings. In addition to his poor eating
habits, he had also begun to drink heavily, starting with a single beer
that would inevitably lead to an afternoon happy hour drink poured
"neat." Even shots of hard liquor became a regular part of his routine,

all in the name of chasing the good times he believed were around the corner. However, the reality of his situation would soon catch up with him.

Throughout his career, he had secured many new and potential clients while unwinding at the bar. It proved to be an effective way to network as they were often on their way home from work, looking to relax after hours of prospecting and talking with people in the real estate market. The overconsumption of alcoholic beverages, unfortunately, would prove to be a detrimental factor in his overall health and well-being.

After enduring two grueling months with no closings, this real estate agent found himself in a crisis, desperately needing to secure a deal in order to avoid financial ruin and potential homelessness. The stress and anxiety of his precarious situation came crashing down one day. While sitting at the bar, nursing a glass of whiskey "neat," he repeated these words to himself: *"I love what I do."* But as he pondered the veracity of his self-talk, doubts began to creep in. ***Did he genuinely love his job, or was he merely trying to convince himself to soldier on in the demanding world of real estate?*** It felt as though he was lost in the sea, floating on a raft and no search party was looking for him. He couldn't simply turn back and return to where he started; he had to keep pushing, but towards what end?

Despite having the experience to juggle multiple transactions at once, he was experiencing financial difficulties because he fell short on marketing to keep the business going. He took pride in his work and was committed to providing the best service possible to his clients.

After weeks of following up with the new home site, the lot that his clients wanted finally became available and his clients were able to secure it with a holding fee. He called his clients and set up an appointment so that they could begin the new home building process for their dream home. In celebration of his hard-earned victory, Mason decided to treat himself to a cocktail at his local bar, located just a few miles from his house. As he approached the bar, he confidently ordered a classic martini, shaken but not stirred, with a twist of lemon. The bartender couldn't help but chuckle and think to himself, *"That makes me want to watch a James Bond movie when I get home!"*

ALWAYS
DRINK
RESPONSIBLY

Glimpsing down at his drink coaster, which was emblazoned with the cautionary message "ALWAYS DRINK RESPONSIBLY" beneath his glass, Mason glanced at his wristwatch, noting that it was already 7:05 pm. After settling his tab and bidding farewell to his favored bartender, he made his way out and climbed into his vehicle. Eager to depart the establishment, he sped off with haste, berating himself for not utilizing the restroom facilities before leaving. As he sped down the road, he caught sight of a police officer positioned on the right-hand side of his vehicle. Despite this, Mason maintained his speed of 60 mph in a 35 mph zone, recklessly ignoring the patrol car to the right of him, now behind him, with its blue flashing lights urging him to pull over. The shrill sound of a police siren, emitting a piercing "WEEE-OOO WEEE-OOO WEEE-OOO," echoed as the patrol car drew closer in the stillness of the evening night air. As Mason pulled over to the side of the road, his heart raced, and his palms began to sweat.

CONVERSATION – TRAFFIC STOP
(With Police Officer Parker and Mason)

Police Officer Parker - *"Do you know why I stopped you?"*
Mason - *"No officer. I don't."*
Police Officer Parker - *"I pulled you over because you were going 60 in a 35 mph zone. License and registration please."*

He took a deep breath, reached into the center console, and retrieved his license and registration. As he handed the documents to the officer, he tried to keep his composure, but his nerves were getting the best of him. The officer took the license and registration and disappeared into his cruiser. Mason anxiously waited for what felt like an eternity. The minutes ticked by slowly as he sat there, staring at his hands, and replaying the events of the evening in his mind. Finally, the officer emerged from the cruiser, making his way back to Mason's car. The officer approached Mason's window and began to speak. However, Mason's mind was racing, and he was becoming increasingly agitated.

Despite his best efforts to appear calm and collected, Mason's speech began to slur, and his eyes took on a glassy appearance. The officer noticed these signs of impairment and began to suspect that Mason had been drinking.

Police Officer Parker - *"Sir, I need you to take a breathalyzer test."*
Mason - *"Can I refuse?"*
Police Officer Parker - *"You can, but that would result in an automatic suspension of your license."*

Mason reluctantly agreed to take the test. Police Officer Parker then proceeded to administer the field sobriety test and have Mason walk heel to toe. Mason stumbled and swayed during the test, further confirming the officer's suspicion. He also took a breathalyzer test that registered his blood alcohol level above the legal limit.

Police Officer Parker - *"Sir, I'm going to have to place you under arrest for driving under the influence. Please turn around and put your hands* *behind your back. You have the right to remain silent, anything you say can be used against you in a court of law...."*

As Mason reflected on his poor decision-making, he realized the gravity of his mistake. His heart raced as he remembered the moments leading up to his arrest, and the fear of the unknown gripped him tightly. The officer's stern expression added to his feelings of guilt and shame. He knew that he had consumed more than two drinks.

Mason was now sitting in a jail cell. He began to think and contemplate the events that led to his current predicament. He had made a grave mistake by getting behind the wheel after having too many drinks at the bar. His reckless actions had not only endangered his life but the lives of others on the road as well. Despite the severity of his actions, Mason knew that this wasn't a permanent setback in his life, but rather a consequence of his behavior. He was now facing a DUI charge and sentencing that would impact his driving record and future plans. However, he was determined to learn from his mistakes and make amends for his actions.

The results that Mason faced following the DUI included paying a hefty fine, being arrested, and having his car impounded. He was also found guilty of driving under the influence. As if that was not enough, he had to install a breathalyzer device in his car, which prompted him to take a "blow test" while driving. He was embarrassed and tried to hide this during his home tours. The device was a constant reminder of his mistake.

Gurus and life coaches encourage individuals to take responsibility for their own lives and to strive for personal growth and positive change. Mason had to be willing to take a long, hard look at himself in the mirror and be honest about where he was, who he was and where he wanted to be. He was looking to improve his business but needed to have humility and ask someone for suggestions and assistance. There are many agents and brokers in real estate offices who are willing to give advice on strategies of how to get to the next level.

Asking for guidance and support from others is ok. It's important to seek mentorship and coaching no matter how long you have been in the game. Technology is changing the game every day. Whether you're looking to improve your business, your health, or your personal relationships, the key is to take action and put the necessary strategies in place to achieve those goals.

THINK BEYOND THE STORY

- What was the cost of this real estate transaction? emotional, physical, or financial

- What do you think about the outcome of this story?

CLOSING POINTS

- Create a follow up strategy

- Remain humble to anyone who could be of assistance with strategies for business improvement

- Use modern technology to improve your strategies for business

- Do not abuse substances that could have a life-altering or life-threatening effect on you or others in order to deal with your issues. Overindulging isn't a clever idea.

33

CHECKING IT TWICE

"In real estate, double-checking is the key to certainty."
ReShawna Leaven

A s the American celebration of Christmas draws near in December, the anticipation among children receiving toys increases. This is fueled by parents using the classic incentive: "Be good if you want Santa Claus to bring presents. This tradition underscores Santa's watchful eye, distinguishing between the naughty and the nice. The events in this narrative unfold amidst this festive atmosphere, echoing the concept of "making a list and checking it twice." Carter Jackson, an experienced real estate agent, realized the need for diligence and thoroughness in handling his client's transaction during this bustling holiday season.

Carter's workload was at an all-time high during this bustling season, despite the fact that it was typically a slow time of year for real estate agents, he was thrilled to have a spreadsheet filled with names of buyers and sellers for the fourth quarter of the year. One week prior to Thanksgiving, Julius Raymond, one of those clients on his roster who had listed his property with Carter, was excited about receiving multiple offers after just one weekend of showings. After receiving an acceptable offer on his place he placed an offer on a new property for purchase right away.

The buyer of Julius' property at 123 Anywhere Lane was subject to a five-day home inspection contingency deadline. To be specific, the home inspection, along with the receipt of the home inspection report and any requested repairs, needed to be received from the buyer by 11:00 pm on Thursday, November 26, which happened to be Thanksgiving Day. However, this task slipped through the cracks. During Carter's busy schedule he failed to submit the addendum and home inspection report on time. It was not submitted until 12:05 pm on the following day, commonly known as "Black Friday." This would make the addendum one day late.

EMAIL (With Jamie Lee to Carter Jackson)

FROM: Jamie Lee (Buyer's Agent)/To: Carter Jackson (Listing Agent)
SUBJECT: Home Inspection Contingency Items - 123 Anywhere Lane

Hi Carter,

My client received the home inspection and would like the seller to repair a few items. The buyer requested the following items from the seller to be addressed: Home Inspection Contingency Items.

- Installation of smoke detectors in every bedroom

- Installation of carbon dioxide detectors on each level (3)

- HVAC to be serviced by a licensed HVAC technician.

I have attached home inspection and the addendum.
Please confirm receipt.
Jamie Lee
123AnywhereLane.PDF

EMAIL (Carter Jackson to Jamie Lee)

FROM: Carter Jackson (Listing Agent)/ TO: Jamie Lee (Buyer's Agent)
SUBJECT: Re: Home Inspection Contingency Items - 123 Anywhere Lane

Good Afternoon, Jamie,

Your email has been received. I will review with my client.

 Please note that your client's contingency expired at 11:00 pm last night.

Thank you,

Carter Jackson

Real estate associations around the country have different deadlines associated with contingency timestamp submissions. If the documents are not submitted by the correct timestamp (Home Inspection Contingency Due on 3/5/2022 7:00 PM ET), the contingency is automatically removed.

After Carter reviewed the requested items, he spoke with his client about the buyer's requests.

PHONE CALL
(With Carter Jackson – Listing Agent and Julius Raymond – Seller)

Carter - *"Hey Julius."*
Julius - *"Hey Carter."*
Carter - *"Julius, I received the home inspection report and the buyers requested repair items. The list is short. I would like to inform you that they submitted the request after the deadline by a few hours."*
Julius - *"Not a problem. What are they requesting to be done?"*
Carter - *"Well... They want smoke detectors installed in every bedroom, carbon dioxide detectors on each level of the home and the HVAC system to be serviced."*
Julius - *"I know that they passed the deadline, however, since it was Thanksgiving Day, I will still take care of the items. These items all seem reasonable."*

After Carter reviewed the requested items, he spoke with his client about the buyer's requests.

Carter promptly notified Jamie, the buyer's agent, that the seller had approved all the items identified in the home inspection report and that he would be sending over the signed addendum later that same afternoon. However, during the course of their conversation, Jamie informed Carter that the closing date would need to be delayed due to courthouse closures for the holiday season.

Unfortunately, during the negotiations and processing of the contract the agents failed to take into account the holiday schedule of the courthouse, and as a result, the closing needed to be extended by two days following the Christmas holiday.

The availability of the land records office during the Christmas holiday season is contingent upon the day of the week on which Christmas Eve and Christmas Day fall. It's worth noting that while it's possible to record deeds online, title companies and banking institutions typically observe the same holiday schedule, which may impact the overall timeline of the transaction. You will see Carter's original closing calendar before he realized the dates that he originally had coordinated for the closing of both properties did not coordinate with the holiday season closings of the courthouse and banking institutions. He had to make calls and reschedule everything (i.e., title companies (2), new buyer, seller)

ORIGINAL #1 – CLOSING CALENDAR
Seller (closing on old home/closing on new home)

DECEMBER						
SUN	MON	TUE	WED	THU	FRI	SAT
19	20	21	22	23 Original closing on 123 Anywhere Lane	24 **CHRISTMAS EVE** Courthouse CLOSED	25 **CHRISTMAS DAY** Courthouse CLOSED
26 Courthouse CLOSED	27 Courthouse CLOSED	28 Deed recorded on seller's home - 123 Anywhere Lane Close on 456 New Home Ave	29	30	31	1 **NEW YEARS DAY**

REVISED #2 – CLOSING CALENDAR
Seller (closing on old home/closing on new home)

DECEMBER						
SUN	MON	TUE	WED	THU	FRI	SAT
19	20 Many people are already taking vacation this week (i.e., schools are on winter vacation)	21 Closing on 123 Anywhere Lane	22 Deed recorded on 123 Anywhere Lane	23 Seller received proceeds from 123 Anywhere Lane	24 **CHRISTMAS EVE** Courthouse CLOSED	25 **CHRISTMAS DAY**
26	27 Courthouse CLOSED	28	29 Close on 456 New Home Ave	30	31 **NEW YEAR'S EVE**	1 **NEW YEAR'S DAY**

Despite successfully closing both of his sales, Carter Jackson encountered a number of challenges that could have been avoided had he been more prudent in his approach. This lack of attention to detail was a recurrent issue in some of his previous transactions involving buyers and sellers, where he sometimes neglected to factor in the closing dates of federal holidays which includes courthouse closures, banking institutions and the other industries associated with a transaction. Hopefully, these experiences will serve as a valuable learning opportunity for Carter and encourage him to take a more mindful approach in the future.

THINK BEYOND THE STORY

- What was the cost of this real estate transaction? emotional, physical, or financial?

- What could the buyer's agent Jamie Lee have done differently?

- What could the listing agent Carter Jackson have done differently?

- What could have happened if parties did not agree to the amendments to the contract?

CLOSING POINTS

- It can be challenging to close a sale and a purchase on the same day. The funds must be released and transferred.

- A suggestion would be to close on the first property on a Monday and the other on a Thursday or Friday

- A client who is participating in selling their home and purchasing a new one should be aware of the risks and pitfalls of this type of transaction.

- Before placing dates on a contract check the calendar for federal holidays

- Consider keeping a calendar of holidays and other events that could impact your closings. Hanging one in your office, placing dates in your electronic calendar, (i.e., Thanksgiving and Christmas).

34

THE TOUCHDOWN

"In divorce sales, a real estate agent transforms into a mediator, a strategic planner, and a problem-solver."
ReShawna Leaven

AT TIMES, A REAL estate agent's role resembles that of a quarterback, orchestrating the transaction and being the leader of the team. Yet they also step in as referees for their clients, when the rules are not being followed to ensure that things are correct when any of the players on the team have made a bad play. This story plays out as a divorce (sale). Emotions run high in divorce-related asset disputes, with happiness often playing a minor role amidst the tumultuous proceedings. Conversely, the weightier aspect lies in the decisions that must be made about the asset of real estate which carries emotional and financial implications for both parties involved.

This tale examines how a real estate agent assisted clients in the middle of a divorce. After receiving one of many postcards that had been mailed, Peter (the homeowner) conducted thorough research of the agent's online presence and reviews. He gave the agent a call and they began to chat about the services needed. Peter divulged that he and his wife were in the process of finding a real estate agent to sell the family home amidst a turbulent divorce, and her contrary nature was likely to complicate the process due to their bitter separation.

PROPERTY ASSESSMENT MEETING
(With Susan – Seller and Lisa – Listing Agent)

Susan calls Peter to include him in the conversation and becomes outraged.

Susan - *"When will you be traveling back to the house to get all these action figures, puzzles and other stuff out of the guest room?" Additional words were exchanged, and the conversation became more intense."*
Peter - *"I'll come when you move out."*
Susan - *"You are the reason why this is happening Peter. You went to California to be what that b*?&*. So, you made things difficult, not me. I am not moving out until I have found a place, and you are going to pay for it. (She took a deep breath) Oh... I am making the realtor nervous. Let me call you back." (She ended the call)*
Lisa - *"Susan, I need to walk around so that I can assess the home. In addition, my home stager will need to make contact with you to assist with a decluttering/redesign plan in the next couple of days. Would that be ok with you?"*
Susan - *"Sure, go right ahead. Is there some paperwork that I can look at while you are walking around the house?"*
Lisa - *"Yes, here's the paperwork."*

With diligence, Lisa conducted a comprehensive assessment of the property, documenting her observations with copious notes and photographs. Upon concluding her meeting with Susan, Lisa promptly contacted Peter while driving to her office to apprise him of the situation.

PHONE CALL
(With Peter – Seller and Lisa – Listing Agent)

Peter - *"Yes, she is bananas which is why I am moving on with my life. I am getting a divorce. Unreasonable expectations."*
Lisa - *"I'm sorry to hear that." (in an empathic voice)*
Peter - *"I agree with everything you stated about getting the house ready for the market. Do whatever you have to do. I will get Susan on board to*

sign the necessary paperwork."

Lisa sent the listing documents to the sellers, and they signed the documents. Afterwards, the home stager created a detailed decluttering/staging plan which included a timeline for listing the home and emailed it to Susan and Peter to begin work.

Several weeks later, Lisa had an appointment to meet with both sellers at the residence. As she parked her car on the street, Susan emerged from the house, clutching her dog tightly and slamming the door shut behind her with an outburst directed at Peter. Despite having met Lisa weeks prior, Susan remained aloof and unresponsive, prompting Lisa to ponder this behavior. Lisa thought *"Hmm, how interesting?"* Lisa emerged from the car and entered the home to meet with Peter.

IN PERSON MEETING
(With Peter and Lisa at the home)

Lisa - *"Hi Peter, nice to meet you."*
Peter - *"Nice to meet you too, Lisa."*
Lisa - *"Wow, there is still a lot of stuff that needs to be packed."*
Peter - *"Yes, she took what she wanted. I have been working on this for four days. I will not be able to complete this. I am leaving today and will be unable to come back to finish. Can you get some junk people to get the rest of these items out of here, because I don't want any of this stuff? Just let me know the cost."*
Lisa - *"Sure, I have a team and a host of other vendors that can assist to remove and get the home ready for the market."*

Lisa took on the responsibility of organizing a contractor to clear the house. Initially, she assessed the contents of each room to identify items that could be sold. Through her efforts of online sales, she successfully managed to generate $1,000 from the sale of various items, including a sofa, game table, golf clubs, tools, and patio furniture, among other things.

Subsequently, Lisa embarked on the task of arranging a skilled paint contractor to revitalize the entire house with a fresh and appealing look. Concurrently, she reached out to her dependable repair person, entrusting him with essential assignments such as replacing light fixtures, repairing kitchen cabinet door hinges, and installing blinds to enhance the functionality and aesthetics of the home.

Finally, Lisa personally acquired some mulch and a selection of flowers, which she strategically placed near the front entrance to enhance the home's curb appeal. This final addition was an enhancement for potential buyers when they arrived for a showing. The home was listed right away, and clients began lining up to view the property. In no time at all a contract was ratified.

Despite encountering a few minor obstacles along the way, the transaction was ultimately proceeding smoothly. However, one particular moment arose as the closing drew near. Susan adamantly refused to sign any closing documents until she was granted confirmation of her total seller proceeds. She firmly stated her entitlement to an equal share of the proceeds as dictated by the court order, declaring, "*I want to make sure everything is 50/50. I will not sign anything until I see that in writing.*"

To resolve this issue, Lisa promptly engaged the services of the title company to draft a document clearly outlining the agreed-upon distribution of the proceeds. This document was carefully designed to require validation by both parties in front of a notary public. Susan was pleased with this outcome and the transaction continued.

To minimize the tension, the closing was conducted by an online notary with Susan and Peter being at independent locations, ensuring the process was both expedient and smooth. Once completed, both parties went their separate ways, and the transaction was successfully concluded.

In this real estate game, our agent was a gridiron guru, playing multiple roles. She was the quarterback, skillfully calling the shots and steering the team towards the end zone. At times, she channeled her inner referee, ensuring fair play and no foul moves in the high stakes match of home selling. Watching from the sidelines, she knew exactly when to be the silent bench warmer, observing the field with a keen eye. Yet, her most impressive play was as the coach, masterminding the strategy to get the house show-ready and appealing to buyers. Throughout this transaction, there were no penalty flags in sight. Our agent adeptly juggled being the coach, player, and even the bench warmer, all to score that ultimate touchdown—a successful sale. In the end, she called all the right plays, advancing us down the field to the sweet victory of a closed deal.

THINK BEYOND THE STORY

- What was the cost of this real estate transaction? emotional, physical, or financial?

- What do you think about the agent's persona during this transaction?

- What are some additional tasks that you think the agent did behind the scenes?

CLOSING POINTS

- Sometimes the agent has to "roll up their sleeves" to get the job done.

- Do not offer martial advice to a couple during a divorce.

- Ask if the sellers would like for the divorce to be final before selling the home.

- You should refer to the property distribution rules in your state for divorce.

- Let the attorney manage the legal matters.

35

WEBS OF THE PAST

"Real estate has many spirals, each one unique and unpredictable in its own way."
- ReShawna Leaven

THE DIMENSION, GEOMETRICAL SHAPE and beauty of a spider's web can captivate a person and be a conversation starter. Observing a spider spinning a web often triggers a thought of how this small creature could create such a strong intricate item. In the realm of real estate, a spider's web can compare a striking resemblance to a real estate deal, where multiple strands are carefully intertwined, and all the parties involved must forge connections to arrive at a satisfactory outcome. It is an intricate web of complexity, with countless unknown variables that can easily ensnare one into "sticky" situations. This was precisely the predicament that surfaced when listing agent Oliver Davis was representing a seller.

Oliver Davis had an upcoming listing. Let's review his process of listing a home.

STEPS OF LISTING A HOME:

- Pre-marketing

- Home listed in MLS (multiple listing service)

- Showing appointments with buyer's agents and their buyer clients

- Offer(s) are submitted and reviewed.

- Offer acceptance (Property now under contract)

- Contract is sent to all parties including the lender and closing company.

- Title work is reviewed.

The title of a home is unequivocally one of the most critical components to consider when selling a property. During this time, a comprehensive investigation is conducted to unearth any encumbrances that may affect the marketability of the property. These could include mortgages, liens, judgments, and other obligations that may be attached to the title. The title company is responsible for unearthing this information by employing a highly skilled title abstractor. This individual uses a keen eye to research the title, scrutinizing records from the present day and extending back 50 years to uncover any potential issues that could impact the transaction. It is imperative to understand that not all sellers possess "squeaky clean" title reports, and an agent should never assume as such. In some instances, sellers may attempt to conceal pertinent information regarding transactions that are tied to the title since they became owners. Alternatively, a previous issue may arise from when the property was initially purchased. Hence, the adage "it's not a problem until it's a problem" holds weight in this regard. As such, it is critical to remain vigilant and proactive in discovering any encumbrances early on to avoid any last-minute surprises or complications during the closing process.

Titles are silent, until the files are opened like the mouth of a talking doll then many voices will be needed to remedy those issues.

"Hi, I'm Title. If you don't fix me, things will go bad. Hahaha"
(Doll voice)

The tale begins with Oliver, the diligent and dedicated listing agent, who is unwinding with a leisurely jog in the serene surroundings in a local park, accompanied by his trusty canine companion. Suddenly, amidst the tranquility, his cell phone erupts into a shrill of ringing. Oliver halts his jog and promptly answers the call, always ready to cater to the needs of his clients, even in the midst of his leisurely pursuits.

PHONE CALL
(With Ramona – Title Company Representative and Oliver Davis – Listing Agent)

The title company calls...

Oliver - *"This is Oliver Davis. How can I help you?"*
Ramona - *"Hi Oliver. This is Ramona at Zero Title. I wanted to update you on your closing. Do you have a few minutes?*
Oliver - *"Hi Ramona. Sure, I have a few minutes."*
Ramona - *"Ok. We found out there were two construction loans on the property when purchased. It looks like they were never released after the project was complete. That's going to affect your client's bottom line."*
Oliver - *"Oh, I see how much the loans are all together."*
Ramona - *"One of the loans is $65,000 and the other is $40,000. This may not be the final figures since we need to contact the company to get the payoff amounts."*
Oliver - *"Wow. That's over $100,000! How much would the seller get with these two additional loans added to his closing cost figures?"*
Ramona - *"This is just a rough estimate but about $85,000 after closing fees and payoff of the existing mortgage on the property."*
Oliver - *"Hmmm. I'm shocked to find this out. What's the next move?"*

Ramona - *"Well if the seller has proof of payment for these liens that would solve the problem. The attorney will still have to review and verify the information submitted before we can move forward. The other solution is to make the payment for the liens from the closing proceeds."*
Oliver - *"Ok. In the meantime, I will speak to my client, but I doubt that he has any documentation. Thank you for calling."*
Ramona - *"You're welcome. I will send you the information that I have from the title abstractor."*
Oliver - *"Ok, thanks. Enjoy your day."*
Ramona - *"You're welcome. You do the same."*

After completing his invigorating jog in the park, Oliver proceeded to his abode to prepare for the day's work ahead. As the day progressed, Oliver immersed himself in the intricacies of the transaction, leaving no stone unturned to ensure a seamless and successful closing process. In the evening, as he deliberated on the latest developments of the transaction, he was prompted to connect with his client.

Just like a spider web with multiple intricate strands, Justin (Oliver's client) has another entanglement that was going to come to light. He has entered into a contract for a newly constructed property without disclosing this to Oliver. This added another thread to the web of complexity. This entanglement looms on the horizon, ready to ensnare any unwary parties in its grasp. Let's dive into this conversation between Justin Edison (the seller) and Oliver Davis (the listing agent) to learn the new discoveries.

PHONE CALL
(With Justin Edison – Seller and Oliver Davis – Listing Agent to discuss the new discoveries)

Oliver - *"Hi, Justin. This is Oliver. How's your day going?"*
Justin - *"All is well Oliver. What's happening?"*
Oliver - *"Well, I spoke with a representative from the title company earlier today and she stated that there were construction loans that have to be paid off in order to close on the home. Were you aware of these loans?"*

Justin - *"Well, when I purchased the home, I had some renovations done with a special program. I was not aware that the loan had to be paid back.*
(Oliver thought to himself "Justin has selective amnesia")
Oliver - *"When you purchased the home, the program parameters should have been explained."*
Typically, the loan is a silent second mortgage loan until the home is refinanced or sold. If you can verify that you paid them off with proof of payment, we can use that paperwork to get the liens released and satisfied. If not, the funds will have to come out of the proceeds at closing to pay for the loans."
Justin - *"I don't have any paperwork stating that I paid them off. (long silence) Well, I guess they will have to come out of the proceeds. How much are the loans?"*
Oliver - *"I will need to find out the details from the processor. It's about $85,000 that you would receive after all your required closing costs. That's the amount that she quoted me when I spoke to her. I will have a firm number once the payoffs are received."*
Justin - *"Oh. Wow! That's a huge difference. I won't be able to get my new house now."*
Oliver - *"New house?"*
Justin - *"Oh, yeah man. I went to this new home site about a few weeks ago. I am supposed to be closing in two weeks. They said they would give me a better deal without an agent."*
Oliver - *"Did you have any contingencies?"*
Justin - *"Contingencies? No, I don't think so."*
Oliver - *"I see. How much will you need to close?"*
Justin - *"Not sure. This is becoming a nightmare. I should have used you for everything."*
Oliver - *"Well, let's get your home sold and I would advise you to talk with your loan officer and the new home sales representative to see what your options are at this point."*
Justin - *"Ok. Thanks."*
Oliver - *"You're welcome."*

Justin and Oliver ended the call. Due to the required loan payoffs needed, the sales contract closing date needed to be extended with the buyer. With any transaction of this nature, unexpected issues can arise, requiring prompt and decisive action to prevent any adverse consequences. In this instance, an addendum or amendment to the original ratified contract was deemed necessary to extend the closing date, avoiding any potential penalties for breaches of contract. Failure to sign this vital document could have resulted in the buyer's lender requesting a new contract, rendering the previous agreement null and void. Thus, the signing of this addendum was a critical component of the transaction, ensuring that all parties were in agreement, so that the closing process could proceed seamlessly.

The proficient efforts of the title company led to the successful gathering of the final payoff figures. Consequently, the title company transmitted the new closing disclosure, revealing that the final amount after paying all real estate fees would be $59,000. These new figures left Justin unable to afford the new home, and he was forced to forfeit his earnest money deposit and seek out a rental due to the sale of his previous home. Once the final figures were confirmed, the closing date was scheduled, all parties signed the necessary documents, and the deed was delivered. It was regrettable that Justin could not secure the home he had set his sights on. This scenario highlights the importance of transparency in any transaction.

During the initial listing consultation, the seller had indicated a preference for renting an apartment for a year before embarking on another home purchase. However, as with a spider's web, clients may suddenly shift course and deviate from their initial intentions. In this case, the seller was caught in the sticky substance of the web and had a difficult time getting out based on his final decision to sell and purchase another home (without consulting his real estate agent).

THINK BEYOND THE STORY

- What was the cost of this real estate transaction? emotional, physical or financial

- What could Oliver have done differently with this seller - before taking the listing?

- How important is getting the title report before a listing?

CLOSING POINTS

- In real estate transactions, it is important to be transparent and forthright with all parties involved.

- Buyers and sellers may have different intentions than what they initially expressed during their consultation.

- Collaborative efforts among all parties, such as the title company, can lead to a successful transaction.

- Even with careful planning and consultation, unexpected developments can arise in real estate transactions, and parties must be prepared to adjust their plans accordingly.

36

THE TRUST IS NOT YOURS

"There is no claim for the uninsured."
ReShawna Leaven

TITLE INSURANCE SHARES MANY similarities with car insurance. Just like car insurance, title insurance involves the payment of premiums and offers a range of coverage items, some included, and others excluded in each policy. Both types of insurance also provide the policyholder with the essential ability to file a claim when necessary. However, it's crucial to emphasize that opting not to invest in insurance coverage can have dire consequences. This decision can put your valuable assets at risk, potentially resulting in the loss of a significant investment, legal disputes, and the worst-case scenario, the forfeiture of everything you've eagerly worked for.

Owner's title insurance plays a pivotal role in shielding property owners from potential claims that may arise due to previous ownership issues. In the realm of real estate, it's absolutely critical to ensure that all past matters have been fully resolved and executed. A prime illustration of this scenario is when a repair is performed on a property but left unpaid by the owner. In such cases, the contractor retains the right to place a "mechanics line" on the property, essentially establishing a claim to receive payment for services. If this payment is not made, the responsibility could inadvertently transfer to the subsequent property owner.

Historically, these issues often surfaced during the title search process, but in the pre-electronic record-keeping era, paperwork had a tendency to go astray (even though this can happen post digital age). Subsequently, owner's title insurance serves as a safety net in such situations, sparing the new owner from the burden of settling the unpaid bill. This vividly illustrates how title insurance proves invaluable in handling complex and potentially ruinous complications and expenses that might otherwise be extremely challenging to overcome.

The significance of obtaining title insurance from a previous sale is exemplified in this chapter, which highlights how a past sale can have reverberating effects on a future sale, as in the case of Barry Bleeker's client. You will glean the importance of prioritizing the purchase of title insurance to mitigate potential risks and ensure a smooth and hassle-free ownership experience.

This chapter begins with the homeowner and agent completing a checklist of items that usually take place during the selling process. The homeowners are preparing for their imminent move by sorting their belongings into keep, donate, and sell boxes. Meanwhile, the listing agent persists in his efforts to maintain communication with the lender and other involved parties to ensure a seamless closing process. Despite his persistent follow-up, unforeseeable predicaments still emerge, which are beyond their control.

Barry had not received any communication from the title company due because the abstractor had not finalized the research. The abstractor was preoccupied with other clients' paperwork which included completion of title commitments, disclosures, closing disclosure balances, and other pertinent documentation, thereby causing a delay in the process.

EMAIL (From 444 Title Group to Listing Agent)

FROM: Gabriel Jenkins/ TO Barry Bleeker

SUBJECT: Title Review - 789 Why Avenue

Hi Barry,

We regret to inform you that your client has an unreleased deed of trust that has to be cleared in order to close. There were three solutions to resolve the issue.

- Find the lender of the $120,000 unreleased Deed of Trust from the previous owner and get the paperwork for a release.

- The owner could use their owner's title insurance to resolve the issue if purchased when the home was purchased.

- The current owner could pay the amount of the deed at closing.

We have already tried to locate the lender and have reached out to the previous title company (they are no longer in business) to request information about the owner's title insurance.

For additional questions, don't hesitate to give me a call.

Gabriel Jenkins

Title Processor

444 Title Group

Barry was left in a state of shock upon receiving the news conveyed in the email. The gravity of the situation made it arduous for him to assimilate and process. He was in a state of disbelief as he repeatedly scrutinized the contents of the email, jotting down notes, and engaging in introspective self-talk to make sense of the situation.

As he engaged in self-talk, Barry vocalized a series of questions to himself, seeking to ascertain the next course of action. He contemplated how to break down the intricate details of the situation in a manner that his client could easily comprehend. He further pondered whether there were sufficient funds to settle the lien or if the specific title company that processed the purchase of the property had completed it with accuracy.

As he formulated a comprehensive list of talking points, Barry prepared to contact his client to discuss the available options. He scrolled through his contact list on his mobile device, locating the contact of interest under the 'R' section and promptly initiated the call by tapping Kathy Reynolds' phone number in his contact list.

PHONE CALL
(With Barry – Listing Agent and Kathy Reynolds – Seller)

Barry - *"Hi Kathy."*
Kathy - *"Hi Barry. I'm well just packing boxes and getting rid of some unnecessary stuff that I don't want to take to the new house. What's new?"*
Barry - *"I'm glad that packing is going well. I received an email from the title company and there is a cloud on the title that needs to be resolved. This snag will cause an issue with closing."*
Kathy - *"What kind of a snag?"*
Barry - *"There is an unreleased deed of trust from when you purchased your home back in 2006. It's about a hundred and twenty thousand ($120,000)."*
Kathy - *"WHAT the heck? What am I supposed to do now?"*
Barry - *"Is it possible that you could have purchased owner's title insurance?"*
Kathy - *"Well... I'm not sure. I'll have to check my paperwork. I think those documents are in my storage. I'll go there this afternoon and let you know. What will happen if I don't find this insurance paperwork?"*
Barry - *"Hopefully, you will. If not, you will have to pay the amount of the unreleased deed of trust."*
Kathy - *"Awww...I can't believe this. This is turning into a nightmare. I have so much to deal with right now on top of moving."*
Barry - *"I'm so sorry Kathy. I hope that you purchased it back in 2006 when you purchased the home. If you need me to come to the storage to help you sort through the boxes, I can."*
Kathy - *"I would love that. You're a lifesaver. That would be extremely helpful Barry. I wouldn't know what I was looking for even if I did come*

*across it. I am so stressed. (*Lighting up a cigarette. Barry could hear the lighter and pause for and inhale as Kathy began to smoke the cigarette). *Barry, I had to light up a cigarette. Please excuse the brief moment of silence. I made a promise to myself that I would put these cigarettes down after the move."*

Barry - *"It will be okay. I will come by your house at 4:30 p.m. and we can ride together to the storage."*

Kathy - *"Ok, that sounds good."*

Upon arrival at the storage facility, Kathy took the initiative to rearrange her possessions to one side of the unit to facilitate ease of access and streamline the search process. Specifically the banker boxes containing important documents, so that she and Barry could begin the search in an organized manner.

CONVERSATION – STORAGE UNIT 276
(With Barry and Kathy)

Barry and Kathy continued their search within storage unit 276 for an hour, sifting through various boxes and documents. Suddenly, Barry's voice broke the silence, *"I think I found it, Kathy. This appears to be what we need. However, it will require verification, but it's a promising start to resolving the issue."*

Kathy breathed a sigh of relief and replied, *"You truly are a blessing, Barry. I couldn't have done this without you."*

Barry humbly responded, *"It's my pleasure, Kathy. As a real estate professional, it's my duty to alleviate any anxiety or stress you may be experiencing. Moving can be a challenging life event, and I understand that everyone copes differently. I have helped many clients through this process before."*

Thanks to their search efforts, a potential financial catastrophe was averted, and the issue was resolved without incurring significant expenses.

EMAIL (From Listing Agent to Processor at 444 Title Group)

FROM: Barry Bleeker/ TO: Gabriel Jenkins
SUBJECT: Title Review - 789 Why Avenue

Hi Gabriel,

I was able to assist my client with locating the supporting documents for the owner's title insurance policy to resolve the unreleased deed of trust. My client purchased title insurance with an enhanced policy when she purchased it in 2006.

Please see the attached documents. I can hand deliver the original documents, if necessary, tomorrow. I would be happy to drop it by.

Barry Bleeker

Empathetic Real Estate Group

Attachment: Title_Insurance_Policy_Kathy_Reynolds.pdf

EMAIL (From 444 Title Group to Listing Agent)

FROM: Gabriel Jenkins/TO: Barry Bleeker
SUBJECT: Re: Title Review - 789 Why Avenue

Hi Barry,

Thank you for sending this information over. This will correct the issue with the title. I will start processing this tomorrow morning when I get into the office. There shouldn't be any delays for closing that I am aware of after this has been resolved.

As far as the delivery of the documents, a hand delivery is not needed. The attachment will suffice. I can use this information to check and verify.

Gabriel Jenkins

444 Title Group

The title company received and carefully reviewed the documentation that was required. It's baffling why the other title company missed the mortgage lien. It's also baffling that the seller had refinanced her home a few years back, and this "cloud on title" was never brought to light.

If the buyer believes that the risk of encountering title issues is low, they might decide to forgo obtaining title insurance, thinking that the potential problems are unlikely to occur. Some individuals may perceive it as an expendable one-time premium fee that may never serve a purpose. In addition, they may forego this optional cost in order to save a few thousand dollars upfront. However, it is important to acknowledge that owner's title insurance is an indispensable component of both resale and new construction transactions. By providing a safeguard against any future claims that may arise during or after ownership. It is an essential investment when acquiring real estate, considering the potential for human error and other unforeseen circumstances. Any legal issues that may arise pertaining to a title inevitably could involve significant financial implications and may lead to emotional turmoil for the parties involved in the future.

THINK BEYOND THE STORY

- What was the cost of this real estate transaction? emotional, physical, or financial?

- Is there anything that could possibly come up on title during the title search? Explain and educate the client on what this means. (i.e., liens, mortgages, HELOCs, solar panels, etc.)

CLOSING POINTS

- After completing, the listing paperwork with the client, order a title search as soon as possible

- Be sure to obtain all necessary paperwork before they start packing. If they don't have a copy of the policy, their closing statement will indicate whether it was purchased.

37

TURBULENCE

*"Sometimes the co-pilot has to take over the wheel to make
sure the plane gets to its destination and makes a safe
landing."*
ReShawna Leaven

IN THE REALM OF real estate, where wealth is accumulated and aspirations lay their cornerstone, there exists a swirling undercurrent of turbulence.

There is an underlying stream of instability in the real estate market, where wealth is amassed, and dreams are anchored. It is within this tempestuous account that two agents, adorned with ambition and armed with expertise, find themselves poised for a clash of wills. As they navigate the intricate dance of negotiations and navigate the treacherous tides of the housing market, their paths intertwine and intensity. Each harboring their own secrets and strategies, these agents stand as formidable adversaries, ready to navigate the stormy seas of opportunity and uncertainty. They cope with a situation in which there is volatility and turbulence. Get ready for an exciting voyage where the difference between success and failure is minuscule. Two agents face off in a battle of wits.

Sally Jefferson, an expert real estate agent with almost two decades of experience set up a showing appointment to show Charlotte's investment listing. THE PRESSURE BEGINS.... as Sally makes a call to Charlotte because she had trouble accessing the property.

PHONE CALL
(With Charlotte – Listing Agent and Sally – Buyer's Agent)

Charlotte - *"Charlotte Locke speaking."*
Sally - *"Hi Charlotte. This is Sally. I have been running around all day, I had to take my dog to the vet and pick up my daughter from school and now I am at your listing and cannot find the lockbox."*
Charlotte - *"The lockbox is located on the end of the realtor rail. Are you at the right location?"* (at many condo locations they create a rail for real estate agents to place lock boxes so that they are in one location)
Sally - *"Oh, I thought it was at the other end. Long day. I apologize."*
(Sally hangs up the phone without even saying goodbye)

Ring, ring (Sally calls back)

Sally - "I can't get into the lockbox. I don't know the combination."
Charlotte - "I texted it to you this morning. Please check your text."
Sally - "Ok. My phone is running out of charge. Could you just give it to me? I will write it down."
Charlotte - "I don't want to say it out loud because your client or others may hear the code and then they will have access to the property. Can you go to a secluded area so I can share it with you?"

Sally went to a secluded area and Charlotte gave her the code to access the property. After Sally showed her client the property, they decided to submit an offer. The turbulent ride begin.

NEGOTIATIONS OF THE CONTRACT

Original List Price: $260,000			
Offer	**Seller's Counteroffer**	**Buyer's Counteroffer**	**Contract Acceptance**
$230,000	**$260,000**	**$250,000**	**$250,000**
Sally's client decided to write an offer on the property, and it was emailed to Charlotte	Charlotte confirmed receipt of the offer and presented it to the seller. The seller reviewed the offer and instructed Charlotte to counter the offer with a new sales price. Charlotte emailed the seller's counter to Sally.	Sally's client countered with a lower price and Sally sent the counteroffer to Charlotte	After careful consideration, Charlotte's client accepted and signed the final changes to the contract and added the date of acceptance which made it ratified.

WIND POCKET #1

As the contract process gets underway, Sally writes her first email to Charlotte. It is highly concerning to observe that all of the email correspondence was written in lowercase letters. This is a clear violation of professional standards. It is unfortunate that the buyers are unaware of the unprofessional manner in which they are being represented by their agent.

EMAIL (From Buyer's Agent to Listing Agent)

FROM: Sally/To: Charlotte
SUBJECT: Addendum

hi charlotte,

i need to access the property on saturday for the home inspection at 1:30

Sally

In reality, the home inspection was supposed to be at 11:30 am. It was a typo (11:30 am not 1:30 pm) time confirmation error on the buyer's agent part. On home inspection day, the tenant was home taking a shower when the buyer's agent and the buyer arrived.

Tenant - *"What are you doing here?"*
Sally - *"We are here for the home inspection."*
Tenant - *"The home inspection is supposed to be at 1:30pm today, not 11:30am."*
Sally - *"We are here now. Let's just get it done since we are here. I think the home inspector has another appointment after this one. (Sally was not apologetic to the owner at all about for her mistake).*

Her level of entitlement was not in line with being a professional in the business for so many years. The tenant was annoyed, but he got dressed and let them proceed anyway. He left and called the listing agent to explain his level of frustration and the unacceptable behavior exhibited by the buyer's agent.

WIND POCKET #2

Another wind pocket of turbulence occurred when Sally inaccurately sent the wrong version of the contract to the lender and title company, with the incorrect sales price. Several weeks into the escrow period, the appraisal was received, and the lender requested that the sale price be increased to $250,000, instead of the $230,000 stated in the contract. During offer negotiations, the contract sales price was altered several times before being finalized.

EMAIL (From Sally to Charlotte)

FROM: Sally/TO: Charlotte
SUBJECT: Addendum

hi charlotte,

i need an addendum to stating the sales price is now $250,000. i have attached the sales addendum needed.

Sally

EMAIL (From Charlotte to Sally)

FROM: Charlotte Locke/ TO: Sally
SUBJECT: Re: Addendum

Hi Sally,

The sales price is already $250,000. Not sure why an addendum is needed. I have attached the ratified contract that shows the sales price of $250,000. I will also reach out to the lender for clarification as well.

Charlotte Locke

Charlotte had to carefully explain to the seller why an addendum to the sales contract was required, even though the original contract had the correct sales price. The seller may have been confused or concerned about this development, so Charlotte had to provide a thorough and satisfactory explanation for the need of an addendum. After all the "I's" were dotted and the "T's" were crossed, the deal closed.

Negotiations in real estate can be similar to turbulence on an airplane. Turbulence can occur at any point during a flight, just as negotiations and other errors (including scheduling) can occur at any stage of a real estate transaction. In both cases, it is important to be prepared and rely on past experiences. In real estate negotiations, an agent who has been in the industry for many years may not necessarily mean they have a professional mode of operating or organizational skills. It is important to be proactive by keeping accurate logs and records of emails and conversations, so that you can address any potential issues with facts and data, if necessary, at a later date.

It is mind-boggling how some agents lack communication skills. Agents do peculiar things during a transaction that make it difficult to communicate particular elements and components of what's going on at a particular moment in time. It's important to keep the communication flowing instead of the "no response to text messages, emails, or voicemails." It's unbelievable how some agents (our colleagues in the field) forget to practice the code of ethics learned during their initial real estate principles course. In addition, they are continuously reminded during continuing education required courses which outlines the importance of communication.

On the other hand, sometimes they share too much information about their past and current business that's irrelevant to the conversation at hand. Sometimes the conversation may include how many years they have been in the business, which has nothing to do with events in that particular transaction or personal information about their daily errands and so on. A good agent should possess the following characteristics in order to bring the "plane" in for a smooth landing. Be knowledgeable of the industry, have good communication skills, have good strategies for negotiating and be adaptable and capable of quickly finding solutions to problems. Last but not least, be ethical and honest.

THINK BEYOND THE STORY

- What was the cost of this real estate transaction? emotional, physical, or financial

- What are some ways that Charlotte could have made the transaction go smoothly?

- How can Sally improve her business practices?

- Will knowing the number of years an agent has been in the business tell you if they are good agents to work with?

- How will you make your transactions run smoothly?

CLOSING POINTS

- Strive to set the standard of excellence in all of your endeavors.

- Adapt your communication style during a transaction as long as it does not compromise professional standards.

- Avoid assuming that others will meet your expectations or share your business practices and processes.

- As a best practice, it is advisable to send the final contract to all parties involved in the transaction, including the lender, title company, agent, and attorney. This ensures that everyone has a copy of the agreement and can refer to it as needed.

- Do not let any additional challenges or obstacles deter you from achieving your objective. Close the deal!

38

H20

"Without all the right elements, a transaction cannot close."
ReShawna Leaven

WATER IS NOT ONLY essential for survival but also is a part of the very essence of life on our planet. Its management and distribution, especially to our homes and businesses, present both advantages and challenges. Ensuring that a property's water-related systems are in optimal working condition is yet another checklist that real estate agents must complete. Those systems and appliances include dishwashers, refrigerators, toilets, sump pumps, hot water tanks, bib hoses among other things that use water as a source to function. Sylvia Marks' professional standards are tested as we delve into this core essential element that we all need. Our exploration begins with a text message between the agents.

TEXT MESSAGE
(With Marybeth – Listing Agent & Sylvia – Buyer's Agent)

"Hi Marybeth. I emailed you the home inspection report with my clients requested repairs. Please confirm receipt." **[Sylvia sent at 8:05 AM]**
"Ok. Thank you. I will look at my email." **[Marybeth sent at 8:37 AM]**

"Thank you." **[Sylvia sent at 8:40 AM]**

"I don't see it in my email. Can you resend it?" **[Marybeth sent at 11:48 AM]**

"Sure." **[Sylvia sent at 12:20 PM]**

"Ok. I have it. I will review and send it to the seller shortly." **[Marybeth sent at 12:30 PM]**

"Thank you so much." **[Sylvia sent at 12:33 PM]**

EMAIL (From Sylvia Marks to Marybeth Lawson)

FROM: Sylvia Marks/TO: Marybeth Lawson

SUBJECT: Re: Seller review needed - 567 Water Street

Hi Marybeth,

The buyers are requesting the following items to be repaired/replaced prior to closing:

1. Repair the dishwasher leak

2. Replace the hot water heater

3. Replace the ice maker. Currently, over cools and freezes ice in the tray

4. Replace the sprinkler system value in the living room and basement

See the home inspection report and contingency removal addendum.

Sylvia Marks

Real Estate Salesperson

The Real Estate Group

Attachments

Home Inspection Report.pdf

Home Inspection Contingency Removal Addendum.pdf

After two days of reviewing the home inspection report and requests, the listing agent emailed the seller's response to the buyer's agent.

EMAIL (From Sylvia Marks to Marybeth Lawson)

FROM: Sylvia Marks/To: Marybeth Lawson

SUBJECT: Re: Seller review needed - 567 Water Street

Hi Sylvia,

The seller is willing to fix all the items per the buyer's request. See the attached signed addendum.

Marybeth Lawson

Associate Broker

123 Real Estate

Attachments

Signed Home Inspection Contingency Removal Addendum.PDF

Ironically, all the repair items are connected to water.

AUGUST 28th - Final Walk -Through Day

During the final walkthrough, Sylvia and her clients checked every aspect of the property. She examined the lights, the HVAC system, and even tried to test the dishwasher, but it had a loud humming sound. Then, she turned on the faucet in the kitchen and the water was off. She thought fast on her feet, *"I need to check the main water shut-off valve in the basement."* When she did, it was in the "on" position. After this discovery, she called the water company and the representative stated that the water had been disconnected at 7 a.m. that morning. Now, Sylvia was faced with a critical question: how could she complete her walk-through checklist with no running water?

In addition to the disconnected water, the following items needed to be resolved:

- Grass was not cut

- HOA violation was corrected: crack in the steps of the stairway leading up to the front door

PHONE CALL
(With Marybeth – Listing Agent & Sylvia – Buyer's Agent)

Sylvia decided to reach out to the listing agent to provide her with an update on the situation. Sylvia dialed the number, she took a deep breath, hoping to find a quick solution to the issue at hand. The phone rang a few times and then someone answered.

Marybeth - "This is Marybeth Campbell. How can I help you?" she inquired in a polite yet professional tone.

Sylvia - *"Hi Marybeth, We're here at the final walkthrough, and the water is off."*

Marybeth - She paused for a moment, then replied with a hint of irritation, *"Your client should have turned on the utilities in their name today."*

Sylvia - *"That's incorrect. All utilities should still be on and in the current homeowner's name. We checked with the water company, and they said the service was canceled by the owner."*

Marybeth - *"Well, that's news to me. I'll have to look into it and get back with you."*

Sylvia - She let out a deep sigh. *"We need to find a solution before settlement. It's imperative that the water supply is restored. In addition to the water being off, the grass has not been cut and the cement has not been repaired per the HOA violation."*

Marybeth - *"I understand, but ultimately it's your client's responsibility to ensure that the utilities are turned on in their name before settlement."*

Sylvia - *"Well the electricity and gas are still on!"*

Marybeth - *"Well..."*

Sylvia - She knew that Marybeth had a point, but she was still frustrated with the situation. *"Well.....I'll speak to my clients and see what we can do to resolve this. We may need to draft an addendum to address this issue."*

Marybeth - *"Yes, let's do that. Keep me updated on what your clients* *decide."*

Marybeth honed in on the water service cessation, deeming it a double victory for her, as she never mentioned the other repairs promised in the inspection addendum. Sylvia began to think about the conversation that just took place and knew she had a lot of work to do to ensure that her clients would not be without water on their closing day and move-in weekend. She was determined to find a solution that would work for everyone involved.

Without delay, she contacted the water company again to inquire about water restoration services. When she called the water company the response added insult to injury when the representative told her that, because it was Friday, that the earliest time for a reconnection was on Monday morning. They had an option to pay an emergency fee of $150 which meant they would send out a technician sometime in the next 12 hours.

The customer service representative instructed Sylvia that she had to go to the water company to make the request in person because their website system was down. Silvia said that she would go to the water company for the buyers because they had to get back to work. She said, *"I need you to fill out this application and sign this authorization form allowing me to assist with setting up your services."* Her clients signed the authorization form and filled out the application and off she went to complete the task of getting the water turned back on.

Following her visit to the water company, Sylvia promptly embarked on a quest to resolve the outstanding issues from the walk-through. She engaged in a collaborative brainstorming session with her broker to explore viable strategies for overcoming this challenge. Ultimately, they devised a solution that entailed the seller depositing funds in escrow to address potential concerns arising when water-dependent items were activated, in addition to the unresolved final walk-through matters.

The buyers requested that the seller give a credit in the amount of

$1,000. (This was back in the day when items could be changed at the last minute before the CFPB (Consumer Finance Protection Bureau required a disclosure three days before closing).

The day of the closing arrived, and Sylvia's tenacity and dedication was evident. The buyers, though initially frustrated, appreciated her unwavering commitment to ensuring their new home was in the best possible condition. The seller, recognizing the oversight, agreed to the credit, and the transaction was finalized. As the keys exchanged hands, Sylvia reflected on the journey. The water, which was the source of so many challenges, symbolized the fluidity and adaptability required in real estate. Just as water is essential to life, so is the ability to navigate challenges and find solutions in the world of property transactions. Sylvia's experience underscored the importance of diligence, communication, and perseverance. As quoted "Without all the right elements, a transaction cannot close." And in this case, water was the element -that tested and ultimately solidified Sylvia's professional perseverance.

THINK BEYOND THE STORY

- What was the cost of this real estate transaction? emotional, physical, or financial

- Who should you talk to when there is an issue in your real estate deal?

CLOSING POINTS

- Give clients a checklist and timeline on how and when to transfer utilities ahead of time

- Never disconnect the utilities, always tell the seller to transfer them.

- Always be aware of your emotional state before making a phone call about negative information

39

READY, WILLING AND ACCOUNT-ABLE

"Placing funds in an escrow account demonstrates the stability of a buyer."
ReShawna Leaven

THE EARNEST MONEY DEPOSIT serves as a tangible demonstration of the buyer's level of commitment. In this chapter we will compare the sturdiness and weight of a ship's anchor to the earnest money deposit funds given by a buyer who commits to perform after signing a contract to purchase a home.

Anchors for a ship come in various types and sizes, each designed for distinct types of vessels and conditions. Common anchor types include the plow anchor, the Danforth anchor, and the mushroom anchor, each with its own advantages and best-use scenarios. The choice of anchor and the proper technique for deploying it depends on the ship's size, the seabed conditions, and the prevailing weather and tidal conditions. Anchors are a critical part of maritime safety and operational procedures, ensuring that ships remain under control and secure in various situations.

The importance of an anchor in preventing a ship from drifting can be likened to the significance of an earnest money deposit in a real estate transaction. In both cases, these elements serve as stabilizing forces. An earnest money deposit, analogous to an anchor, is typically accepted by the seller to instill confidence in the commitment to the deal. When the deposit is substantial and heavy like an anchor, it dissuades the buyer from entertaining the thought of withdrawing from the transaction without just cause.

However, in many lines of business, there are those who try to take shortcuts or find non-conventional and unscrupulous means to achieve their goals. As you will find out in this story, Emily Adams' client Henry Thomas turns out to be a person who exhibits such characteristics.

On a delightful afternoon, Emily embarked on a jog with her loyal canine companion, Roxy, at a bustling dog park near her home. As she savored the picturesque surroundings, Emily paused momentarily to take a well-deserved respite, settling upon a sturdy bench to quench her thirst with a sip of cool water. Ever mindful of Roxy's needs, she thoughtfully poured water into her faithful friend's bowl, ensuring that both of them were hydrated and refreshed.

As Emily basked in the tranquility of the surroundings, her peaceful reverie was suddenly interrupted by the jarring sound of her phone's ringtone. With a touch of curiosity and apprehension, she answered the call, recognizing the voice on the other end as that of her college roommate from sophomore year, Sabrina Gills.

PHONE CALL
(With Emily Adams and Sabrina Gills)

Emily - *"Hello."*
Sabrina - *"Hey Emily. It's Sabrina. I got a new number. How are you?"*
Emily - *"Oh hey Sabrina. I'm good. I almost didn't answer when you called because of your new number."*
Sabrina - *"I am doing well. I have a friend, well he's actually an ex-boyfriend and he is looking to buy a home. Are you still a real estate agent?"*
Emily - *"Yes, I am still in the business."*
Sabrina - *"Awesome. Do you think you can help him? He was unhappy*

with the last agent and reached out to me to see if I knew anyone."
Emily - *"Sure. I would be happy to help him. Sorry that it didn't work with you two."*
Sabrina - *"Oh girl. He's nice, just not nice for me. Long story. We'll have to catch up after you sell him the house and I will tell you about it."*
Emily - *"Sure, it's a date then. After, I sell him a house, we'll get together and you can tell me the story. It's been too long since we've spent time together anyway. Send me his info and I will connect with him."*
Sabrina - *"Sounds good. I'll share his contact card from my phone. Enjoy your weekend."*
Emily - *"Thank you, same to you."*

Emily was overjoyed upon receiving a referral from a former college friend. As the story unfolds, her enthusiasm and excitement for this new opportunity propelled her forward. She was so excited that perhaps it caused her to overlook certain crucial aspects of the home buying process in her eagerness to impress and please her client.

Emily's client was very "easy-going" during the beginning of the process, she had to pinch herself to confirm that this was not just a figment of her imagination. With a pre-approval letter in hand from a well-established and reputable lender, Henry was poised to secure a VA loan of up to $400,000, a fact that further cemented Emily's confidence in his ability to make this a seamless and successful transaction.

He had a willingness to explore various property options, so Emily made sure to clarify the crucial criteria that had to be met for the property to be considered viable. For example, if a property was a condominium, it had to appear on the list of approved VA condos to be eligible for purchase. This attention to detail was indicative of Emily's unwavering commitment to ensure that her clients were fully informed and knowledgeable about every aspect of the process. Emily continued to guide Henry through each step of the process, leaving no stone unturned in her quest to provide a superlative experience for him. As they embarked on home tours, she demonstrated a level of expertise and professionalism that left Henry feeling fully satisfied and confident during this process.

Henry viewed several homes over a period of six weeks. He kept a rating sheet created by Emily to score the pros and cons of each home. This data would be of good use later in assisting him with finalizing a decision on a suitable match for his discerning tastes and preferences. Despite the time and effort invested by Emily in these showings, it wasn't clear if any of these properties resonated with him in a way that warranted a serious offer. Undeterred Emily remained steadfast in her mission to continue with the tours in hopes that Henry would find the perfect home.

WEEK SIX OF LOOKING AT HOMES

Emily - *"So what do you think? Do you like any of these homes we saw today?"*
Henry - *"Yes. I like the property on 333 Access Way. I think that home has the best features and a positive vibe for me. Plus, it has a fenced yard for privacy. I think that this is the one. What are the next steps? I want to place an offer."*
Emily - *"You will need to submit an offer. If the seller accepts your offer, then you will need to place your earnest money deposit into escrow once the contract is accepted."*
Henry - *"Ok, how much does that need to be?"*
Emily - *"It's typically 1% of the sales price. For this home that would be $3,500."*
Henry - *"Oh, I thought that with a VA loan, there was no money down."*
Emily - *"Yes, you are correct that with a VA loan you do get 100% financing, however, you have to show the seller your good faith to purchase the home as well. All contracts need to have consideration for an offer to be valid."*
Henry - *"Ok. Let's write the offer and see what the seller says."*

She was so excited about writing the offer she forgot to get the earnest funds and ask Henry to write the check. Emily assumed the funds were in his checking and/or savings account and continued with the transaction. The next day she gave Henry a call.

Emily - *"Hi Henry. Will you have the earnest money deposit available in the next 48 hours if the contract is accepted?"*
Henry - *"Emily, I will have to see how much money I have left on my credit card and see if my friend will let me borrow the money."*
Emily - *"Hmmm...You won't be able to get the funds from a friend or use funds from a credit card. Both of those options will increase your liabilities which increases your debt in the eyes of the lender. Do you have savings or a 401K that you can tap into for the funds?"*
Henry - *"Oh, I wasn't aware about the earnest money requirements. Let me get my thoughts together and get back to you."*
Emily - *"Ok, Henry. I am here when you need to talk."*

Emily was met with a disappointing reality when she learned that her client, Henry, did not have the funds necessary to move forward. During their phone conversation, Henry divulged that he was considering borrowing money from a friend or using his credit card to cover the remainder of the cost. Emily knew all too well the perils of such an ill-advised approach and was quick to intervene.

In no uncertain terms, Emily made it clear that this was not an acceptable solution. She explained to Henry that the earnest money deposit process must be conducted in a proper and professional manner and that borrowing funds in such a haphazard way would only lead to more problems down the line. She advised him to focus on saving up the necessary funds and wait until he had the proper resources to move forward with the process.

After the earnest money conversation, Emily ended her buyer agency agreement with Henry. She gave him an action plan to begin the buying process at a later time in the future. There was no need to continue viewing homes as he was not truly ready to buy a home. Remember, in Principles of Real Estate "ready, willing and able" is the ability to purchase.

EMAIL (From Buyer's Agent to Buyer)

FROM: Emily Adams/TO: Henry Scott
SUBJECT: Termination of Agreement and Working Relationship

Dear [Recipient's Name],

I hope this email finds you well. After careful consideration, I have come to the decision to terminate our agreement and working relationship at this time. It is important to me that we operate in an environment where both parties are fully committed and prepared to enter the real estate market.

While I understand that circumstances may have led to this decision, I believe it is best for both of us to pause our collaboration until you are fully ready to proceed. Please know that I am open to revisiting our partnership in the future should you decide to re-engage in the real estate market. To assist you in your future endeavors, I would like to propose an action plan that can help you prepare for your return to the real estate market:

- Save for earnest money deposit: I recommend setting aside $250 per month towards your earnest money deposit. This will help you accumulate the necessary funds for securing a property when the time is right.

- Save for closing costs: It is essential to plan for closing costs associated with purchasing a property. I suggest saving $250 per month specifically for covering these expenses.

By following this action plan, you will be better equipped financially when you decide to reenter the real estate market. Should you have any questions or require further guidance in the future, please feel free to reach out to me. I genuinely appreciate the opportunity that I have had to work with you thus far, and I am confident that your return to the real estate market will be a successful one. Until that time, I wish you all the best in your preparations and endeavors.

Sincerely,
Emily Adams
Real Estate Agent
123 Real Estate Co.

You cannot borrow from a friend,
Nor can you borrow it from kin,

Your checking account's the only play,
It's the debit route that saves the day.

Turn to your savings, it's true,
Even your 401K will do!

PHONE CALL
(With Emily Adams and Sabrina Gills)

Emily: *"Hi Sabrina, how are you doing today?"*
Sabrina: *"I'm doing well, thanks for asking. How about you, Emily?"*
Emily: *"I'm good, thank you. I wanted to talk to you about the client you referred to me."*
Sabrina: *"Sure, what's going on?"*
Emily: *"Unfortunately, I won't be able to assist your friend with his home purchase."*
Sabrina: *"Oh no, what happened?"*
Emily: *"It's a bit of an unfortunate situation."*
Sabrina: *"I see. So, what's the next step?"*
Emily: *"I provided your friend with an action plan to begin the buying process at a later time. I explained that there was no need to continue viewing homes if he was not ready and able to purchase at this time."*
Sabrina: *"That makes sense. I'm sorry that it didn't work out this time."*
Emily: *"It's unfortunate, but I appreciate the referral and hope to assist your friend in the future when he is ready to move forward with the purchase."*

Maintaining open communication with the referral source throughout a transaction is essential in establishing trust and ensuring that they are aware of the progress being made. However, it's equally important to exercise caution when sharing information to prevent any breaches of confidentiality. As a real estate agent, it's important to strike a balance between keeping the source of business informed and protecting the privacy of the client even if it is a close friend.

When a homebuyer makes a purchase, the lender verifies whether the escrow deposit has been received and funded. In this digital age, this process is mostly conducted electronically through applications like Zoccam or wire transfers. The earnest money should be sourced honestly, meaning that it must be obtained solely from the buyer, unless purchasing with someone else and even that will need to be sourced. It is recommended that the funds come from the same account that was submitted to the lender to avoid any additional inquiries. Failure to comply with these guidelines can result in a denied transaction. Nowadays, it is common to see earnest money deposits as high as 20% of the sales price in today's competitive market. The earnest money deposit is an indicator of the buyer's commitment to the transaction and how they intend to proceed with the purchase.

In summary, the comparison between an earnest money deposit and an anchor primarily serves to illustrate that both situations involve creating stability. Just as an anchor secures a ship in place, preventing it from drifting away, an earnest money deposit holds a real estate deal steady. It reassures the seller that the buyer is serious and committed, much like how an anchor ensures that a vessel remains where it's intended. This deposit acts as a firm grip in the unpredictable seas of property transactions, providing a sense of security and trust for both parties involved.

THINK BEYOND THE STORY

- What was the cost of this real estate transaction? emotional, physical, or financial

- How do you manage earnest money deposits? Do you know the options available to you?

CLOSING POINTS

- During a buyer consultation, before looking at homes, before offer submission has the earnest money deposit conversation

- Explain when the funds are due

- The earnest money can be a personal check, certified check, money order, wire transfer or mobile deposit via an app.

- Explain that the funds must be their own and they must be sourced and verified

40

STILL EMPLOYED?

"Be prepared because not every deal will close."
ReShawna Leaven

T HIS CHAPTER RESEMBLES THE process of auditioning for a leading role in a Hollywood blockbuster. In order to excel, a prospective real estate agent must first immerse themselves in research and training, honing their language and persuasive techniques. They must then impress potential clients with their knowledge of the industry and the art of negotiation, earning the privilege of being entrusted with the client's needs. Once hired, the real estate agent's performance is under scrutiny, as they work diligently to secure a successful sale that meets all parties' needs. Ultimately, their success is measured not only by the satisfaction of their clients but also by the endorsements and recommendations that follow, similar to receiving a coveted academy award.

We will begin this story with introductions of the buyer, Hunter Lewis. Hunter was a person who exuded a relaxed, laissez-faire attitude and was seeking to purchase a home. He sought the guidance of Olivia Pressley, a seasoned real estate professional who had honed the art of relationship building with her clients. As with all her clients, Olivia began the consultation by getting to know Hunter on a personal level. They met at a local coffee shop, and Olivia probed into his childhood, hobbies, and occupation, using the information to create a personal connection with him.

Hunter, in turn, spoke candidly about his demanding job and how he felt unappreciated and overworked. Olivia listened attentively, without interrupting, as he shared his feelings. After establishing a sense of trust and familiarity, Olivia then turned to discussing Hunter's preferences for his new home. She encouraged him to outline his "deal breakers," to which he responded that he was looking for a home that was within his budget, required little yard maintenance, and was conveniently located near his workplace since he relied on public transportation. With Hunter's needs and wants in mind, Olivia set out to find him the perfect home. Her tenacity paid off when she found a home that clicked all of Hunter's boxes and fulfilled his wishlist.

Our story commences during the week of the much-anticipated closing date. The arduous process of verifying employment details had been conducted for a second time, and the loan had been granted clearance to proceed with the final stages of the sale. As it was a split settlement, the seller had already signed all necessary documents a day prior to the official closing date.

On the day of settlement, the buyer, Hunter Lewis, was accompanied by the closing agent, who meticulously reviewed all the pertinent documents with him. It was a momentous occasion, filled with the gravity of the transaction and the anticipation of its successful completion. With precision and care, the closing agent ensured that Hunter understood every aspect of the documents, leaving no stone unturned.

Documents

Closing Statement	Reviewed and signed
Deed	Reviewed and signed
Deed of Trust	Reviewed and signed
Promissory Note	Reviewed and signed

A host of other documents were signed and now they came to the loan application. As soon as the closing agent moved on to the loan application, things took a sharp turn.

AT THE CLOSING TABLE
(With The Closing Agent, Buyer and Buyer's Agent)

Closing Agent - *Ok, Mr. Lewis. Here is the mortgage application with your address, place of work and it highlights your debts and liabilities at the time of your application. It's essentially a snapshot in time when you applied for the loan.*
Hunter - *"Oh, I don't work there anymore."*
Closing Agent - *"I'm sorry, Sir. What did you say?"*
Hunter - *"I don't work at that place anymore as of last night."*
Olivia - *"Hunter, you are joking right?"*
Hunter - *"No, I am not joking. I quit."*
Olivia - *(spit out her water after she realized that her client was very serious and not joking) "I am so sorry. Do you have some paper towels, so I can clean this up?"*
Closing Agent - *"We have a ladies room across the hall where you can find paper towels. Okay. We are going to have to stop closing and I will have to inform the lender of this change and the closing has been canceled."*
Olivia - While in the restroom, Olivia looked in the mirror and thought to herself. *"I'm getting too old for this" (Lethal Weapon 1987). The fact that he left his job when we were closing today is unbelievable to*

me. What am I going to do now?"

To begin with, she faced the daunting task of contacting the listing agent and divulging the unfortunate turn of events. The mere thought of this conversation sent shivers down her spine, leaving her to ponder its outcome with trepidation. The news was daunting, knowing that it could potentially cause a ripple effect of repercussions.

Moreover, she had to return the keys to the lockbox, a symbolic gesture that marked the end of the failed endeavor. To make matters worse, her hopes of receiving a hard-earned commission check was squashed, as the sale had fallen through.

The conversation with the listing agent over the phone was an excruciatingly unpleasant experience, to say the least. The sellers were understandably irate, and the tension in the air was palpable, leaving everyone involved in a state of disappointment and frustration. The ramifications of the failed sale were far-reaching and left a trail of negative emotions in its wake.

However, Hunter appeared to be the only person unaffected by the distressing situation. He was at ease, having achieved his goal of freeing himself from a job that had caused him considerable distress. It was a hollow victory, as it came at the expense of others, leaving behind a bitter aftertaste of resentment and ill will.

The sellers were not willing to let Hunter off the hook so easily and threatened to take legal action against him for specific performance due to his intentional act of quitting his job, which they saw as a clear violation of the contract terms. However, they soon realized that litigation would not be a viable option, as it would tie up their home in legal proceedings and prevent them from selling it on the market.

Instead, the sellers decided to keep the earnest money deposit as compensation for the damages incurred. They also chose to cut ties with their previous agent and hire a new one to sell their home, hoping for a fresh start. Their decision paid off, as the home sold quickly to a cash buyer, according to MLS records.

Unfortunately, both agents involved in this transaction lost out, as the deal fell through due to Hunter's actions. It's a harsh reality of the real estate industry that not every transaction will be successful, and one must be prepared to face the consequences of a failed deal. Even though the sellers terminated their listing agreement and hired a new agent, it was not the listing agent's fault for the unfortunate turn of events.

In conclusion, every deal, whether successful or not, serves as a learning experience in the game of real estate. It takes strength, perseverance, and resilience to survive in this industry, and one must always strive to be better. Success cannot be taken for granted, and one should never count the money that they haven't yet received, as not every deal will close.

THINK BEYOND THE STORY

- What was the cost of this real estate transaction? emotional, physical, or financial

- Is the agent still due a commission even though the sale did not close?

- What would have happened if Hunter had not mentioned quitting his job?

CLOSING POINTS

- You are never in control of a person's actions even after building a good rapport.

- You should always have a backup offer (if you are representing the seller)

- In most cases agents are compensated after closing. That means the deal has been signed, sealed, and delivered.

- Make sure your client knows not to change employment type (i.e., teacher to entrepreneur); or quit their job before closing.

- Don't let many of the things that are required during a transaction to be inferred (i.e., quitting his job)

ABOUT THE AUTHOR

In the dynamic world of real estate, few names resonate with the depth of experience, passion for teaching, and commitment to mentorship quite like ReShawna Leaven. With a career spanning over two decades, ReShawna has carved a niche for herself as not just a real estate professional, but as a luminary guiding others through the often complex landscape of property buying, selling, and investment.

ReShawna's journey in real estate began at the turn of the millennium, a period that has seen her evolve alongside the industry's numerous transformations. Her firsthand experiences during the boom and bust cycles have endowed her with unparalleled insights into the market's nuances, making her advice not just relevant but invaluable. ReShawna's expertise is not confined to transactions; it is a comprehensive blend of knowledge accumulated through years of hands-on involvement in various facets of real estate.

A fervent advocate for education, ReShawna has dedicated a significant part of her career to training and teaching. Her background includes teaching Principles of Real Estate, presenting workshops and mentoring novice agents. This is a testament to her belief in empowerment through knowledge. She has an innate ability to use strategies to solve complex concepts, making them accessible to novice agents and seasoned professionals alike. Her educational programs are crafted with a keen understanding of the industry's changing dynamics, ensuring her students are well-equipped to navigate the market confidently.

The culmination of ReShawna's experiences, her passion for teaching, and her commitment to mentorship is encapsulated in her latest work, "The Cost to Close." This book is not just a guide; it's a companion for anyone looking to understand the real estate market. Through humor, wisdom, and practical advice, ReShawna offers readers a front-row seat to the lessons learned over two decades. "The Cost to Close" is more than a book; it's an invitation to journey with a seasoned guide through the complexities of real estate, making the path to closing not just successful, but enlightening.

Thank you for purchasing The Cost to Close. Be sure to share your experience with others by leaving a review. Visit www.costtoclose.com for additional resources that compliment this book. I appreciate your support and wish you the best with your real estate endeavors.

9 798985 197310